Porsche 911

The Ultimate Sportscar as Cultural Icon

by Ulf Poschardt

gestalten

S HK 4343

Contents

Prelude

A Visit to the Shrink

The psychoanalyst was kindly disposed to the man on the couch. "No, there is no need to worry just because you love a car. Especially when it's a car with feminine curves, a voluptuous rear, and a décolleté that softens even the hearts of car-haters." Such forms answer a basic anthropological need, and in the first place, the world of forms is a feminine world, even if this isn't apparent with the majority of cars.

Anyone who has fallen in love with a car as a young boy would have never have expected one of their earliest conscious passions to survive into adulthood. But with the 911 this is possible. The car grows up along with you, and in a quasi-miraculous way appears to escape the usual aging process. The Porsche 911 was unveiled at the Frankfurt Motor Show in 1963, and since then has stayed with us. That makes it unique. No existing sports car is so old.

"You shouldn't blame everything on childhood," commented Professor Rainer Kaus in his calm and friendly manner, surrounded by the mass of books, pictures, and *In-Treatment* DVD boxes crammed into his office. "When young men pull up in front of the university in a Porsche with screeching tires, then the psychodynamic implications remain their secret." But the experienced psychoanalyst has a few ideas. It is simply about the intoxication of speed, and the intoxication itself. The sports car becomes a sex object that we use to arouse both ourselves and others. And to crown it all, there is the allure of envy. The arousal of envy should not be seen as a destructive force, but as a provocation designed to set one's environment in motion, to lend it dynamism. Everyone is envious and produces envy. Unfortunately our society fails to deal with it productively.

Driving a Porsche is something very positive, continued the nice gentleman. The idea of sitting in a tight cockpit, intimately connected to the vehicle, is a symbiotic experience that everyone is actually in search of. Symbiosis is like a bath that one can immerse oneself in. The important thing is that one doesn't sink or become so entangled with the object that separation is impossible. Becoming frozen in symbiosis could be problematic. Symbiosis includes the desire to let oneself fall. The engine propels us through the world at high speed, and in the process we can let ourselves fall. In answer to the question from the couch as to whether this isn't perhaps dangerous or questionable, the psychoanalyst quietly responded: "One must keep an eye on the technical things." Which means? "Okay, I regress, I enter into a symbiosis with the vehicle, the intoxication, the speed, but I don't lose control, and that also applies to my feeling of pleasure. Intoxication, regression, and symbiosis are important pleasure-generating principles; however, they need to be set limits to prevent potential self-harm." He looked at me earnestly. "There are people who submit to intoxication, regression, and symbiosis with abandon, and they don't care what happens to them. Every regression requires an instant of reversal." The Porsche driver knows instantly what he is talking about: an unsuccessful reversal that had already brought him close to death and dispatched the beautiful sports car to the junkyard. Not every piece of information has to be processed during the first session, though.

S-J 6547

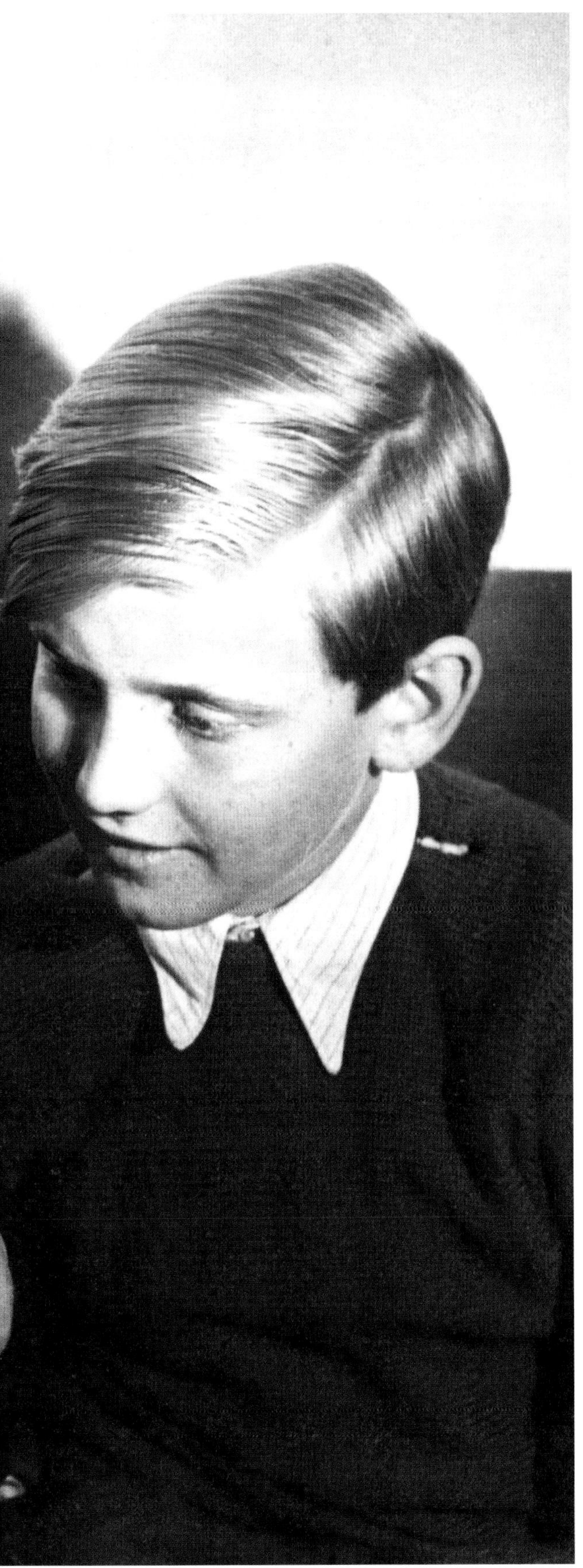

The 911 grows up along with one, and in an almost miraculous way appears to escape the usual aging process.

« Ferdinand Porsche showing grandchildren Ferdinand Alexander Porsche (left) and Ferdinand Piëch (right) a Porsche 356 no. 1 model in 1949.

The psychoanalyst takes a close look at the patient. "One has to be lucky. For example, having a partner who reminds one of one's responsibility and is capable of saying: 'That's enough. It's OK.' This generates an internalized sense of responsibility."

And what about the death instinct? The psychoanalyst considers this somewhat overrated. It doesn't really help to explain things. Intoxication is connected to happiness, not least because nearly everyone knows how to stop things when they reach a certain point. Everyone has the freedom to live out their feelings of intoxication, regression, and symbiosis, and being able to stop them completes the happiness. And turning to the ideas of the French ethnologist and anthropologist Georges Devereux, Kaus has also found an explanation for the behavior of the notorious speed merchants. In his magnum opus, Devereux explained that the less fear one has when observing something, the more one is capable of seeing. In this sense, the Porsche improves one's perception, assuming one is not a coward. The less fearful the driver, the better he is at steering the car.

Professor Kaus is the ideal psychoanalyst for Porsche drivers. His couch is low-slung and he has an inquiring mind completely devoid of prejudice. Ideally a sports car should be driven "leisurely." "When we rush and hurry all the time we generate pressure. And too much pressure is not good for the psychosomatics. Nor is unresolved envy." Instead of feeling the need to defend myself, Professor Kaus turns me into a reasonable, well-adjusted member of society. A healthy narcissism is important for an unneurotic sense of personal worth. If narcissism is understood less as a form of pathological self-love—a popular prejudice of Protestantism—and more as an appropriate form of self-care, then it does one good—relaxes, stimulates—and can help generate new ideas. Just as desire and arousal are necessary for people to develop fantasies, so narcissism promotes activity and dynamism. And of course, a certain pleasure in self-presentation is also necessary. "Essentially," remarked Professor Kaus, coolly, "people consider this a precondition for displaying solidarity with their fellow human beings."

Prehistory

The German Car: Porsche Before Porsche

"What a Krautwagen!" gushed Boris Johnson on seeing the Porsche 911 Targa parked outside his house for a test drive. Back then, in 2003, Boris Johnson was an influential opposition politician and member of the Tory party. In 2008 he was elected Mayor of London, was a key player in the British voting to leave the EU, and has since become foreign secretary. In addition he is also an active man of letters, free thinker, eccentric, and car lover.

For Johnson, a Brit, the Porsche 911 was and is, first and foremost, a very German car whose name—after the terrorist attack of September 11—sounds as ridiculous as a Nissan Obama or a Datsun Pearl Harbor. Towards the end of his test drive for the British *GQ* magazine, and after all the ridicule and jokes about the name, he praised the 911 with an almost un-British effusiveness, ordering his readers to buy one immediately. This somewhat martial gesture is an ironic allusion to the Prussian spirit assumed to reside in the 911.

Other Brits took a less friendly approach. Jeremy Clarkson, for example. The man who is arguably the world's most famous car journalist hates the Porsche. "If the Porsche 911 were a woman, then it would be Brunhilde, if it were a building it would be a bunker, and if it were food then it would be meat pie," conjectured Clarkson in a now infamous film available on the internet and a source of amusement for 911 fans to this day. It features Clarkson as he attempts to murder a Porsche. Dejected, he is forced to conclude that it is not just a rumor that this car is made from granite. An old piano crashes onto the aged red 911, leaving only a dent. Then it is smashed against a house, which destroys the brickwork but not the Porsche's roadworthiness. He shoots at the 911, pours acid over the motor. It is no good. Finally, he drops the 911 onto a camper van filled with gas from a 10 m (33 ft.) crane, blowing it up.

Thus this act of destruction unwittingly turns into a British homage to the quality of this "supercar," which is actually too robust for this exotic motor engineering niche. In another program Clarkson expends less effort demonstrating his antipathy. The Porsche 911, he gibes, is actually a VW Beetle with sports shoes. The rear motor is an absurdity, as if horses were hitched up to the back of a carriage and required to push people and luggage around. The car's idiosyncratic, monstrous Teutonism is feared, admired, and marveled at. On the other side of the planet, the car's exoticism is raised to a new level. In Japan a chain-smoking tuner transforms elderly and more youthful 911s into Haikus with the aid of the German language. The abbreviation for Akira Nakai's company is RWB. The three majuscules stand for "Rauh Welt Begriff" (Rough World Concept), a line of concrete poetry that would cause confusion back in Germany, but in Japan stands for the most free-spirited form of car tuning. While the tuning scene familiar from films such as *The Fast and the Furious* specializes in the modification of Asian vehicles, the Porsche 911 has a double portion of exoticism. It is not just European, but German. On the massive rear spoiler of the RWB Porsches, inscribed in fantasy German, is the slogan "Sekund Entwicklung" (Second Development). And all of the cars tuned by Akira Nakai have a sticker on the top edge of the front windscreen that reads "Rauh Welt." The sculptural redesign of the

» A 1948 Porsche 356 coupe in production in Gmünd, Austria.

Porsche's life was shaped by the attempt to bridge the gap between everyday motoring and the racetrack.

» In the summer of 1944 the Porsche design company relocated to a former sawmill in Gmünd, Austria (↓), until after the end of the Second World War in 1948. After this, production of the Porsche 356 (↑) began.

wider, deeper, and hysterically ennobled Porsche 911 is augmented by a theatrical language that only a few employees at the Goethe Institute in Tokyo or students of German philology could possibly understand. However, Johnson, Clarkson, and Akira Nakai are united by a common sense of excitement in the face of a product that is not just unique but uniquely "German." For the tuner, who tends to be somewhat taciturn in interviews, German has become a cubic capacity upgrade for his fantasy and revs up the mythologization of a sports car that is considered one of the world's top five motor sport legends. Akira Nakai liberates the vehicle from the severity of its Teutonic puritanism, transforming it into a mythical creature with monstrous rear spoilers, hub caps, and ultra-wide slicks, which, in a misjudgment of reality, mistakes the streets of this world for an unending racetrack. Something quintessentially German is transformed into a global bird of paradise.

The 911 proudly cultivates its German core, which, due to its historical links to the darker corners of history, is not without its difficulties. As a result, Porsche also succeeds in accessing difficult markets such as the American East and West Coasts, where the freelance, creative, and adventurous clientele is frequently of Jewish origin. "I am half Austrian and—so to speak—have a special aesthetic connection to these cars," explained Jerry Seinfeld. "When I look at a Porsche, it awakens feelings in me like no other car. I love the history of Porsche and have built up the collection so that it also tells this history. From the beginnings in Gmünd to the latest models." For the actor who emphasizes his Jewish identity in his work, the company's Nazi roots are not a problem: "I find the Nazis themselves more unsettling than the cars that were developed in this period. For me the VW Beetle was almost like a reparation paid to the rest of the world."

The 911 never made any bones about its origins, on the contrary: the genealogical tree of the most successful sports car of all time extends directly back to the early 1930s when the tragedy first descended on Germany, and from there to the rest of the world. In the middle of the world economic crisis the renowned engineer Ferdinand Porsche opened an engineering office in Stuttgart, which in April 1931 became the "Dr. Ing. h. c. F. Porsche Limited Company for Engine and Vehicle Design and Construction." Together with his son-in-law Anton Piëch, shortly followed by his son Ferry, he worked as an engineering consultant for car companies such as Wanderer, NSU, and Zündapp. For the latter he was contracted to develop a small car designed to sell well even in times of crisis. At the other end of the spectrum stood the design of high-performance engines and the development of a formula racing car for the Auto Union company. Porsche was always interested in both, though as an engineer at Austro-Daimler and Mercedes-Benz his preference for sporty vehicles was always apparent. According to his grandson Ferdinand Piëch, he was especially impressed by Bugatti's ability to combine lightweight racing cars with powerful engines, uniting the best of both worlds. For Austro-Daimler, Porsche built the Sascha, a racing car employing a lightweight construction and equipped with an engine with a spartan 1.1 L cubic capacity. This car, christened after Count Sascha Kolowrat-Krakowsky, was a decisive milestone in the development of the later Volkswagen. From an early stage Porsche's life was shaped by the attempt to bridge the gap between everyday motoring and the racetrack, which from 1948 found its ideal consummation in Porsche's first sports car—and the continuation of his life's work by his son Ferry.

The development of low-priced small vehicles and exclusive racing cars in the engineering office in Stuttgart resulted in an accumulation of know-how uniting diverse elements. Ferdinand Porsche sensed that the combination of these car genres, which up to now had largely been treated as disparate entities, could be an opportunity. However, the time wasn't ripe. The basic concept for the first Porsche, which in 1948 would carry the designer's name, was already contained in the design for a small car for NSU called Type 32. It was equipped with a fastback and a rear-mounted four-cylinder boxer engine with air-cooling. In January 1934, following the seizure of power by the Nazis and their car-mad leader, Ferdinand Porsche presented his idea for a *Deutscher Volkswagen* (German people's car). In addition to a streamlined form, technical innovation, and an affordable price, the focus was on a new, fundamental reinterpretation of the Volkswagen concept. As Porsche stated in an expose for the Reich Ministry of Transport, it shouldn't just be a scaled-down version of a large car, but something completely distinct, in keeping with the times. Military applications were only hinted at in an aside. A short time later, following the self-confident pitch, the small Stuttgart-based manufacturer was awarded a contract from the Reich Association of the German Automobile Industry (RDA) to build a small car. Thanks to the countless preliminary models and prototypes Porsche had designed to date, a form of archetypal Beetle could be presented within the space of a year. In 1935 the first and second test vehicles were presented to Hitler in Munich, who proved very enthusiastic.

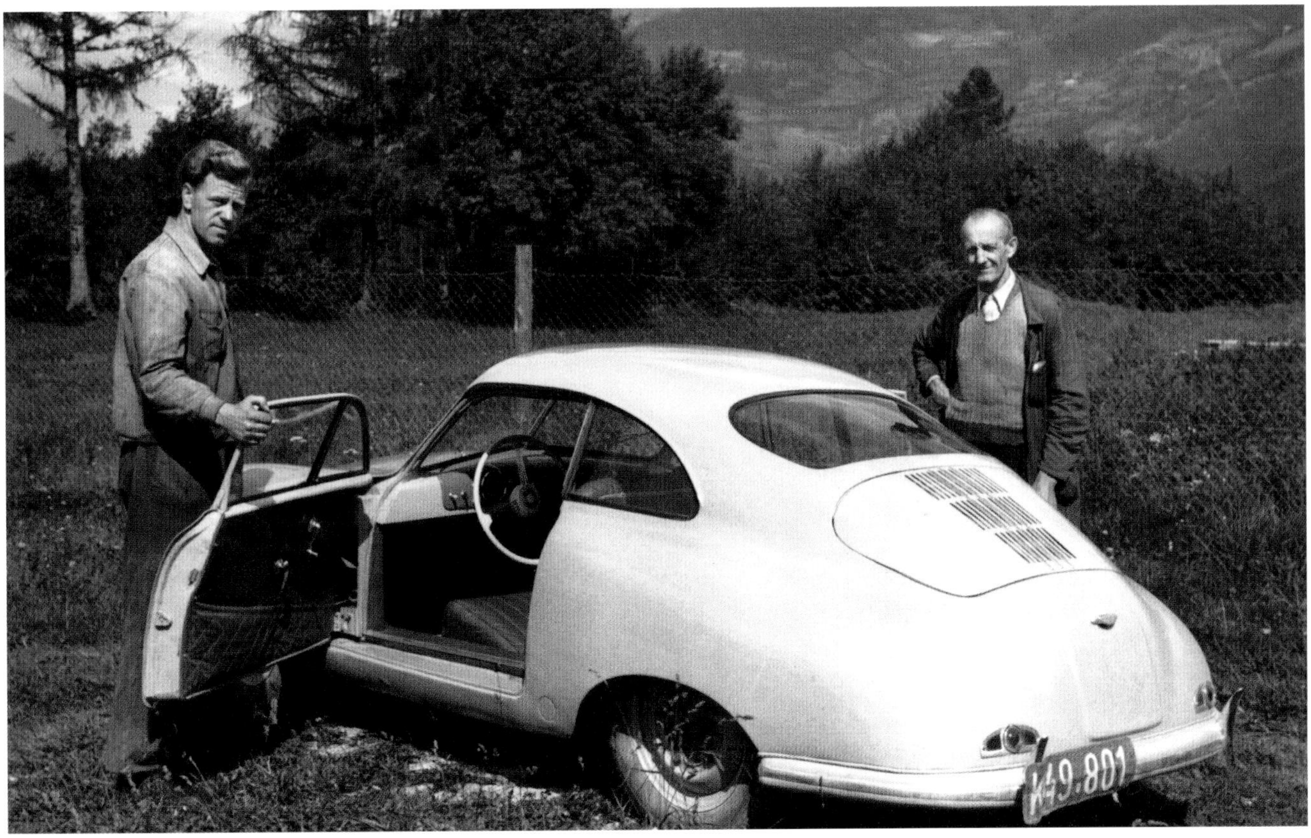

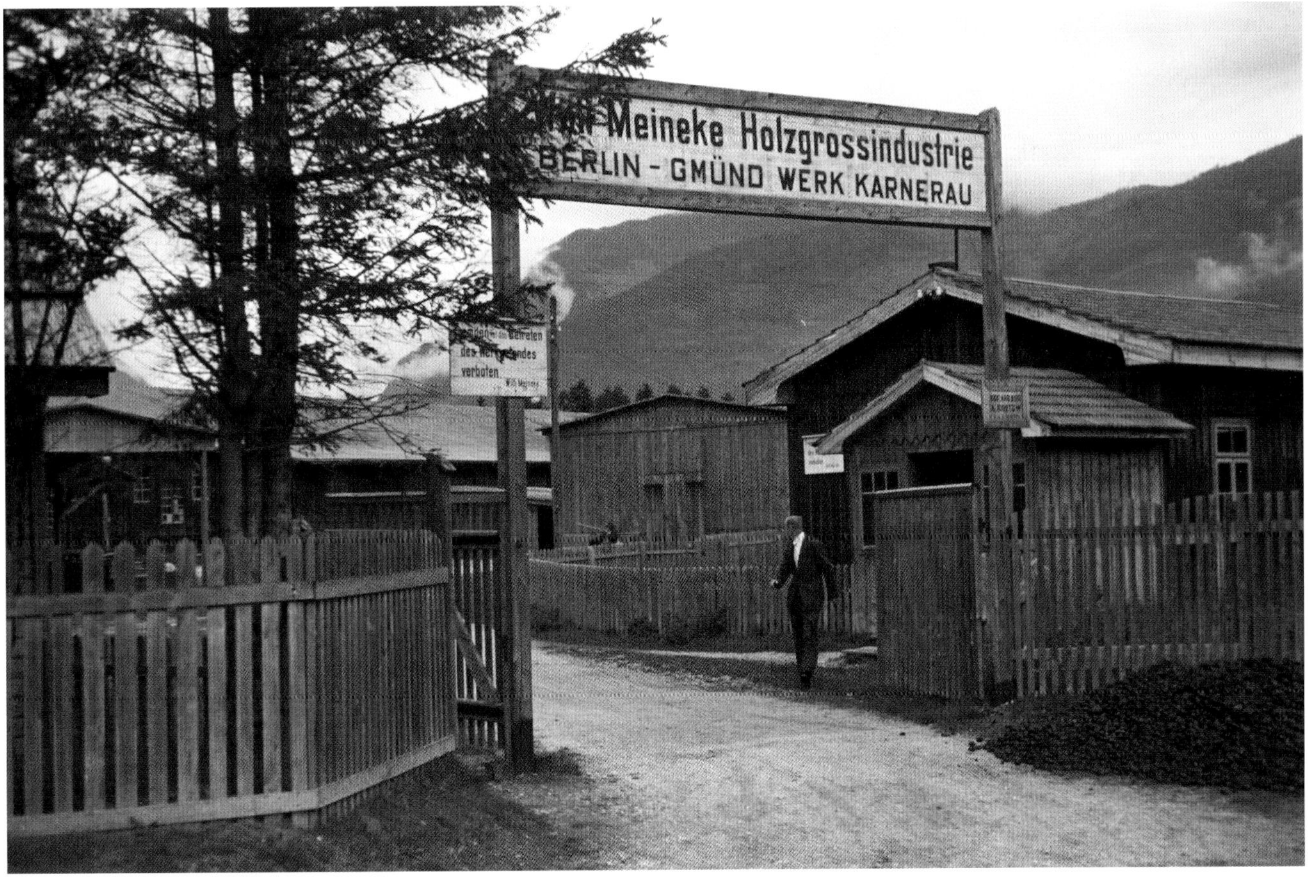
Meineke Holzgrossindustrie
BERLIN - GMÜND WERK KARNERAU

IIIA-0427

Ferry Porsche, in very German fashion, attempted to keep out of politics ... He never wore a uniform and pursued a pragmatic approach in his relations with the Nazi state, while resisting the pressure to mutate into an enthusiastic follower.

« Ferry Porsche and his cousin Herbert Kaes among Porsche engineers, test-driving the Porsche Type 60 during Easter 1936.

However, the competition were less enthusiastic about the Führer's new darling and the tiny little engineering office in Stuttgart that was about to secure possibly the biggest contract of the 1930s. Their jealously hardly bothered Porsche. Unperturbed, he visited Ford and General Motors in the United States to study their methods for the quick and efficient production of small cars. May 1937 saw the founding of the Association for the Preparation of the German People's Car, for short GeZuVor. Ferdinand Porsche was appointed one of the three managing directors with responsibility for planning and technology in the soon-to-be-built Volkswagen factory.

However, Porsche's energies are not completely absorbed with the launch of VW. The Stuttgart-based Porsche KG, as the company is now known, continues to expand. In 1938 the firm moves to Zuffenhausen, Baden-Württemberg, where the Porsche-Werk 1 factory would later be built. A year before the outbreak of the war, the Volkswagen is finished, and in May the foundation stone for the Volkswagen factory is laid near Fallersleben, Wolfsburg. Ferry Porsche recalled that Hitler suggested it be named the "Porsche-Werk," but Ferdinand declined the honor. There are a number of political rumors concerning these events; however, Porsche, in a very German fashion, attempted to keep out of politics. For this reason, his grandson Ferdinand Piëch described him as politically naive, "like a child," portraying him as a boffin almost exclusively concerned with technical matters. Porsche never wore a uniform and pursued a pragmatic approach in his relations with the Nazi state, while resisting the pressure to mutate into an enthusiastic follower. He always referred to the Führer as "Mr Hitler." The world of the engineer was to remain insulated from the Holocaust, the annihilation of the Jews, and the concentration camps. Nevertheless, it was the German automobile and defense industry that proved to be the main beneficiary of the forced laborers and concentration camp

Compared to the other small cars of the time the Beetle was an elegant, well-proportioned five-seater, whose anthropomorphic countenance, with its big eyes and high forehead, displayed all the childlike features that would be one of the factors in its forthcoming global, decades-long popularity.

» The Type 32 designed by Porsche for NSU parked in Stuttgart in around 1934 (↓), and a 1940 *Kübelwagen*—offroad vehicle used by the German military (↑).

prisoners conscripted to work in the factories under inhumane conditions. Adolf Rosenberger's exit from the company marked a particularly dark chapter. In 1935 the firm's commercial manager and once close friend of Porsche was arrested on a charge of racial defilement and deported to a concentration camp, from which he was released a few days later. From there he fled to America via Switzerland—thanks to the help of the Porsches, as they claim in their memoirs. Rosenberger saw it differently. After the war he demanded compensation for the shares he ceded to Ferry, which he received in the form of 50,000 reichsmarks and a Porsche.

The Beetle has its origins in the bleakest period of German history, though one wouldn't think so to look at it. Compared to the other small cars of the time it was an elegant, well-proportioned five-seater, whose anthropomorphic countenance, with its big eyes and high forehead, displayed all the childlike features that would become part of its forthcoming global, decades-long popularity. The Beetle even looked cheerful in its standard black paintwork. As if anticipating its fame in future times of peace, it remained a car apart from the despotic, aggressive Mercedes cabriolets and limousines. According to the car journalist Wolfgang Blaube, in addition to his small car concept, Porsche also presented the Reich leadership with a proposal for a KdF-Wagen,[1] a sports car designed to help shape the free time of the German people. However, the leaders had other plans. Instead of bringing happiness to industrious small families, the ancestral Beetles were initially transformed into *Kübelwagen* (offroad vehicles) for the armed forces. The Porsche office profited from the military build-up that was conducted on an enormous scale at the outbreak of the Second World War. In Zuffenhausen, tanks, amphibious all-terrain vehicles, and even a people's tractor were developed. Ferdinand Porsche was appointed director of the Tank Commission at the Reich Ministry for Armaments and Ammunition. Prior to this, and still under commission from the Volkswagen factory, Porsche had planned and built a racing car, whose beating heart was a highly tuned 33 hp VW boxer engine, packed into an extremely streamlined body with a top speed of almost 150 km/h (93 mph). The Type 64, or "Berlin-Rome Car," is considered the first thoroughbred Porsche. It had the silhouette of the later Porsches, a rear-mounted engine, and was extremely lightweight at only 545 kg (1,200 lb.). After the war its low-slung nose would finally be emblazoned with those seven letters which that complete its status as the "first Porsche."

In 1943 Albert Speer, in his capacity as Minister of Armaments, removed Porsche from his office as director of the Tank Commission. At this time, the Germans are in the process of losing the war, and the allies are concentrating their bombing raids on factories where tanks and military equipment are being built or designed. The Wehrmacht's Armaments Division advises Porsche to transfer operations to Carinthia in Austria. In Gmünd, at the heart of the gently rolling Lieser valley, 749 m (2,457 ft.) above sea level, makeshift workshops are established in the drafty halls of a former sawmill. At the end of the war the Americans requisition the Porsche factory in Stuttgart, or more correctly, what is left of it, using it as a base for repairing their lorries. In Gmünd Porsche is granted a provisional license to resume work, exclusively for the design of civilian products.

At the beginning of August Ferdinand Porsche is arrested and transported from Carinthia to the eastern region of Hintertaunus in Germany. An interrogation center, known as the "Dustbin," has been established in Kransberg Castle, where war criminals and scientists are questioned. After a number of witnesses testify in Porsche's favor, he is released in September. A short time later he is arrested again by the French. The reasons for that are complex. Louis Renault was accused of collaborating with the Germans and his company taken into state ownership. Consequently, in an attempt to divert attention from their own collaboration with the Nazis—or so the story goes—the Peugeot family launched a series of attacks on Porsche. Today, this remains speculation until French records are released after 100 years under lock and key. What is certain is that Porsche was accused of bringing Peugeot employees to Germany as forced labor.

Together with his son Ferry and son-in-law Anton Piëch he is first interrogated in Baden-Baden and then taken to Paris on May 3, 1946. After three months in detention Ferry is released, as he was not a member of the management board at the VW factory. The eldest Porsche is kept in detention, even though he

[1] KdF stands for *Kraft durch Freude* (Strength through Joy) and was a Nazi organization created to enforce conformity in the population during their leisure time.

Built in 1939, the Porsche Type 64 was also known as the "Berlin-Rome Car" after the long-distance race planned for that year. The race never took place because of the outbreak of the Second World War.

"We had a vision of a small, agile, lightweight vehicle that could outperform a large, powerful car."

↳ Ferry Porsche in his 1974 anniversary speech.

⇑ From left to right: Fiat Topolino (used for comparing the competition), and Porsche Types 8, 32, and 7 at the Porsche Villa in Stuttgart.

is plagued by severe attacks of biliary colic. The French, in the person of a Lieutenant LeComte, decide to import the idea of the Volkswagen into France. As the state-owned Renault factory has designed its own Volkswagen in the shape of the 4 CV, Ferdinand Porsche is forced to work on the project. There are varying accounts of the extent of Porsche's collaboration. In February 1947 Porsche and Piëch are transferred to the prison in Dijon. The 71-year-old is visibly deteriorating. With the change in the political climate in Paris and the exit of the communists from government, Peugeot loses its fear of nationalization and withdraws its charges against Porsche. However, Porsche's dream of producing his Volkswagen in Germany as chief factory director and overseeing its market launch has been overtaken by events.

In 1946 the first Beetle rolled off the assembly line in Wolfsburg, the newly christened Volkswagen production plant. Initially, Porsche was to receive one Reichsmark in licensing fees for every VW, a short while later it was five marks. For Porsche this source of income would serve as both a decisive financial boost on the road to independence and a form of secret life insurance for periods when the often volatile car market generated fewer sales, or when an important new innovation for serial production or the racing sector resulted in high development costs. From an analysis of the extent of Porsche know-how employed by VW in the construction of its bestseller, it is clear that the licensing fee was comparatively meager. As late as the 1960s the engineers in Wolfsburg restricted themselves to merely updating the pre-war ideas of Ferdinand Porsche and his team. At around the same time car production resumed in Gmünd. A Swiss contract for the development of a four-seater car was assigned the type number 352, which in its original form looked very similar to the 356. It was designed by Erwin Komenda, who had worked for Porsche since the early days and was responsible for the construction of the car bodies. Back then there were no designers. Form was a natural product of function. At the beginning of 1948 the aluminum body parts for the first 356 were hammered into shape by hand over a wooden block. Komenda's routine and his sense of form lent the first Porsches an expression appropriate to the technology. The coachbuilder's modesty fitted well to the young company, not to mention the times. The megalomaniacal, flag waving, column-lined Germany had perished, and with it the proclivity for bombastic gestures. The first series of Porsche bodies were proud expressions of humility, full of elegance. Ferry Porsche, who in his father's absence had matured into a corporate figurehead at the works in Gmünd, developed a feeling for the age and the appropriate forms. He harbored artistic ambitions, secretly painted watercolors, and could even imagine becoming an architect.

In the original prototype for the 356 the motor was situated in the center; however, for the serial model the four-cylinder engine was shifted to the rear. The 356 had something spartan and sober about it. It refused the grand gestures. It was fast and compact: the antithesis of the mighty compressor-engined Mercedes of the Nazis, which looked as if they had emerged from the studio of Arno Breker.[2] The Porsche 356 wanted to leave all that behind it. It was the Volkswagen for the people's elite, while remaining closely connected to the whole with which it was inseparably linked and interwoven. It was bolted together from its metal, but with a little more finesse and precision. It was Brâncusi instead of Breker. It was a break with the zeitgeist of the Nazis and a challenge to the new age in which a luxury product such as a sports car appeared to be out of step with the Calvinist spirit of reconstruction. The souped-up Beetle motor demonstrated that, with a little more passion, much more was possible than a simple bread and butter existence.

The contract work to develop a Grand Prix car for Cisitalia proved so lucrative that Ferry was able to secure the release of company founder Ferdinand and his brother-in-law Piëch for a sum of one million francs. The once so proud and autocratic patriarch returned to Gmünd on his release from prison a broken man. On witnessing the 356 in the final stages before serial production, he raised virtually no objections. Gravely weakened by imprisonment, Ferdinand was delighted by his son's assumption of the reigns at Porsche. Although so much of the first Porsche was based on his preliminary work, the car was primarily a product of the young Ferry's ideas. On the father's return it quickly became apparent that the old man was no longer fit enough to make a contribution: "I was on my own," Ferry remarked succinctly. But this also had its positive side. The Porsche was entirely his car. The aerodynamics were optimized by employing the simplest of means. Ferdinand Piëch recalls how a 356 fitted with threads attached with glue was driven at top speed beneath a bridge while Ferdinand Porsche and the engineer Josef Mickl took photographs from above. As early as June 1948 the first genuine Porsche, the "Roadster Gmünd" was authorized. A short while later it made an appearance at a race in Innsbruck, with a top speed of 130 km/h (81 mph) and weighing in at 600 kg (1,323 lb.). The first orders quickly followed.

With the founding of the Federal Republic of Germany, Porsche officially started production. The company motto *Fahren in seiner schönsten Form* (Driving in its most beautiful form) was an aesthetic promise, which, in the immediate post-war period, held out the prospect of idealistic pleasure as opposed to any obvious utility. Immediately following its first public appearance, Porsche became a site of longing for the enthusiastic Germans — though not just Germans — a trademark for dreams in an age primarily concerned with escaping the horror of the past. Naturally the 356 also offered such escapism. The Porsche trick was to be found in its gesture of modesty and reduction. "We had a vision," recalled Ferry Porsche in his anniversary speech from 1974, "of a small, agile, lightweight vehicle that could outperform a large, powerful car." This also conceals a political message. The interior of the 356 was no less spartan. The leather and steel surfaces gave it the appearance of a laboratory or a clinic. It was a cool, uncomfortable car — businesslike in the extreme.

Initially a modest 50 cars were planned. The production conditions in Gmünd were absurd. A sports car, highly innovative for its time, was being built between mountains, far from any infrastructure. The vehicles were painted in the open air, which, according to car experts, resulted in blemishes. It quickly became clear that the company would only amount to something if it moved to a larger city. Furthermore, Austria was threatening to expropriate German companies on its soil. For the Porsches, moving could only mean one thing — returning to Stuttgart. As the American occupying forces had commandeered the old Porsche factory in Zuffenhausen, the small sports car manufacturer found refuge in the Reutter coachwork factory. The 356s produced there would be the last that Ferdinand Porsche would see. He had subjected the first models to a thorough inspection, in the final stages seated on a stool in front of the coupe. "The bodywork will have to go back to the workshop," he declared. "It is not right, it is not symmetrical!" The old man was correct, as the measurements proved. The bodywork had slipped to the right by a total of 2 cm (3/4 in.). Porsche had built his life's work on this instinct for precision, now it was up to the son to continue the legacy. This heritage was taken up, and this pledge was exacted. The management staff worked from the Porsches' private villa, in the same room where the idea for the Volkswagen was born. Professor Albert Prinzing, the company's first authorized representative and schoolfriend of Ferry, recalls with a laugh how the management

[2] Sculptor endorsed by the Nazis and known for his public works. The opposite of the abstract, "degenerate" art of the expressionists.

staff at Porsche used to work in the old cook's room, crammed into 18 square meters (193 sq. ft). The meetings were held in the courtyard due to lack of space.

There is a snapshot taken in Gmünd in 1949 that reveals a great deal, and anticipates much more. The old, mellow-looking übergrandfather Ferdinand holds a model of a 356 Roadster in his hands. Seated next to him are his grandsons Butzi and Burli. Thirteen years later one would design the 911, and the other would refine its six-cylinder boxer. Butzi, christened Ferdinand Alexander Porsche, was Ferdinand Piëch's favorite cousin. Together the two young members of the clan would assume the challenge of somehow living up to the family's genius. Psychologists speak of the responsibility that parents, often unconsciously, pass on to their children: the task of doing justice to their heritage, and, more frequently, completing what the parents have strived for but were unable to complete. "I was brought up on gasoline and ended up devoting my whole life to automobiles," recalled Ferry Porsche. For Ferry the Austro-Daimler factory was a playground. At the age of 11 he was given a child's car with an air-cooled, six horsepower, two-cylinder engine capable of a top speed of 60 km/h (37 mph). A short while later he entered a driving competition organized by the Vienna Automobile Club in his mini Austro-Daimler, and recorded the fastest time. The family history of the Porsches and Piëchs is full of such anecdotes. In this respect, the history of the Porsches can be read as a relay race. Ferdinand passed over to Ferry and Ferry to Ferdinand Alexander. The situation was similar with Ferdinand Piëch. In her opulent homage *Ferrytales*, Susanne Porsche, who married into the family, wrote that obtaining the approval of their father was important for all the sons "even though this was rarely vocalized and sometimes hard for the sons to recognize."

When the Porsches moved to Stuttgart, Ferdinand Alexander—the first son of Ferry Porsche and his one and only true love, Dodo—returned to the place where he first saw the light of day in 1935: the villa on Feuerbacher Weg. At the time the whole family lived under one roof, and as a consequence functioned like a form of genetic excellence cluster, where, it goes without saying, exchanging knowledge of automobile construction dominated daily life, from the breakfast table to the evening fireside talks. If Augustine is correct and the life of the parents is the book from which the children read, then for the Porsche offspring there was no escaping the ideas and goals of the parents and grandparents. As a consequence, the development of the 356, alongside its economic necessity, was a mission that the two adolescents had internalized. It is only thanks to this upbringing that F. A. Porsche, along with Ferdinand Piëch, could exercise such a decisive influence on the development of the 911 at such a young age. They received the necessary education and competence from childhood on.

» Ferry Porsche in his 356/2 with his nephews Ferdinand Piëch (left) and Michel Piëch (right), and the son of his private secretary, Ghislaine Kaes (middle).

Emancipation, Revolt, and Noblesse: The World of the Porsche Driver

In the beginning Porsche was something reserved for the very few. Accordingly, being a Porsche driver was completely different to what it is now at the beginning of the twenty-first century. Nevertheless, anyone who wants to understand the Porsche myth must know who its first adherents and propagandists were. They were wealthy self-made individuals and those born into riches, all of whom, despite their privileges, wanted something from life that at the time they had to create themselves. They were unruly spirits, activists, fanatics, go-getters, adventurers, idealists, bon viveurs, connoisseurs, speed lovers, and individualists.

Switzerland, which escaped the war and its destruction, would become Porsche's pioneer market. The first serially produced 356 was bought by Jolanda Tschudi, an emancipated woman far removed from the Nazi ideal of motherhood, who set records as a glider pilot and survived a series of risky African expeditions as a co-pilot, including seven emergency landings. The wiry little sports car appealed to individualists, to those who didn't need a car of baroque proportions to assert themselves. From the very start this included women, who also used the Porsche, a comparatively dainty car devoid of macho posturing, as a driving force for emancipation. They were sporty, self-confident, often tomboyish ladies of a provocatively natural type who were determined to define their own roles, rather than have them dictated by society. They were independent in every sense, including financially. As daredevils and risk takers they competed in motor races, frequently beating the men, who, back then, were as incapable of dealing with this shame as their fellow men 70 years later.

Gilberte Thirion had a model for a mother and a motor racing-obsessed industrialist for a father. During her first racing trials in a Porsche 356 SL, her father sat in the co-driver seat and assisted his courageous daughter. A highly unusual role allocation for a successful businessman at the beginning of the 1950s. Nevertheless, it fitted the image of that privileged, liberal milieu where Porsche found its first and increasingly loyal customers. Thirion worked as a PR woman for Champion spark plugs and surprised journalists with her technical knowledge, which was unusual for a woman at that time. In 1953 she had a bad accident during a race in France, lay in hospital for over a month, and was confined to bed for a further four weeks. This failed to cure her of her passion for speed, however. Like many racing drivers of the time Thirion competed in both road races and rallies. For the 1954 season she shared a Gordini Roadster with Annie Bousquet, nee Schaffer, a native of Vienna who was even more uninhibited than Thirion. Having met her French husband when he was a prisoner in Austria, Bousquet began to take an interest in motor racing, when, after a skiing accident in Sestriere, she met the then famous racing driver Alberto Ascari at the hotel bar who engaged her on the spot as a co-driver for his next rally. Like Thirion, Annie Bousquet competed in rallies and circuit races. Both racing drivers paid little attention to male

» Count Paul von Metternich with a 356 1500 S cabriolet at the Carrera Panamericana race in November 1952.

» Montlhéry, France, 1955: French racing driver Annie Bousquet with her Porsche 550 Spyder.

expectations. Instead, unimpressed by the male competition, they created their own style, both in their public appearances and driving. As if feeling the need to contrapuntally augment Simone de Beauvoir's theses on the social and cultural construction of the woman, which were heatedly discussed at the time, they deconstructed both the role of the woman and the racing driver, reassembling them to create a new construct. These women refused to pull over to the right for men, voluntarily allow themselves to be overtaken, or, heaven forbid, relinquish a head start. However, they did brake for men. That was all. If one is not born a woman but made into one, then resistance is a duty—an act that attained a special symbolic significance on this parade ground of patriarchal heroism. It is the time when Margaret Thatcher, although already active in the Tory party, is sent from the room as a woman, when, following dinner in the upper middle class villas, the men gathered in the drawing room to talk about politics. It is the beginning of the end of male autocratic rule.

Motorsport at this time was still quite a dangerous affair. Annie Bousquet set a world speed record with her 550 Spyder and then crashed due to a burst tire at 230 km/h (143 mph) while attempting to add a one hour record. Two years previously she had spent a month in hospital following a serious racing accident. Her husband Pierre was killed in a car accident soon after. In June 1956 she took part in the Reims 12-hour race. Shortly before the start she decided to travel to Zuffenhausen to have her beloved (lavender) blue 550 adjusted. Immediately after the service check she got back into the car and drove to Reims. By the start of the race she hadn't slept for one, if not two nights in a row. On the seventeenth lap her left-hand front and rear wheels left the track, the Spyder jack-knifed, overturned, and flew into the mown wheat fields at high speed. Annie Bousquet was pulled out of the Porsche with a broken neck. Although she was quickly transferred to hospital, she was declared dead on arrival. From the pictures of the wrecked Spyder with the number 32, it was clear that Bousquet didn't stand a chance of surviving the accident. The wreck bore a strong resemblance to James Dean's tattered car, a Porsche of the same model, in which he was killed the previous year. Bousquet's friend and rival Gilberte Thirion ended her racing career following this fatal accident. A number of observers speculated that after the death of her husband, Bousquet began to drive even more recklessly—a somewhat romantic notion. France's all-male racing sport officials used the death of the sportswoman to impose an immediate ban on women competing in the country's major races. It was only lifted in 1971. Porsche's publicity material cultivated a conservative image of women in its catalogs, billboards, and trade fair appearances. Women tended to be portrayed as accessories, as opposed to the tamers of potent sports cars and male fantasies. It was only in the pages of the Porsche magazine *Christophorus,* that its Amazons were presented without the usual chauvinistic overtones.

The front cover of the first edition in 1952 featured a sporty, emancipated woman parking her Porsche in the snow next to the piste before attaching her skis. Her dark hair is tied back in an austere ponytail, she is wearing a brightly colored striped pullover, a classic pair of sunglasses, and lipstick as red as the Porsche's leather seats. She has nothing of the blond, pliable mother type of the Nazis, and little of the functional severity of the *Trümmerfrauen*.[3] This woman doesn't need a man to accompany her up the mountain in the lift, or guide her on the steep descent into the valley. There is no wedding ring in sight; no children. This woman bought the Porsche herself and she uses it to amplify her autonomy, beyond the streets and well-worn role models.

These women were not just PR or magazine fantasies — logically enough they also existed in reality. For example, the doctor of medicine Hedda Heuser, who in 1962 became the youngest female parliamentarian at the age of 35 as a representative of the liberal FDP in the German Bundestag. The tall, former competitive athlete was a challenging figure. As a health professional she was one of the first to call for an uninhibited approach to sexual education according to the Scandinavian model. *Life* magazine made her famous in America with a major expose, following which, in 1964, *Die Zeit* newspaper named her the "glamour girl" of German politics. Almost a little stereotypical, portraits of the liberal Dr. Heuser were fond of highlighting that she drove a Porsche, and wore modern gold jewelry and a fur coat. In the tight-laced, nagging egalitarianism of the Bonn Republic, she was both an ambassador for liberal-mindedness and a cultivated provocation. As president of the Association of Women Doctors she embarked on a high-speed campaign to secure the benefits of an emancipated life for her female colleagues. The issues were part-time advanced training, professional reintegration, and reconciling family and job. The socially committed politician cultivated a fast-paced lifestyle, admitting to *Christophorus* that she liked driving at speed. This fitted perfectly.

Surprisingly, the first catalog for the 911, which at the time was still called the 901, got by without featuring a man at the steering wheel. However, the blond lady, a Swabian Doris Day look-alike in a casually androgynous outfit, between plaid bags and suitcases in front of the open boot, looked more like the wife who had packed for a weekend trip than an Amazon of the fast lane. In the advertising for the 356 the woman was already reduced to a male trophy. It is the year 1960: "On the tennis court I recently saw a young lady with delicately chiseled features. A beautiful figure. She held two greyhounds on a lead. And then she got into a PORSCHE. A wonderful picture, I said to myself. It couldn't be any other way. Every one a thoroughbred, as revealed in their beauty and quality." However, the consumers were ahead of the game. And Richard von Frankenberg, progressive aristocrat and editor-in-chief of *Christophorus*, ensured that the conservative bourgeois sensibility didn't run riot, at least during his reign at the company magazine, which ended with his death in 1973.

"On the tennis court I recently saw a young lady with delicately chiseled features. A beautiful figure. She held two greyhounds on a lead. And then she got into a PORSCHE. A wonderful picture, I said to myself. It couldn't be any other way."

↳ Richard von Frankenberg, racing driver and journalist.

» *Christophorus*, the Porsche customer magazine, published its first issue in 1952, which featured an emancipated woman alone on a snowy piste with her Porsche.

In the official Porsche advertising the woman found her place on the front passenger seat, preferably admiring the male driver, or stroking the car — an erotic act performed on the motorized prosthesis of the beloved husband and breadwinner. A low point in this, at best, archaic view of the world, was the advertising for the Porsche Carrera RS, a supposedly male car. In the advert from 1972 it stated: "The Porsche Carrera RS: Only 500 men will drive it." Three years later red lipstick graced the rear of a Carrera. Nevertheless, famous, and in some cases openly homosexual, women such as Jil Sander, Countess Dönhoff,[4] or Martina Navrátilová, also identified with the 911's liberatory potential, which in the egalitarian vernacular was still understood as masculine dominance. The author Ralf Bönt, who in 2012 wrote a controversial manifesto for men entitled the *The Dishonored Sex*, was delighted when the equal opportunities officer for the city of Ulm picked him up from the station in a 911 to drive him to the reading. He: "Chic car." She: "My man buys the cars. But it's practical, it's got 4-wheel drive." The woman herself also had style, added Bönt, who prior to studying physics completed an apprenticeship as a car mechanic. For Bönt it is only a question of time before more women than men will be driving a 911, which, like smoking before it, is now a sign of emancipation and freedom. Furthermore, the economic realities are shifting. In the United States in 2010 women in the category of unmarried, childless wage earners under the age of 30 already took home between 12 and 25 percent more than men in the same group.

[3] Women who cleared the rubble from Germany's ruined streets after the Second World War.

[4] Marion Countess Dönhoff was born into Prussian nobility, a member of the Nazi resistance, a cutting-edge journalist, and joint-publisher of the liberal *Die Zeit* newspaper.

Christophorus
ZEITSCHRIFT FÜR DIE FREUNDE
DES HAUSES PORSCHE
W58-3284
Nr. 1 / 1952

» At the Mitternachtssonne rally in Stuttgart, 1950. Left to right: Prince Joachim zu Fürstenberg, Ferry Porsche, Count Constantin von Berckheim, Count Günther von Hardenberg, and Prince Friedrich zu Fürstenberg.

B 31 - 3605

» A woman's place: catalog pages from the 1960s highlight Porsche's male-dominated target group.
» "The Porsche Carrera RS: Only 500 men will drive it"—advert for the 911 T 2.0 coupe in 1968.

Der Porsche Carrera RS: Nur 500 Männer werden ihn fahren.

Denn Deutschlands schnellstes Auto wird nur 500mal gebaut.

Die wenigen, die ihn fahren, werden allerdings einen Sportwagen besitzen, wie ihn Porsche nie zuvor in Serie gebaut hat:

210 PS leistet der 6-Zylinder-Einspritzmotor mit 2,7 Liter Hubraum.

Sein Leistungsgewicht von 4,5 kg/PS ermöglicht eine Beschleunigung von 0 auf 100 in 5,8 sec.

Höchstgeschwindigkeit 245 km/h.

Ein Frontspoiler sowie ein augenfälliger Heckspoiler verbessern den Anpreßdruck der Räder und die Richtungsstabilität des Wagens.

Der Porsche Carrera bringt damit beste Voraussetzungen für den sportlichen Einsatz mit. Aber auch auf der Straße kann er sich sehen lassen. Der elastische Motor ermöglicht problemloses Fahren selbst im Stadtverkehr. Ein 85 Liter-Tank gibt ihm einen großen Aktionsradius. Zudem kann der Carrera wie alle Porsche mit Normalbenzin gefahren werden.

Einen Porsche wie den Carrera gibt es nicht alle Tage. Und 500 Stück sind nicht viel. Sie mussen also schon sehr schnell sein, wenn Sie ihn fahren möchten. Es sei denn, Sie interessieren sich für die weiter verfeinerten und verbesserten Porsche 911 T, E und S: Deutschlands erfolgreichste Sportwagen.

PORSCHE

VW Porsche Vertriebsgesellschaft mbH, 714 Ludwigsburg, Postfach 1108

Die Dr.-Ing. h. c. F. Porsche KG. hat mit dem Typ 901 ein wirtschaftliches und schnelles Automobil geschaffen, das unter Berücksichtigung der typischen Porsche-Linie alle Vorzüge der bewährten 356-Modelle und die langjährigen Erfahrungen seiner Konstrukteure und Versuchsingenieure in sich vereint. Es rundet das gegenwärtige Verkaufs-Programm nach oben ab. Im Gewicht und Temperament dem Carrera 2000 GS ebenbürtig, in den Endgeschwindigkeitswerten ihn noch übertreffend, wird der Typ 901 die alte Porsche-Formel „Fahren in seiner schönsten Form" von neuem beweisen. Dieses Modell stellt ein Optimum an Fahrkomfort, Straßenlage und Fahrsicherheit dar, wie es der anspruchsvolle Porsche-Kunde seit Erscheinen des ersten Porsche-Wagens gewöhnt war.

Der Motor ist ein luftgekühlter 6-Zylinder-Boxer-Motor mit je einer obenliegenden Nockenwelle, bei dessen Konstruktion die Erfahrungen der Grand-Prix- und Sportmotorenentwicklung verwertet wurden. Die Kurbelwelle ist achtfach gelagert. Für die Bauteile wurde weitgehend Leichtmetall verwendet. Konstruktiv ist der Motor so ausgelegt, daß er im Rahmen seiner Entwicklungsstufen für Sportzwecke verwendet werden kann. Die beiden Nockenwellen werden, erstmals bei Porsche, über Ketten angetrieben. Für das Fahrzeug wurde ein neues Getriebe entwickelt, welches in seiner Funktion dem bisherigen gleicht, jedoch wegen des großen Geschwindigkeitsbereiches 5 Vorwärtsgänge besitzt. Die vordere Radaufhängung und Führung erfolgt durch untenliegende Querlenker und die beiden Stoßdämpfer, die Abfederung durch längsliegende Torsionsstäbe. Aufhängung und Führung der Hinterräder werden von Längslenkern übernommen, die über querliegende Drehstäbe abgestützt sind. Der Antrieb erfolgt über Doppelgelenkwellen.

Die Lenkung arbeitet nach dem Zahnstangenprinzip und wurde vorn in der Fahrzeugmitte angeordnet. Diese Bauweise ermöglichte es, einen wesentlichen Beitrag zur inneren Sicherheit zu leisten, da durch den Einbau der Umlenkungen die Verwendung einer starren Lenksäule vermieden werden konnte. Das Fahrzeug ist an allen vier Rädern mit Scheibenbremsen ausgestattet.

Für die Karosserie ergab sich nun die Notwendigkeit, die neuen Aggregate zu einer Einheit zusammenzufassen und bei den äußeren Abmessungen, die den Typ 356 lediglich in der Länge um 120 mm übertreffen, während in der Breite eine Einsparung von 70 mm erzielt werden konnte, einen größeren Innenraum zu schaffen. Gleichzeitig wurden, den heutigen Forderungen entsprechend, größere Fensterflächen geschaffen.

Der Vordersitzraum konnte in den Innenabmessungen trotz geringerer Fahrzeugbreite vergrößert werden. Im Prinzip wurde die heutige Sitzposition, die guten Komfort bei langen Reisen bietet, übernommen. Der Fußraum hinter den Vordersitzen wurde um etwa 6 cm verlängert. Zur Erleichterung bei Instandsetzungsarbeiten können die vorderen Kotflügel ausgewechselt werden. Um bei der Belüftung des Fahrgastraumes den heutigen Ansprüchen gerecht zu werden, wurde der Lösung dieser Frage besondere Aufmerksamkeit geschenkt. Unter der Vorderhaube ist reichlich Raum für die Unterbringung von Koffern und sonstigen Gepäckstücken.

901

Technische Daten

Motor	
Zylinderzahl	6
Bohrung	80 mm
Hub	66 mm
Hubraum tatsächlich	1991 cm³
Verdichtungsverhältnis	9 : 1
Leistung	130 PS (DIN) bei 6200 U/min
Höchstes Drehmoment	16,5 mkg bei 4600 U/min
Literleistung	65 PS/l
Motorkonstruktion	
Bauart	Viertakt-Vergasermotor mit je drei sich gegenüberliegenden Zylindern (Boxer)
Kühlung	Luftkühlung
Kurbelgehäuse	Leichtmetall
Zylinder	Grauguß
Zylinderkopf	Leichtmetall
Anzahl der Ventile (je Zylinder)	1 Einlaßventil 1 Auslaßventil
Anordnung der Ventile	hängend V-förmig
Nockenwelle	im Zylinderkopf, obenliegend
Ventilsteuerung	über Kipphebel
Nockenwellenantrieb	Kettentrieb
Kurbelwelle	geschmiedet, 8 Gleitlager
Pleuellager	Gleitlager
Gebläseantrieb	Keilriemen
Schmierung	Trockensumpfschmierung (getrennter Öltank) mit Saug- und Druckpumpe, Ölkühler und Ölfeinfilter im Hauptstrom
Kraftstoff-Förderung	elektrische Kraftstoffpumpe
Elektrische Anlage	12 Volt Batterie 45 Ah
Entstörgrad	fernentstört nach VDE 0879 Teil 1
Lichtmaschine	360 W strom- und spannungsgeregelt
Zündung	Batteriezündung
Kraftübertragung	
Lage des Motors im Fahrzeug	Heck hinter der Hinterachse
Kupplung	Einscheiben-Trockenkupplung
Schaltgetriebe	Porsche Sperrsynchrongetriebe
Anzahl der Gänge	5 vorwärts, 1 rückwärts
Synchronisierte Gänge	1 bis 5
Schalthebel Anordnung	neben dem Fahrersitz
Achsantrieb	spiralverzahntes Kegelradgetriebe mit Kegelradausgleichgetriebe oder Sperrdifferential
Achsenübersetzung	7 : 31, i = 4,428
Übersetzungsverhältnis	(siehe nachstehende Aufstellung)
Fahrgestell, Radaufhängung	
[illegible]	
Vorderradaufhängung	Einzelradaufhängung an Querlenker und Geradeführungen
Vorderradfederung	durch Drehfederstäbe und Gummihohlfedern
Hinterradaufhängung	Einzelradaufhängung an Längslenkern
Hinterradfederung	durch Drehfederstäbe und Gummihohlfedern
Stoßdämpfer	vorn und hinten doppelwirkende hydraulische Teleskopstoßdämpfer
Fußbremse	Scheibenbremse hydraulisch auf alle 4 Räder wirkend
Handbremse	mechanisch auf die Hinterräder wirkend
Wirksamer Bremsscheiben Ø vorn	227 mm
hinten	243 mm
Bremsbelagfläche je Rad vorn	52,5 cm²
hinten	40,0 cm²
Wirksame Bremsfläche ges.	185 cm²
Handbrems-Trommel Ø	180 mm
Wirksame Bremsfläche ges.	194 cm²
Reifen	165–15 Gürtel
Felgen	4½ J x 15
Lenkung	Zahnstangenlenkung, Lenkungsdämpfer, Sicherheitslenksäule
Lenkübersetzung	1 : 17
Tankinhalt	ca. 68 ltr.
Fahrleistungen	
Höchstgeschwindigkeit	ca. 210 km/h
Leistungsgewicht (fahrbereit)	7,7 kg/PS
Kraftstoffverbrauch	11–14 ltr./100 km
Beschleunigungszeit von 0–100	9,1 sec.
von 0–160	21,9 sec.
Fahrzeit für 1 km	29,9 sec. bei stehendem Start
für 400 m	16,4 sec.
Abmessungen	
Radstand	2204 mm
[illegible]	1272 mm
Spurweite hinten	1312 mm
Länge	4135 mm
Breite	1600 mm
Höhe	1273 mm
Bodenfreiheit	118 mm
Wendekreis	10 m
Getriebe-Übersetzungen	
5-Ganggetriebe	1. Gang (11 : 34) i = 3,09 2. Gang (18 : 34) i = 1,89 3. Gang (22 : 29) i = 1,32 4. Gang (26 : 26) i = 1,0 5. Gang (29 : 22) i = 0,758 Weitere Zahnradpaarungen sind lieferbar.

Sonderdruck anläßlich „30 Jahre Porsche 911"

W 221 Printed in Germany Änderungen vorbehalten August 1963

An equally important and formative clientele in the early years were the aristocrats. The first international rally triumph in the form of a double-victory at the Mid-Summer Rally in Sweden was secured by two blue-blooded teams. Prince Joachim zu Fürstenberg won with Count Berckheim, and Prince Fritzi zu Fürstenberg was second with Count Hardenberg. The next victories went to Huschke von Hanstein, Paul von Guillaume, and Count von der Mühle. There is a photograph of the latter two in front of their silver 356 with short trousers, tight T-shirts, silk scarves, and gaunt torsos. Their appearance and physique are more reminiscent of Bohemian society and the university than the mansion or castle. In the Porsche the aristocracy showed its modern face. On the other side were gentlemen such as Huschke von Hanstein, style icons who lent the sporting nonchalance of the Porsche a cosmopolitanism that was somewhat underrepresented among the Swabian engineers.

Porsche also embodied a decidedly analog mechanization of the noble activity of horse riding. The thin civilizing shell, especially in the cabriolet, provided a romantic experience of a nature similar to that of horseback. This is also how Donald von Frankenberg described it in his reminiscences of his father Richard: "The German nobility was running out of horses. The Gotha [genealogical directory of the nobility] drove the 356;" it was also the title he gave to the small chapter on the predilection for Porsche of the nobility, who, almost without exception, used their sports cars for racing. The down-to-earth test driver at the Stuttgart factory, Hans Herrmann, recalls that at Porsche it sometimes looked like a club for the nobility.

The Porsche 356 was an unpretentious sports car. According to Ferry Porsche, the company would never have been so successful without its aristocratic "VIPs," as he called them. His sense of pride at the royal buyers shines through in his memoirs. That the Egyptian Prince Abd el-Moneim bought one of the first lightweight metal coupes in 1949 was as much a source of delight as the allegiance of aristocratic male drivers such as Prince Bertil of Sweden and Prince Paul von Metternich-Winneburg.

The Ruhr nobility also loved Porsche. Every year, beginning in 1952, Alfried Krupp von Bohlen und Halbach bought the latest Porsche model, which considering his size and that of his

bank account, appeared rather modest. That Krupp preferred to drive his little runabout, instead of being chauffeured in a stretch limousine from Daimler — as was more appropriate to his stature — fitted well to this type of businessman, as well as an age in which Germans attempted, without too much fuss and by virtue of the work of their hands, to forget the disgrace of the Nazi barbarism and the two world wars they were to blame for. The journalist Wolfgang Mache reported that from his manager's office on the third floor Krupp had an unobstructed view of parking space no. 1, where a Porsche with the number plate E-RZ was parked. His last purchase, as Ferry remembers with sadness, was a 911 with the number plate E-RZ 3. For Ferry Porsche there was only one famous woman who enjoyed the same status as these noble individuals: Madame Claude Pompidou. She first purchased a 356, then a 911, before her husband became president. As a result of this passion the president at the time made an unusual confession to Ferry Porsche at the Paris Motor Show. "Monsieur, we are actually old friends. My wife has driven two of your fabulous cars!"

Apart from social privilege, was there another common denominator? If one believes the historical documents, then it was the body mass index. The customers' lean and wiry physiques found their mechanical counterpart in the vehicle's light frame. According to the writer and 911 driver Ralf Bönt, "What definitely doesn't work is a pot-belly in a 911." For Bönt the 911 contains an aesthetic and ethical imperative: "Driver and car must be tailored to one another."

The first Porsche customers recognized themselves in the car's understated muscularity. The biopolitics of the sports car privileges light, wiry people. As a rule racing drivers are significantly smaller than the average. A sports car is generally an imposition for overweight people. That applied to the Porsche 356, and, to an extent, still applies to the 911. Although positively spacious compared to a two-seater like the 550 Spyder, the idea of a compact, lightweight sports car also places limits on the physique of the driver and front passenger — not to mention the children on the jump seats. For anyone who cultivates a fetish for lightweight construction like Ferdinand Piëch, being overweight is virtually intolerable on psychological grounds alone. On top of this comes the definition of the Porsche as a sports car, which, especially in the early years, was essentially a racing vehicle. And as the sports cars of this time lacked any kind of driving assistance system, motorsport was grueling in the extreme.

While prosperity in Germany, as in the West as a whole, spread rapidly in the 1950s, and along with it the emergence of the affluence belly and double chin as status symbols of a life of pleasure, Porsche projected quite a different picture of itself and its customers, which was also embodied in the representatives of the Porsche family. Neither Ferry nor his sons, nor the ascetic-looking Ferdinand Piëch, display the slightest signs of the corpulence that comes with affluence. The aristocratic racing drivers and company representatives who gave the make its public face, such as Huschke von Hanstein or Richard von Frankenberg, also exuded chivalric elegance — despite all their differences. Huschke von Hanstein had been an enthusiastic Nazi and member of the SS, and as a racing driver had prominently displayed their runes on his BMWs. Von Frankenberg was the son of a Jewish writer who was sentenced to death by the Nazis in 1945, but succeeded in fleeing to England at the last minute. With his reckless driving style and frequent, sometimes terrible accidents, Frankenberg, nicknamed Schreckensteiner, had his place in Porsche's pantheon of heroes, which, despite the brand's popularization, helped preserve its careening, core intensity. A self-cultivated athleticism was also an integral part of the image of the speeding aristocrats. Porsche was an exercise machine for the existential arts in the spirit of the French philosopher Michel Foucault. Himself a sports car driver, Foucault championed the idea of life as a work striving for style and beauty, a philosophy that can also be read autobiographically — including its motorized aspects — as a form of individualized, liberatory gesture, an emancipation from the biopolitics of fatuous standardization.

Porsche's customer base was soon joined by mavericks and eccentrics. From an early age James Dean combined his lust for freedom with a motorized need for speed. The actor's pop existentialism, his restless melancholy, found its objectification in the two Porsches he bought in the year of his death. The Dean myth was an accelerated death wish that found its all-too-fitting end in an accident on the way to a motor race. However, careful investigations revealed that James Dean did not ram the 23-year-old Donald Turnupseed's Ford indiscriminately, or even wantonly. Instead, Turnupseed had taken his right of way on that twilit stretch of the California State Route. Turnupseed didn't see Dean's Porsche coming, as he later explained. This in turn contributed to the Porsche myth. The 550 Spyder was a compact, flat car and relatively small compared to the American steel-plate colossi of the time. On top of that, Dean had not turned on his headlights. Dean smashed into the Ford without braking, the front passenger Rolf Wütherich, the Porsche mechanic, broke his legs and jaw. James Dean died at the site of the accident. The photo of the shattered 550 went around the world, proclaiming the vulnerability of the speed merchant when journeying in such a fragile, and for the time, high-powered vehicle. However, Dean's speed at the time of the accident was anything but suicidal. He was driving between 89 and 97 km/h (55–60 mph).

The first Porsche customers recognized themselves in the car's understated muscularity. The biopolitics of the sports car privileges light, wiry people.

« Richard von Frankenberg and his cars: a 645 Spyder "Micky Maus" on the Avus, the first racetrack in Germany, in 1956 (↑) and a Porsche 550 Spyder at Le Mans 1955 (↓).

Everyday mythology transformed the accident into a variant of Russian roulette. His last words have been passed down to us as "He's got to see us," an expression of the stubborn-headedness of a Hollywood star who could drive directors livid with rage. On the rear engine hood, directly beneath the Porsche lettering, painted in cursive writing, stood "Little Bastard," Dean's nickname on the set of *Giant*.

With this existentialist cowboy and cinematic rebel, Porsche succeeded in enlisting the individualist-anarchistic hedonists and self-promoters in its cause. They appeared to be people who found it hard fitting in, or were outright nonconformists. Nevertheless, with Porsche they discovered their own make, which radiated both the kudos of the established and the spirit of rebellion. Shortly before the fiftieth anniversary of the Porsche 911, that which began with James Dean and ended in catastrophe with Andreas Baader found its expression in the hymn of a bald-headed, 150 kg (330 lb.) gangster rapper with full body tattoos named Rick Ross, who saw Porsche as a symbol of life according to the "survival of the fittest." The song "911" was released in 2012, and its video, which looks like an Afro-American paraphrase of an otherwise rather white Porsche advertising strategy, describes a lifestyle of limitless freedom along with the associated sense of having made it — albeit an "it" that agitates, intensifies, and sharpens one's own inner disquiet, the inner motor, the restless drive. For Rick Ross, 911 is the number of the devil, of the inner demons struggling for status, recognition, supremacy, and lawless pleasure. The 911 is transformed into a weapon wielded by gangster rappers to keep their own appetite for risk alive.

The Long Road to the 911

When Ferdinand Alexander Porsche entered the family business in 1958 he filled a gap that up until then had not even been recognized as such. A designer appeared—in a very Protestant fashion—to be more of a cost factor than a money earner. Thus, Ferdinand Alexander began his design work in the engineering office as an exoticism. However, because he had spent his childhood in, on, or next to Porsches, knew the factory like his nursery, and received a great deal of knowledge from his father, the young man didn't remain an outsider for long and was quickly taken seriously. His brother Wolfgang, who as a pupil at a boarding school could only take part in the discussions at the weekends, related how there was no such thing as closing time for the Porsche family—especially when it came to replacing the 356 without upsetting the stalwarts. Maybe it was the socialization in that familial excellence cluster that enabled a man of just 27 to design a car that would appear to so effortlessly outlive its creator: the Porsche 911.

It is both an epochal break and a smooth transition from the 356 to the 911. If the father's legacy were to be given human form, then one could say that the 911 is the more athletic, better-built son of the 356, though the similarity to the father is still clear to see. The sloping back, the rounded rear window, and the circular headlights on the convex fenders—features which Susanne Porsche termed the Ferry style.

Ferdinand Alexander grew up a free individual. While the family suffered under the grandfather's temperament, his son Ferry preferred a quieter, gentler parental style. Unlike the plumber's son Ferdinand, Ferry was no proud self-made man, but the junior manager of a prospering family company. This position gave him a natural aplomb, which the father, continually struggling for recognition, could never have. On the Saturdays when there was no school, Ferry drove his sons to the factory to inspect the production of the sports cars. In a mixture of family and works outings, the Porsches' heritage and legacy was continually celebrated and cultivated. As is the case with all family companies, sustained success was only conceivable if the generational bond remained intact: if the children and grandchildren were infected with a passion for the work of their parents and grandparents from an early age. The pictures from the family album often show the children in the proximity of cars, engines, and Vespa scooters. The garage frequently replaced the living room. For Ferry it was similar, accompanying his father to motor races as a young boy to watch his creations compete. Ferdinand Alexander had a sense of what would be expected of him as the first-born and went his own way at an early age—which his father also tolerated. He attended an independent Waldorf school in Stuttgart from where he transferred to the Ulm School of Design, a style-defining institute that set out to continue the bauhaus legacy in post-war Germany. He only stayed for two semesters, after which he had seen enough. Not that the ever-courteous "F. A.", as he was called, would have ever said it, but there was little he found challenging

» A dramatic display at the Max Hoffman showrooms designed by Frank Lloyd Wright on New York's Park Avenue around 1954/55.

» Ferry Porsche with his son Ferdinand Alexander in the Zuffenhausen factory yard in 1964.

« The interior of a functionalist manifesto: the dashboard of a slate-gray 1958 Porsche 356A.

among the design purists compared with what he knew from his grandfather's or father's engineering and R&D offices.

Porsche was a company without designers. The self-confident engineers considered it superficial and something of a luxury to think about design. The first Porsche, the 356, was a functionalist manifesto. The first prestigious Porsche sales room on Park Avenue in New York was designed by the elderly Frank Lloyd Wright, whose final works also included a house for the Porsche importer Max Hoffmann built at the gates of New York. In pictures featuring a Porsche in front of Wright's late work, the colors and forms of both house and sports car appear related. They were messengers of a new age that had already begun and whose victory was imminent.

It is part of the self-image of Porsche that it cannot tolerate being overtaken anywhere by anything: whether on the fast lane of the freeway, at the start of a race, or while performing a bold parking maneuver in front of the opera.

« A prototype Porsche 530 four-seater from circa 1952/53 (↑), and a Porsche Type 695 being configured in the Zuffenhausen design department (↓).

The aerodynamics, the lightweight material, and the maximum economy in the dimensioning of the vehicle had shaped the design. When Ferdinand Porsche, known in the family as Butzi, began working in Zuffenhausen, Erwin Komenda was the recognized authority when it came to bodywork construction. Three years previously Ferry Porsche had promoted him to chief engineer, so it appeared natural enough to the sober-minded man in his mid-fifties that he would be responsible for the form of the 356's successor. Since the end of the 1950s it had been clear that the small, lightweight sports car, directly descended from the Beetle, had reached the end of the road technically. A completely new car was needed with more room, more power, and more contemporary technology. At the end of the 1950s there were faster cars on the freeway. An unacceptable thought, not just for Ferry Porsche, but also for the small, sworn circle of Porsche drivers who back then still greeted each other with hand or blinker signals and had begun to organize themselves into Porsche clubs. It is part of the self-image of Porsche that it cannot tolerate being overtaken anywhere by anything: whether that is on the fast lane of the freeway, at the start of a race, or while performing a bold parking maneuver in front of the opera.

Back in 1951 Erwin Komenda had designed a four-seater version of the 356. In a somewhat brutal fashion he extended the wheelbase of the delicate sports car by 30 cm (12 in.) and exchanged the previously compact doors with massively proportioned versions, enabling future passengers to comfortably climb into the coupe's rear compartment. The experiment was called type 530 and lacked the charm of minimalist sculpture. The creature looked bulky and erratic. Furthermore, the car was too heavy for the souped-up four-cylinder. The idea of putting it into serial production was dismissed out of hand. However, the question of whether a new Porsche should be a full-blown four-seater or a smaller 2+2 remained open. Ferry Porsche was uncertain on this issue for some time. During the entire second half of the 1950s Ferry Porsche commissioned designs that allowed for sufficient seating comfort in the rear as well as a larger trunk. When one looks back at these false starts it becomes apparent just how uncertain Porsche's future was at the time.

The quasi-natural evolution of the 356 from the Beetle threatened to become a dead end, an automotive cul-de-sac without a living heir. The bodywork manufacturers, Reutter in Stuttgart and Beutler in Thun, Switzerland, received contracts to construct elongated 356s. After the designs and suggestions from these companies failed to produce any convincing results, Ferry Porsche invited the "hippest" car designer of the time, Count Albrecht von Goertz, to design the new Porsche. This was also a capitulation to the zeitgeist, that demanded flamboyant designs and a break with the autopoiesis of Porsche's non-design. With the BMW 507, presented at the IAA in 1955, Count Goertz had created a roadster that set new standards in the combination of elegance and sportiness. With its 150 hp, eight-cylinder engine, and its gentle, Mediterranean forms, the BMW was a serious rival to the 356, which in comparison looked almost dainty. Heady with success, Count Goertz designed a prestigious, muscular sports car for the Zuffenhausen-based company that was more reminiscent of a Ferrari or a Maserati. At the front the car was fitted with hyper-thyroidal double headlights while the rear was lit up by six small flashing lights. In addition there were massive, by Porsche standards, almost baroque bumpers. What Count Goertz presented, in a rather theatrical form, was the glitter and glamour of the 1950s, and for this reason it was rejected by the down-to-earth Porsches. The aristocrat, who worked for Raymond Loewy in New York after the war, had designed a "very beautiful car;" nevertheless, Louise Piëch and Ferry Porsche were in agreement: it was a Goertz, but not a Porsche.

The Goertzian design was in love with the grand gesture. The same year Roland Barthes declared the car to be the equivalent of the great Gothic cathedrals, and in his popular and shamelessly cited work *Mythologies,* considered it a major creation of the epoch, passionately conceived by numerous nameless artists. In the style of pop art, Barthes enacted an intellectual and cultural upgrading of the automobile, without the hyper-modern pathos of the futurists. The Citroën DS—automotive darling of the French post-structuralists—with the pompous nickname Déesse, meaning goddess, offered such bold theses a generously dimensioned sounding board. As if descended from heaven, it appeared to the poet as a superlative object: completely new and without origin, slick, science fiction. The DS, with its streamlined bodywork and hydropneumatic suspension, was without doubt an innovative car; however, it was innovative in a brash, comparatively obvious fashion. Like Goertz's design, there was something theatrical about the way this Citroën paraded its inner and outer qualities. "NEW" was written above both of them in huge, brightly lit letters. It was the antithesis of the compact functionalism and traditionalism of Porsche. The idea that innovation and the new were dependent on a gift from heaven appeared absurd to the mechanics in Zuffenhausen and the Porsche family. Naturally every innovation has a prehistory and a Porsche should always reflect the tradition of innovative work that has gone into its making.

What Count Goertz presented, in a rather theatrical form, was the glitter and glamour of the 1950s, and for this reason it was rejected by the down-to-earth Porsches.

« The development of the Count Goertz-designed Porsche Type 695 in February 1958.
⇑ Porsche's designers Willi Vetter, Karl Vettel, Georg Urbanczik, Rudi Maier, and Walter Huettich in 1958.

In his memoirs Count Goertz took things lightly. "I asked myself whether I hadn't been given the wrong instructions—but when

The 911 began as a coupe whose road presence would exude a natural functionality and confidence derived from its performance. (The Porsche didn't need to, and didn't want to prove anything to anybody.)

» The Type 754 T7 in 1961/62 (↑). The car was conceptualized by F.A. Porsche and became the framework for the 911's design (↓).

was a briefing ever perfect?" He risked a second design, christened "Junior," so that Porsche ended up rejecting two of Goertz's ideas—"and that was the end of my collaboration with Porsche," as the nobleman concluded, almost amused. Nevertheless, he remained on good terms with the Porsches privately, even claiming to have lured Ferdinand Alexander Porsche into the family business from the Ulm School of Design.

At the age of 22 Ferdinand Alexander Porsche, encouraged in his free creativity by the Waldorf school, entered Erwin Komenda's design department. As well-known as Count Goertz may have been, the ultimate authority in the department was Komenda, but not for long. Ferdinand Alexander had completed a two-year internship at Bosch before starting his studies in Ulm, so he had no problems tackling design concepts dominated by technical issues. On the contrary, the young man had a sense that he would encounter the aesthetic functionalism of the Ulm school in its purest form in Porsche's engineering offices. Furthermore, the intellectualism and theorizing cultivated in Ulm was not his thing anyway. He wanted to create, not talk. A colleague from the model department named Heinrich Klie suggested a few details during the preliminary work that Ferdinand Alexander could build on, and he intended to. They concerned the relatively high fenders compared to the 356 and the integrated headlights, as well as the austere chrome strip on the front hood. The young Porsche grandchild was not only confident enough to use the department's preliminary work, but also the employees. Thanks to his familiarity with these people and their work, an intimacy that he had shared since childhood, he had a certain natural affection for them. They worked in his family's company and were thus somehow part of the clan. At any rate this feeling of intimacy and trust was something cultivated by the father, Ferry Porsche. For Ferdinand and Ferry Porsche the employees were "their people, members of their family," recalls Herbert Linge who was awarded his apprenticeship by Professor Porsche personally and remained loyal to the company until his retirement.

There came a point when Ferry, who had brooded and puzzled over the definition of the 356's successor for a long time, recognized to his horror that the road to more room led away from the recently established myth of the compact and light sports car. For Ferry Porsche it was clear that "We occupy a very nice niche," and that others are better at producing limousines, which is why he decided to hone Porsche's freshly acquired core-competence. His son understood him instinctively and the most clearly of all. Ferdinand Alexander's type 754 T7 was produced in the space of a few weeks between the end of August and the beginning of October 1959. At the time the "designer" was not even 24-years-old. The front section was almost identical to the later serial version of the first 911s. As the T7 was still mounted on a four-seater chassis, the silhouette still lacked the compactness and the rear the elegance of the later 911. However, this quickly changed.

Ferry Porsche was happy and not a little proud of his son's design. However, he had the feeling that the young man and his design weren't taken seriously by everyone in the bodywork department. In his memoirs he described it idiosyncratically as an undesirable development that came from the offices—against his will. His employees justified the fact that the car was getting bigger and heavier with platitudes such as "The whole of humanity is getting bigger, the car has to be bigger too."

After countless discussions the wheelbase was reduced by 10 cm (4 in.) again. This lent the Porsche more harmonious proportions. In addition, the bulky protrusion on the tail, designed to give rear passengers more headroom, disappeared. Porsche relinquished the idea of a sports car that provided travel comfort or even an acceptable seating position for four adults. Finally, Ferdinand Alexander was commissioned to design a coupe on the basis of the T7, which, instead of containing four seats ,would provide just two proper seats and two jump seats. The new Porsche was to be powered by an air-cooled, six-cylinder motor with overhead camshaft, and have the road performance of the 356 Carrera 2, which extracted 130 hp from the four-cylinder boxer engine and had a top speed of 210 km/h (130 mph).

The T8 was developed, and Ferdinand Porsche enlisted two technicians into his team to prevent the designs lapsing into the artistic. The humility of the son in the face of the engineering spirit of his father and grandfather was not reverential but constructive. He made the engineers his allies in the development of the design ideas. In his excellent history of the 901, Jürgen Lewandowski describes how the door was always open between the design and development departments. The result quickly proved worth seeing. It was the first Porsche 911—the form had been found. The model already had the side window architecture

that has remained to this day. The roofline had found its proportions, the relationship between the raised fenders and hood had been established. This topography above the hood dramatized the tendencies that could already be detected in the profile of the 356. Now the lamps had become gun barrels, as the designers in Weissach say, or that décolleté which makes the hearts of millions of men—and also women—beat faster. The forms were gentle and the car's face was benevolent. The 911 dispensed with an aggressive aesthetic and began as a coupe whose road presence would exude a natural functionality and confidence derived from its performance. The Porsche didn't need and didn't want to prove anything to anybody. Following the completion of the first model, the work merely consisted of refining a successful form, which, no one could have predicted at the time, would endure for over half a century. The first one-to-one model followed a short while later, constructed from wood and sheet metal. It was presented to the management board on April 16, 1962, and accepted. The same year the first prototype in the form of the 901-1 was built. The collaboration between father and son had born fruit. "Back then," recalled Ferdinand Alexander Porsche, "when I was constructing the 911, he stood right behind me from the beginning. Not because I was his son, but because he was convinced. He always had a highly developed sense of form; he never liked extreme colors and forms." Father and son looked at the 911 and both saw themselves in it. An ideal case for a family business.

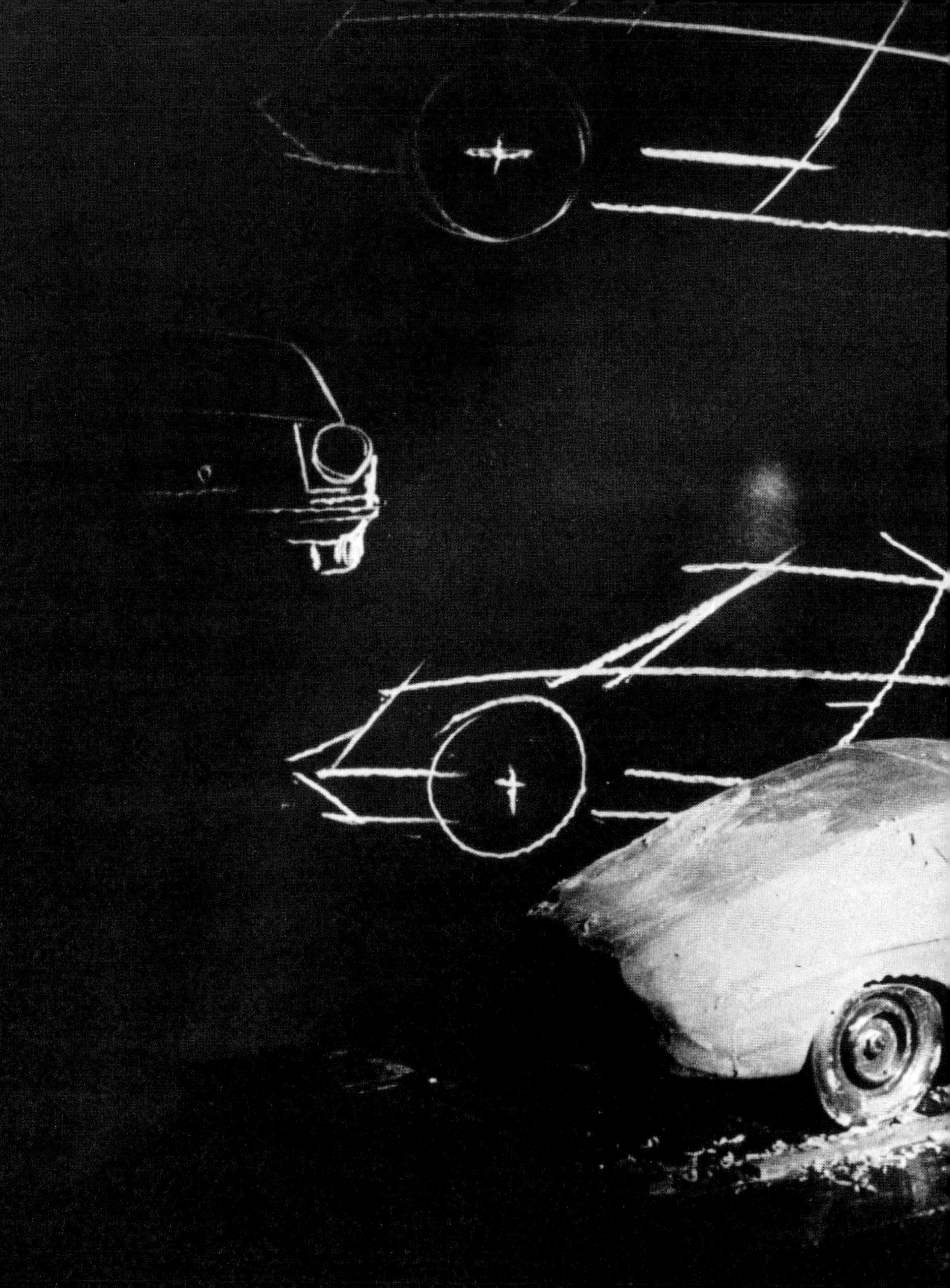

« Ferdinand Alexander Porsche working on a model of the Type 911 in 1968.

The Ideal Form

With his design, Ferdinand Alexander brought the Porsche tradition in tune with the design ethos of the time, something that remained largely hidden to the other German car manufacturers. It was an ideal generation change: the most important product was designed by the youngest operationally active representative of the clan. Ferdinand Alexander Porsche appeared to be a very fastidious child of his time. At around the same time Dieter Rams, his senior by just two years, designed his first objects for Braun. The radio-record player combination with the technical name SK 4, known colloquially as "Snow White's Coffin," was a masterpiece of minimalist elegance, which, when unveiled in 1956, changed product design in Germany.

This reductionism was less an appendix to bauhaus than a prelude to minimalism that emerged at the beginning of the 1960s in art, music, and architecture as an antidote to abstract realism, the twelve-tone principle, and gaunt functionalism.

Looking back, Rams defined 10 theses for a good design, which the Porsche 911 fulfilled almost as a matter of course. Good design must be innovative and make a product usable. It should be aesthetic and make a product understandable. In the case of the 911 this was exemplified by the contouring of the rear as the site of the motor and the power transmission to the road. The bold, voluptuous, and muscular tail of the 911 was the ideal sculpture for a rear-engine car. Good design must be unobtrusive and elegant. This meant the avoidance of all kinds of showiness, which would only disappoint serious customers. The Porsche should not appear more innovative (see DS), more powerful (see Goertz's design), or precious (see DS and Goertz) than it was in reality. Good design has to be durable, rigorously conceived down to the last detail, environmentally friendly, and as little "Design" as possible. With these brief and clever theses Rams described the essence of the 911's form. The last point was especially important to Ferdinand Alexander Porsche. Less design is more, Rams concluded; it enables one to concentrate on the essentials instead of weighing down the product with superfluities.

It is for this reason that the Porsche 911 is a favorite car of architects, designers, and artists. The 911 calmly resists the urge to design. In a mysterious way it is as neutral as it is emotional, both functional and elegant. If one asks children to sketch a Porsche they generally produce a 911. Why? Because this car is a contemporary development of the childlike features of the Beetle and the noble simplicity of the 356, coolly and rigorously communicating the power under the bodywork without a trace of humor. Less affected than a house by Adolf Loos,[5] the 911 declares from the start, in accessible language, that ornament is a crime—at least when it comes to making cars. That was a radical counter-concept at a time when limousines had wings, sports cars had gull-wing doors, and American runabouts had metallic outgrowths. The 911 was a contemporary of Braun design and the Chancellor's Bungalow by

[5] Austrian and Czech architect and theorist famed for his essay *Ornament and Crime*, which argued for clean surfaces in opposition to the decorative art nouveau of the time. Paved the way for the bauhaus school.

Sports cars, and especially Porsches, were luxury items, constructed and sold in the spirit of a refined modesty. Anyone looking for something brasher would have to turn to the Italian or English competition.

» Ferry Porsche (right) with race engineer Wilhelm Hild (center) and race mechanic Hubert Mimler in Zuffenhausen, 1955.

Sep Ruf.[6] For a designer such as Otl Aicher the 911 was like a form of futuristic sculpture. "It is also in motion when stationary," stated Aicher.

One of the reasons for the success of Porsche in a post-war Germany attuned to equality and moderation was its gentle aesthetic distinction. Sports cars, and especially Porsches, were luxury items, but they were constructed and sold in the spirit of a refined modesty. Anyone looking for something brasher would have to turn to the Italian or English competition. The Porsche was a product of Rhenish capitalism and social partnership. In this respect it was a socially compatible vehicle from the outset: it announced that the country's wealthy elite valued the functionalist ideals of the majority as highly as the gesture of humility and modesty so central to the postwar federal republic. Anyone wanting to loudly proclaim social difference would not be happy with the 911.

Porsche did very little advertising. Ferry Porsche decided that outstanding motor racing achievements were the best form of advertising. In this respect, performance was the only marketing that Porsche was interested in. The 911 was less concerned with generating a furor with pomp or grandiloquence than convincing through its technical brilliance. It was about being and not appearance—effectively an affront to every designer.

But not for Ferdinand Alexander Porsche, who also tended to be self-effacing and unostentatious in his personal dealings. Privately the stoic was also a friend of moderation. Like his father he married his childhood sweetheart and remained, if one believes the reports about the couple, happy. Like his father and grandfather before him he stayed faithful to his Southern German-Austrian homeland. Ferdinand Alexander Porsche cultivated an unassuming biography and lifestyle. He despised fashions. That fits to his work—as well as the social compatibility of his designs. He didn't live in a parallel universe like many other designers who had lost contact with people's everyday lives.

The appearance of the 911, its design, contained a compelling logic. Everything was where it belonged. Nothing was added for the sake of show or for design reasons. It was a classic modernist car on the road, fitting to an international style. A serious car, as the designer Peter Schmidt emphasized. He suspected that no one smiled during the design of this sports car. While the German art of engineering as manifested in Miele washing machines and Braun shavers was sometimes a little boring, the 911 was more keenly formulated. The neutrality that Ferdinand Alexander Porsche aspired to resulted in a clear design that served as an ideal projection screen. With its emotional asceticism, Porsche was in keeping with the times. The idea that the observer constructs the object of desire in the act of observation rose to prominence within cultural theory. If the object offers a clear form, then the observer can easily construct this object, resulting in a special emotional connection. However, the case was different with sports cars such as those from Pininfarina, which were equipped with over two dozen finely designed details, all of which absorbed the observer's concentration, and thus their ability to construct this object of desire.

From the outset the 911 offered a balanced mixture of a memorable form and a large projection surface. Porsche's goal of a harmonious bodywork lent the form a naturalism, even though its dynamic elegance betrayed a certain audacity. In contrast to the German cliché of plush snugness as the preferred environment for Teutonic happiness, this car, despite its close confines, was no cozy domicile. The interior styling was cool. For many prospective buyers, its refinement was even a little too cold.

The social acceptance of the 911, its popularity, even among those who generally cultivate feelings of envy, was due to the young designer's avoidance of obscenities in his products. Another reason was to be found in the family business' not infrequent, deep-rooted sense of responsibility for the welfare of its own employees. This was not just lived out on an everyday basis when Ferry Porsche shook the oil-smeared hands of his employees and asked them how they were doing. It was also apparent in the unusually generous social benefits. Above and beyond government and wage agreements, the company paid the equivalent of an extra month's wages in bonuses and treated employees and salaried staff completely equally. The company founder took an interest in social cohesion—in a fashion that not only allowed for differences, but treated them as an asset. According to the Stuttgart-based architect, former Porsche driver, and businessman

[6] Architect and designer in the bauhaus movement. Created the flat-roofed Chancellor's Bungalow in Bonn out of two concrete blocks, the smaller for living and the larger for official events. It was the chancellor's residence from 1963/4 to 1999.

Werner Sobek, it was a way of manufacturing "typical for small and medium-sized businesses in Baden-Württemberg" that shaped the Porsche. The high social quality of Porsche's products, the exemplary payment, training, and qualification of its employees, all contributed to the success of the 911. According to Sobek "It is the solid foundation which invisibly strengthens the make." The social quality of the 911 lends its beauty an idealistic twist. The good strives for the true and the beautiful.

The Apple designer Jonathan Ive, who hardly misses an opportunity in interviews to emphasize how impressed he is by the functional design of postwar Germany, described design as the most direct route to implanting products in the consciousness of buyers: as a dream, a promise, a vision of a more beautiful world. His predecessor at Apple, the Swabian Hartmut Esslinger, was, and remains to this day, a die-hard, self-confessed 911 driver and fan. He was also responsible for introducing Steve Jobs to the Porsche kick in the 1980s. In his employment contract Esslinger had to agree in writing that he would not drive his Porsche faster than 200 km/h, which was completely incomprehensible to Apple's lawyers in the USA, where speeds equivalent to 125 mph were only permitted on the racetrack. Naturally, as a Porsche fan Esslinger didn't keep to the agreement.

There is a well-known anecdote about Esslinger taking Steve Jobs on a high-speed drive from an appointment in Germany to Frankfurt airport. It is July 1986 and the American airforce has just bombed Libya in retaliation for the Lockerby attack and Jobs has to return to Apple's headquarters immediately. Esslinger steps on the gas and Jobs expresses his gratitude with the words:

"Thank you for showing me what a Porsche is capable of." On landing in San Francisco he rings up to confess that the flight was relatively boring compared to the furious drive in the 911. In those days Jobs also delighted in driving at speed. His 911 was black, Esslinger's white—in Apple design. Apple's functional minimalism is a relative of Porsche's no-frills design.

"A typical Porsche is there to be touched," declared Ferdinand Alexander. "It has a body. He is a she." With this statement, a challenge to gender theorists, he succinctly described the bewildering attraction of a Porsche and the markedly human-like 911. It was a powerful man in the guise of a woman. For Ralf Bönt, the 911 is more reminiscent of a big cat, regardless of whether it happens to be on a lower gear, sleepily lumbering around, or charging at full speed, greedy to be at one with the world flowing around it. The hips of the 911 are a masterpiece, declared Bönt, a passionate 911 driver. Compared to a 911 an E-type Jaguar looks like a clown's shoe, and a Ferrari like a squashed cheese grater.

Esslinger always emphasized that the designers of his generation, which also included Rams and Ferdinand Alexander Porsche, regarded "form follows function" less as a design requirement than as a fundamental design principle. The phrase was derived from an observation of nature, and from the knowledge that within this very same nature form always follows function as a matter of survival. In the words of Steve Jobs: "Design is not just what it looks like and feels like. Design is how it works." It was an evolutionary reinterpretation of the aesthetic idealism of classical modernism, which gave objects a character identical to nature. But that wasn't all: when Esslinger was designing for Apple in the 1980s, the goal was to make computers like living organisms or an extension of one's own self. Jobs' role model, together with Esslinger, was a Porsche-like design.

It should be mentioned at this point that Jobs also drove a silver 928. When Jobs withdrew from Apple he remained loyal to Porsche, and the 911 in particular. Other masterminds of the digital revolution also became Porsche customers. In 1979 the 22-year-old Bill Gates bought a Porsche 911 Turbo in metallic turquoise, and in 1988 a 959. The other Microsoft founder, Paul Allen, also chose to drive this analog product born of the basic research conducted in Weissach. As the 959 was not approved for American roads, the country's president at the time had to sign a law specially drafted to permit such exotic vehicles.

For Gates, like Jobs, "usability" defined the quality of both software and hardware. Technology requires ideal interfaces to meet the biomechanics of the human body. However, until the ideal of a total merger has been achieved, it is sufficient to think of the product and the user as a unity. The futuristic idea was that humans should adapt to technology (or in Heidegger's words, the dominance of enframing). A far more modern idea, though, was that the most innovative technical concepts should take on a biomorphic form. To this day designers at Porsche speak of the 911's shoulders and voluptuous rear, while world-weary old men light up at the sight of the latest 911. He is a muscular woman full of life. Michael Mauer, designer of the twenty-first century's Porsches, also cultivates a telltale semantics. The linguistic images employed by the wiry and humorous designer when referring to his design are anthropomorphic throughout. He speaks of the raised shoulder line, the well-proportioned rear, and the fenders' sinuous muscles.

Designers and architects like things that conform to their ethos, which unite form and function—and curate the objects in their life accordingly.

« Ferdinand Alexander Porsche looking stern behind a model of the 911 S Targa in 1968. Despite Porsche's reservations about the car's wide roll bar, the racing feature would help give the car its motorsport-inspired name.

However, the weakness of designers and architects for the 911 can also be traced to less exalted reasons than this partial human likeness. For the Munich-based designer Thomas Elsner, who has driven Porsches for decades, this sports car provides relief. "As my job requires me to think a great deal about design on a daily basis, I like to surround myself with things that have an aesthetic perfection," states Elsner, "otherwise I would be continually thinking how I could improve their form." The synthesis of the biomorphic shell and the aesthetics of reduction finds their common denominator in the 911's functionalism and essentialism. As in evolution, the successful creations are those that function—and survive.

The product's manufacturing history also corresponds to contemporary ideas of minimalism. The ancestral Porsche, as it is essentially a remix of VW parts, is a manifestation of maximum inherent necessity, or, in the words of the American artist Matthew Barney, maximum "drawing restraints." That a design of such elegance and poise could emerge from the narrow corridor of possibilities defined by manufacturing costs, functionality, and the pressures of serial production, is what Elsner describes as a classic design challenge. He also considers this one of the reasons why the 911 proves so attractive to this milieu. Designers and architects like things that conform to their ethos, which unite form and function—and curate the objects in their life accordingly.

1963
1973

» The classic *Elfer* in a vibrant shade brightened up the landscape of the 1960s.

The Classic 911

The Benchmark

The women wear dark skirts and jackets and black fur caps; their pearl necklaces glint in the spotlights along with rectangular, lacquered handbags. The men all wear dark suits, white shirts, and severe ties at the Porsche stand at the 1963 Frankfurt Motor Show. "Typ 901" is emblazoned on the license plate of the light yellow coupe, which, in the middle of September, appears like a harbinger of spring, a signal of change, of gaiety and clarity, ...

amidst the smartly-dressed manifestations of success—which makes the new sports car appear even more wayward. With narrow 165 tires, the short wheelbase, and the tight dimensions of its predecessor, the 901—from the slim bumpers and smooth wing mirrors to the modestly dimensioned exhaust pipe—was a delicate creature compared to the neo-baroque steel-plate colossi with tail fins being sold as the cars of the future at numerous other stands. Mercedes unveiled the 600, which as a Pullman was over 6 m (20 ft.) long and equipped with a 6.3 L engine with 250 hp. The 901 appeared minute, and not just in comparison: 1.60 m (5 ft. 3 in.) wide, just over 4 m (13 ft.) long, and 1.32 m (4 ft. 4 in.) high. Even in the interior the car's anti-feudalism appeared to take on a programmatic character. The brochure for the 901 featured a sparsely populated dashboard behind a filigree steering wheel—a completely unfamiliar austerity program for 911 fans: just two circular instruments, the speedometer, and the rev counter.

« A viper green 911 S 2.0 Targa camouflages into the landscape in 1967.
↓ The dashboard of the 911 T 2.4 coupe.

When the Porsche 911 was unveiled in the guise of the 901, it was far from being the undisputed star of the Frankfurt Motor Show. Mercedes launched the Pagode as the successor to both the 300 SL and the 190 SL, and Aston Martin presented one of the most elegant British sports cars of all time in the form of the DB5. Incidentally, the designer of the Pagode, Paul Bracq, was also the enthusiastic driver of a wine-red 356, and thus the Pagode was given its form by a Porsche fan. 1963 marked a civilizational leap in the history of car building. The construction and design of sports cars passed through a phase of pure beauty, ravishing formal language, and groundbreaking automotive concepts. However, what people couldn't see at the time was that car manufacture was experiencing its high renaissance. Compared to the Pagode or the DB5, the 911, at 1,080 kg (2,830 lb.), was a lightweight car. The British gran turismo weighed in at 1,465 kg (3,230 lb.); the Mercedes Benz 230 SL, just over 60 kg (132 lb.) less. Furthermore, the driving experience in a Porsche was significantly louder, more authentic, and rawer. The car presented at the 1963 Frankfurt Motor Show was a prototype that still had a long way to go before serial production. This pre-emptive strike on the part of Porsche was designed to prevent the competition from entering its market.

Thanks to its 130 hp engine the dainty 911 had a top speed of 210 km/h (130 mph). The press release described its acceleration as "quick as lightening." Porsche was forced to relinquish the name 901 because Peugeot (Peugeot again) had secured the rights to serial numbers with a zero in the middle in France. That is why only a few prototypes with the model name 901 were built. One must be thankful to Peugeot to this day when one considers how clumsy and scientific the pet name "zero one" would have sounded (*Nulleinser* rather than *Elfer* in German). "Just add a ten to it", commented Ferry dryly. With Swabian stoicism the 901 was henceforth called the 911. The reason was entirely pragmatic: the metal numerals 9 and 1 had already been produced. The 1 was simply used twice. Conspiracy theorists would point out that this abbreviation corresponded to a fateful day in German history: November 9th.[1]

Shortly before the start of serial production the instrument panel was expanded to create a backdrop, which, up until the 996, would impress every 911 driver. The arched dashboard now featured a central rev counter, a fuel gauge and oil level indicator to the left, followed by oil temperature and oil pressure ganges. To the right of the rev counter was the speedometer and on the far right the clock. The sequence of indicators from left to right followed a dramaturgy that began with the sports car's blood circulation and heart rate, and then proceeded to connect the beating of the boxer motor with the space-time continuum as expressed in speed and time. With the 911, oil temperature and pressure were monitored continually. In the case of the classic 911 it was not uncommon for the oil level to be checked mechanically at the rear every 1000 kilometers. To this day, the first thing a 911 driver does in the morning is take a look under the engine to check for oil leaks. Even the coarsest 911 driver, male or female, ensures that the 9 L of oil from the dry-sump circuit are gently warmed before they really hit the gas pedal. "Barbarians" who rev up their 911s when still cold are treated with disdain and opprobrium by the community and punished with the withdrawal of affection.

Anyone who has had the pleasure of driving one of the last fast 356s knows how faithful the classic 911 has remained to its ancestors. The myth of uncontrollability persists, although it only applies to a narrow threshold of vehicles. Otherwise these cars can be driven unbelievably fast, and thanks to their light weight—and despite the horsepower rating, meager by today's standards—are extremely agile. A rear engine gives traction, but nevertheless, up into the 1990s, the 911s were notorious for the tail breaking loose around curves and in the wet. The car oversteered dramatically, but the majority of 911 pilots transformed the initial shock at this instability into a delight in making the sports car dance. The first 911s had a terrible straightline performance. In order to balance this out, scrap metal was inserted into the corners of the bumpers, which at that time provoked a furious reaction from Ferdinand Piëch. The Belgian racing driver Paul Frère referred to the estimated 20 kg (44 lb.) of lead in the front bumper as a "not particularly elegant solution;" however it reduced the car's sensitivity to wind. In addition there was the "botch" with the suspension struts, which could not be adjusted at the top. Piëch was so incensed that Porsche's technical director had to go, allowing Piëch to personally take care of the sports car's weight distribution and balance. Despite these challenges, which were ever-present for drivers of the Porsche 911, the pleasure of piloting this sports car was enormous. There was no car tester that didn't agree.

When Porsche invited car journalists from around the world to Stuttgart at the beginning of 2013 to experience the various type series on the test track, the reporters were impressed by the driving dynamics of these, by today's standards, seemingly underpowered classic 911s. Porsche specified the acceleration time for 0–100 km/h (62 mph) as 9.1 seconds; other testers such as Paul Frère managed this in under nine seconds; and Count von Brockdorff as quick as 8.5. Even though, half a century later, every generously motorized small car is capable of similar performance statistics, the critics were impressed. For Count Brockdorff the acceleration was reminiscent of a "supersonic jet fighter," thanks not least to the barrage of noise generated by the six-cylinder boxer, which would provide the 911 with its characteristic sound from then on. The elferclassix Lounge fan website ranked the sound of the boxer no. 1 among its 50 reasons for driving a Porsche 911.

[1] This *Schicksalstag* (Fateful day) has been the date of several historic events, including *Reichspogromnacht* (also known as Night of Broken Glass) in 1938 and the fall of the Berlin Wall in 1989.

» A glimpse inside the Porsche Werk factory in Zuffenhausen: the production of the Porsche 911 2.0 coupe and the 912 coupe in 1965.

Asked what is special about the 911, drivers, co-drivers, pedestrians, aficionados, and the merely curious invariably answer that this sports car has an unmistakable sound.

To this day this sound, along with the form and the principle of the rear motor, has remained a constant, even though the car has undergone considerable changes with the uninterrupted growth in cubic capacity and the switch from air to water cooling in 1998. The source of the noise was to be found in the outside camshaft. The author and playwright Moritz Rinke recalls: "When I was a child an admirer of my mother drove down the Worpswede approach road to our house in a 911. It was dark blue and had this beautiful old form. It was love at first sight. My mother, however, stayed a while longer with my father, even though he drove a Volvo." Asked what he remembers most clearly from this magical encounter, Rinke's answer is clear: "The exciting sound of the engine. You have to imagine, virtually the only thing we heard on our farm were animal noises. Chickens, horses, dogs, and then suddenly this uniquely beautiful sound with the dark blue curves and the admirer. Later, many years later, I saw *Woyzeck* at the theatre, and when the drum major with the dark menacing voice appeared to the beating of the tattoo and stole Marie away from Woyzeck, it made me think of the Porsche that drove down our approach road."

The sound of the 911 tended to become deeper with increasing cubic capacity, though it remained almost identical until the G model. It was only with the 964 that the car acquired a completely different sound. From the moment of its market launch in 1964 the sports car was caught up in a continual process of optimization. And it was precisely because of its unmistakable character that the Porsche could be continually altered. In somewhat philosophical terms, one could say that identity and difference stood in a complex relationship to one another, that the identity allowed for a plethora of difference. The variations of the 911 looked like organic mutations of the coupe's biomorphic shell. A number of changes were virtually imperceptible from the outside. In order to appeal to the lower market segment, Porsche launched a less expensive version of the 911 in April 1965 that was fitted with a dated four-cylinder engine and christened the 912. In the serial version the dashboard lacked both a clock and a combined instrument, leaving just three circular dials. Anyone wanting the older brother's full instrument panel had to pay extra. The sports car, which from the outside was almost indistinguishable from its bigger brother, needed 13 seconds for the standard acceleration test. Due to its rather unspectacular road performance the car failed to generate much enthusiasm. In the major study on Porsche 911 drivers published in the *Spiegel* magazine in 1966, 912 drivers expressed a sense of disappointment at their Porsches' sporting virility. In contrast to the American market, the German freeway provided a hunting ground where top speeds were also decisive in determining the pecking order in the fast lane. It was only with the introduction of the 911 T as starter model that the 912 could be retired. The 911 T was equipped with a less expensive, tame six-cylinder engine generating a mere 110 hp.

"Whoever drives this Porsche over the course of decades develops an intimacy with the object that helps keep one calm even in hairy situations."

↳ Rainer Schlegelmilch, motorsport photographer

» Speeding in style: in 1968 the Porsche 911 Targa was trialed as the car for policing Austria's autobahn. This was short-lived as the cars proved too expensive and too small for the equipment.

Even more important than the launch of the 912 was the unveiling of the 911 Targa in September 1965. Alarmed by discussions about new safety standards for cabriolets in the United States, the most important market for the 911, Porsche's engineers and designers had already begun working on a completely different solution by the time the coupe was launched. A roll bar with a width of over 20 cm (8 in.) was incorporated into the design to the safety of passengers in the open-top car—without sacrificing too much of the cabriolet feeling. That was why the rear windscreen in the first models was made from plastic and equipped with a zipper for removal. Unfortunately this touching attempt to combine safety and outdoor cabriolet flair proved impractical. The "soft window" provided poor rear vision, was an open invitation for car thieves, and ultimately resulted in poorer torsional stiffness, which was problematic for such an agile car. That is why the 1970 Targas were fitted with a rear windscreen made from glass.

Understandably, Ferdinand Alexander Porsche had his reservations concerning the rather clumsy solution of the wide roll bar, not least due to the considerable disruption to the coupe's lines. However, his colleagues from sales insisted on an open-top 911, especially for the sun-worshipping buyers in the south and west of the United States market. The discussion over the new vehicle, which was neither a full-blooded convertible nor a coupe, quickly led into a pragmatic debate on a name for this body form. Harald Wagner, the national sales director, came up with the name almost in passing. At Porsche it was clear that this form of open-top car should be named after a racing track; as Le Mans and Monza were already taken, this left Targa Florio. Luckily the idea of calling the creature "Flori" was rejected. "Why don't we just call it Targa?" asked Wagner, and so the car was christened. That Targa actually means "shield" in Italian was

unknown to him at the time. This was first discovered by the advertising copywriters at Porsche, who also emphasized that its type of roll bar was used in motor racing and was commonly fitted to Grand Prix cars. Despite the casual manner in which this sports car subspecies received its name, Porsche was highly focused when it came to further development of the classic 911. In 1966 a top of the range model was launched in the form of the S model sporting 160 hp—an impressive power output requiring an engine speed of 6,600 rpm, which propelled it through the streets with its high-rev scream. In 1968 the wheelbase was extended by 5.7 cm (2¼ in.) in order to improve straight-line stability. In the process the rear fenders were made a shade wider and the wheel arches modified. Under the hood the boxer grew. In 1969 the cubic capacity was increased from 2 to 2.2 L and in 1971 was raised again to 2.4. Every increase in cubic capacity improved the pulling power and performance figures of the six-cylinder boxer, which throughout the period formed the basis for countless motor racing engines tuned to produce an output of up to 850 hp. The most spectacular serial Porsche was the Carrera RS 2.7 with 210 hp, which was so fast that the engineers had to equip it with a front and rear spoiler in the form of a ducktail. Designed as a special model for motor sport homologation, the roadworthy racing machine sold surprisingly well.

Even after almost 10 years of product optimization, the 911's technical imperfections continued to cause problems. In the early 1970s Rainer Schlegelmilch—whose car Andreas Baader would later steal—could only enjoy the top speed of his 911 S Targa for short periods. After just over two minutes the temperature rose so alarmingly that he had to take his foot off the gas immediately. Cruising speeds of 190 to 200 km/h (118 to 124 mph) were less problematic. "It is only since the introduction of water cooling that the 911 can be driven foot-to-the-floor," explained the photographer and loyal 911 driver who started driving his eleventh 911 in 2012. Schlegelmilch is aware that his opinion is not shared by all 911 fans, though: "A number of them have the feeling that the last real Porsche was the model with air-cooling." Schlegelmilch is a pragmatic representative of the 911 clan. That "touch of genius" that characterizes the 911 for Schlegelmilch is its ability to provide, over decades, a new driving experience with each model, while remaining familiar in a different way each time. Thus for 911 veterans of his ilk the car offers a feeling of complete familiarity: "Whoever drives this Porsche over the course of decades develops an intimacy with the object that helps keep one calm even in hairy situations." Furthermore, this sports car is absolutely reliable. He has never broken down in over 40 years. Consequently, this car can prove less fatiguing than a marriage.

Carrera
CH
ZH·52177

» The Porsche 911 takes a plunge in the drop test in 1966. The graphic patterns on the car helped highlight the depth of the damage.

» German cool: 911 coupes in 1968—statement cars for the man about town or the woman in the country.

SF-N 99

» The colors of a decade: a vibrant display at the Geneva Motor Show in 1973.

PORSCHE
37
INTERMECCANICA
OPEL
HALLE
3
Motors
VW-PORSCHE
914 2.0
Carrera
PORSCHE
Carrera RS

» Porsche Targa featuring a removable soft rear window (a feature later discontinued) parked illegally in front of the New York skyline in 1967.

END
NO
PARKING
ANY
TIME

The Filmstar

» Car fanatic Steve McQueen at Le Mans 1970. His rival in the film of the same name, Erwin Strahler, was played by Siegfried Rauch. The two developed a close friendship, with McQueen often visiting Rauch at home in Bavaria.

Among cineastes, *Le Départ* is considered a little gem. During a period of approaching civil-war-like disturbances and cultural upheaval, the young Polish director Jerzy Skolimowski created a light, carefree film about a 19-year-old trainee barber who was determined to become a great rally driver—behind the wheel of a Porsche 911 S.

In this anarchic feature film the 911 S, completely new at the time, played the role of an object of desire for a rebellious, fun-loving adventurer. The film begins with a joyride through nighttime Brussels in a classic white 911 that Marc has stolen from his boss' garage. Following the frenzied drive with his best friend, he refuels the Porsche with the gasoline he has brought along, mechanically rewinds the kilometers on the speedometer, lovingly washes the car, and can't avoid checking the trunk and engine compartment in an overcautious reflex. Finally he checks the oil level, at which point his friend calls him to his senses. Thus the film begins with an erotic encounter, which, in a relatively unsubtle fashion, announces the theme, while the plot itself largely consists of a 48-hour search for a Porsche 911 that Marc can use to compete in his first rally.

The fast-paced scenes of the predominately underhanded attempts to gain possession of a 911 are set against the backdrop of Krzysztof Komeda's cool and racy soundtrack—which lends the Porsche-obsessed hero's attitude to life both a romantic spirit and a contemporary modernity. The protagonists' hastily delivered monologues, the hectic movements of the young eccentric, the impelling music—nearly every element of the film contains the promise of speed, which for the hero, can only be fulfilled by a Porsche 911. Largely misunderstood by contemporary film critics, it transformed the stylish car-fanatic into a quintessential hero of his time: aimless wanderer. One year after Godard's *Masculin Féminin,* from which Skolimowski borrowed the two lead figures (played by Jean-Pierre Léaud and Catherine Duport), this film de-ideologized the youth at precisely the time they were becoming radicalized in the schools and universities. At no point in Skolimowski's film do the figures see themselves as political subjects of revolutionary change. Instead, blindly searching for meaning, they flee every profundity in a state of dizzying pursuit.

If, almost 50 years later, one asks the director how a Pole ended up making a film in Belgium about a steel-plate hero from Baden-Württemberg, the answer is quite simple: "At this time the Porsche 911 was the most beautiful car in the world for me." Furthermore, his producer was married to the publisher of a major Belgian car magazine, and so he had easy access to brand new sports cars. For Skolimowski, himself a young car fanatic, the 911 was an electrifying symbol of freedom and anarchy. Although dirt poor and unable to afford a Porsche, one year after completing his film studies he invested the proceeds from *Le Départ* in a similarly emblematic sports car: a Ford Mustang. In a Polish gesture, in search of Western freedom he ignored the more obvious German variant, opting instead for that pony car that stood in a direct mythological relation to the wagon trains of the wild west era. Skolimowski derived great pleasure from driving the Porsche during shooting, and to this day the sound of the classic 911 continues to ring in his ears. This was also an important element in the sports car's cinematic presence, accentuated and dramatized by the soundtrack from his close friend Krzysztof Komeda.

The film retains its subversive quality to this day, with its wild antics destroying libidinous conventions. The hero stops at nothing. He wants a Porsche 911. It is his destiny. He flirts with women as old as his mother, sells all his belongings, destroys friendships,

PERNOD
SUZE
SHELL

For Marc in *Le Départ*, the 911, as a wild and impetuous car, appears to be the ideal automotive extension of his self.

» Some of the Porsche team mixing with the stars at the Sebring race in Florida, 1970: Kurt Mayer, Steve McQueen, Gerd Schmid, and Dieter Wurster.

and betrays everything and everybody for a ride in a Porsche 911. While on a nighttime drive with an older customer in her Mercedes Pagode, he starts rhapsodizing about the Porsche until she begins pleasuring him orally in order to shut him up. The satisfaction is short-lived and the search for a Porsche 911 S, the physical manifestation of his longing, continues. As a by-product of his search for the car, he meets a beautiful blond girl who becomes his faithful hunting companion.

At around the same time Skolimowski's role model, Jean-Luc Godard, used car travel as a metaphor for the failure of the Western lifestyle: in *Weekend,* the consumption of mobility ends up in a bloodbath. In contrast, one year before the student revolts, *Le Départ* depicts youths who are able to live out their excessive fantasies of adventure, luxury, and transgression in a comparatively unproblematic fashion. It is anti-authoritarian because the authorities (boss, police, the rich) have lost their ability to inspire fear long ago. Marc's actions contain an auto-destructive streak, when, in a fit of pubescent masochism, he allows someone to give him a bloody nose, sticks a safety pin in his arm in a proto-punk gesture, and cuts his throat with a razor blade—while his driving of the revved up 911 represents a quintessential act of existential self-harm. And it is not just the hero who continually drives the 911 to the brink of destruction. The classic 911 skids through the narrow hairpins of old Brussels and drifts over the country roads around the Belgian capital. The 911s featured in the film are either in a constant state of drift or stand like uncompromisingly elegant sculptures in a Brussels that frequently resembles a Polish city. It is Skolimowski's first film in Western Europe. The film won the Golden Bear at the Berlinale, and, historically, can be seen as the immediate precursor to May Spils' *Go for It, Baby,*[2] which appeared in the cinemas one year later.

Skolimowski paints a loving portrait of the 911. Its curves are always dramatically lit. The white Porsche at the beginning of the film has a pristine sheen in the light of the streetlamps. The images reflect Marc's intoxication. Jean-Pierre Léaud, who also looks a little like the young director, is quite obviously the artist's double. Even on their first night together Marc performs a mime lying in front of his lover's bed, imagining he is behind the wheel of a 911. The film ends here a short while later. Somehow nowhere. No happy ending. None. In principle *Le Départ* was a film that anticipated the mindset of the youth after the rebellion. Just over ten years later, in *American Gigolo,* Marc's post-heroic hedonism would become mainstream.

The film's hero is like an ADHD patient who can never sit still; his inner disquiet compels him to get behind the wheel of a Porsche. He is only at rest when driving at speed—and it is only in such scenes that the film acquires its lyrical peace. The skidding car transforms Léaud's inner restlessness into a monumental ballet performed on public thoroughfares. Like the protagonist, the sports car, with its tendency to break out at the rear, found no balance or purchase. Together they glide through a world that appears too slow, too un-heroic, too restrictive. From another perspective, the Porsche and the young man in search of meaning provide each other with a form of unstable, mutual support. More than the new girlfriend, the Porsche 911 offers meaning in material form, while in exchange Marc allows the car to live out its wickedness, which the respectable 911 owners with their cultivated scruples—such as Marc's boss or the Porsche dealer—no longer do. For Marc the 911, as a wild and impetuous car, appears to be the ideal automotive extension of his self. Its respectable appearance is merely skin deep, while its essence calls for a rebellion against the routine of the status quo.

Marc and his girlfriend's search for a 911 that they can steal is like the hunt for a rare treasure. Even in a wealthy city like Brussels, the Porsche is not a car you find on every street corner. What is remarkable is the extent to which the 911 is seen as an urban phenomenon, not something hidden away in castles and country estates. It is a young car that cries out for a 19-year-old driver, while the Pagode, as the film shows, finds its rightful owner in the form of an ageing vamp.

Despite the disrespectful manner in which the car is obtained, it is treated lovingly. Even an anarchist like Marc recognizes authorities, and the Porsche is such an authority. Marc's devotion to the automobile is in sharp contrast to his otherwise pervasive irreverence. A similar construction is used in the TV series *Californication* to characterize the notoriously unfaithful womanizer Hank Moody. His one true love, to whom he remains faithful, is a black Porsche 911 cabriolet. Moody also sees himself as an apolitical anarchist. He rails against the prevailing conditions without embracing a social alternative. He is a radical individualist.

[2] A.k.a *Zur Sache, Schätzchen,* a comedy that captured the youthful rebellion in West Germany, and provided a breakthrough role for Bavarian actress Uschi Glas, who thereafter was referred to as *Schätzchen.*

At the end of *Le Départ* it remains open whether the hero is more in love with the car or the girl: they both appear equally seductive.

With the figure of Marc, Skolimowski created the archetypal cinematic Porsche driver. It is a car for hyper-individualists and speed addicts. In 1970 a Porsche 911 S received its first lead role in the racing driver film *Le Mans*. In the film Steve McQueen drives a slate-gray model through the French backwoods to the Le Mans racetrack. Once again, the director, Lee Katzin, employs the 911 as the hero's double. McQueen lines up alingside a Ferrari-driving German, with the somewhat Tentonic name at Erwin Strahler, and racer to overcome the death of his racing driver friend for which he feels responsible. The melancholy classic 911 with a matt paint-job is the everyday companion of a sensitive daredevil. Following this film the 911 would remain an automotive accessory for individualists and loners. The forensic psychologist Alex Cross, played by Morgan Freeman, drives a classic black 911, a type of Batmobile for intellectuals, when he sets out to nail psychopathic serial killers. In the two film adaptations of the James Patterson novels *Kiss the Girls* and *Along Came a Spider,* the black 911, model year 1974, represents a steel-plate extension of the protagonists' self. Like his car, Morgan Freeman is dressed in black from head to foot. A brooding existentialist, he paces and drives between tight-laced policemen who treat the successful scientist and author like an alien. That the psychologist is an Afro-American intensifies his status as an outsider, which he turns to his advantage during the course of the books and films to become the center of events. His Porsche is a protective shell and a place where he can gather strength, as well proclaiming an elegant athleticism. An equally enigmatic figure is played by Robert Redford in *Spy Game*. A CIA agent organizing an illicit rescue mission in China, he succeeds in fleeing the high security compound in Langley in his green metallic 911 classic shortly before his cover is blown. It is not surprising that Hollywood stars from Paul Newman and Steve McQueen to Patrick Dempsey (who has also driven for Porsche in Le Mans). The choice of car would seem to announce that they believe in their own individuality—and want to look good in the process.

The Revolutionary's Car

The end of the RAF was lurking in Gustav-Freytag-Straße. Andreas Baader drove past the almost new yellow Porsche 911 S Targa with the black anodized chrome parts,numerous times before he decided this would be his next getaway vehicle and prestige object. The Frankfurt-based photographer Rainer Schlegelmilch acquired his third 911 in June 1971 after his last 911 was rammed by a lorry in 1969 at a set of lights in Bellinzona, Switzerland, close to the Italian border, and subsequently scrapped. Schlegelmilch's girlfriend received a shock and retired to the hotel. The photographer flew to Frankfurt where he leased a Porsche 912, the "ladies" Porsche as he called it, from the car rental company Hertz. The same day he drove back to Bellinzona, picked up the girlfriend, and arrived into Monte Carlo a day later to photograph the Grand Prix. The insurance company received notification of a total write-off, together with a car rental bill for over 5,000 deutsche marks, which back then was a horrendous sum; however, it was paid immediately.

Back in Frankfurt Schlegelmilch ordered a new 911 S Targa without delay—in the same special yellow and with the ample motorization that made this 911 the most powerful in the program. The "S" was considered a car for aficionados and real men. "Jjjumm" was the onomatopoeic title of the *Spiegel* article from 1966 introducing the sports car, which back then sported 160 hp, had a top speed of around 230 km/h (143 mph), and cost just under 25,000 deutsche marks (five times the price of a Beetle). According to Porsche's chief press officer and race director, Huschke von Hanstein, this car wasn't about speed maximization but greater acceleration "when danger threatened." The car accelerated from 0–100 km/h (62 mph) in less than 7 seconds. A jurist in Munich warned at the time that such a road performance was criminal. Maybe Baader had read this. Not suitable for learner drivers, was the comment in the owner's manual. When Baader discovered the "S" in Gustav-Freytag-Straße, the car had 190 hp under the hood and a top speed of over 230 km/h (143 mph). It wasn't the first 911 that Baader had stolen, but it would be his last. At the beginning of the 1970s a 911 was a very special car—and the highly motorized "S" was a real eye catcher, and not just for experts. Baader had the Targa re-sprayed violet—quite appalling, as the original owner was forced to admit on identifying it in the garage of the Federal Office of Criminal Investigation (BKA) in Wiesbaden. Initially the BKA took a very close look at the photographer. With his long hair and artistic, unconventional lifestyle, he could have easily been a member of the sympathizer scene. "Me, happily casual in jeans and braces and with pistols on the wall that I had bought in Portugal," recalls Schlegelmilch. That the old pistols required a gun license was of not interest to the high-ranking BKA officials. They wanted to know everything about the Porsche and the photographer's lifestyle.

He realized how serious the situation was shortly after the arrest of Andreas Baader. At the time he was on his way to the Belgian Grand Prix when, just after Aachen, he was first followed by a police car and then stopped on the road by three officers who aimed their machine guns at the photographer and his girlfriend. "Just don't call me Andreas," joked Schlegelmilch to his girlfriend, who he had often called "Ulrike" in fun. That was the

» Photographer Rainer Schlegelmilch and his 911 Targa, which was returned to him after it had been stolen by the Baader-Meinhof gang and repainted purple.

Hessian way of dealing with the madness of the RAF terror. After checking their papers, the police waved them on. This was when Schlegelmilch realized that the arrest of Andreas Baader in the vicinity of a Porsche could have something to do with his much beloved Targa S.

It was thanks to Baader's love for Porsche that 911 drivers became the focus of police investigations for a few days in June 1972. Schlegelmilch recalls that a colleague was stopped by the police because a police helicopter had spotted a Novoflex pistol grip lens with their binoculars—which from above resembled a machine gun.

Schlegelmilch had always dreamed of a 911. In the past he had owned a Volvo, a Beetle with 24.5 hp—and at the beginning of his driving career—a Zündapp Janus with 13 hp. It was in this four-seater microcar, powered by a single cylinder two-stroke engine, that he drove from Frankfurt to his first motor race in Monza "over the Gotthard Pass at 15 km/h [9 mph]," as he recalled. When it came to his first Porsche Schlegelmilch had the pleasure of discussing his purchase with no less a figure than Ferdinand Piëch himself. At the time the adroit photojournalist met him, he was the Porsche race director at the Targa Florio. After explaining that he was about to order a 911, Piëch told him to be patient. "'Wait a few more weeks, a new version with a folding spare wheel allowing for a larger tank is coming out.' And that is what I did." Back then the Targa with 130 hp cost around 23,000 deutsche marks. This was the beginning of a life-long passion. In 2012 Schlegelmilch began driving his eleventh 911.

For Andreas Baader, Schlegelmilch's 911 would be his undoing. Early in the morning of June 1, 1972, four months after the theft, BKA investigators were surprised by an eggplant-colored 911 Targa roaring towards them down a one-way street close to the site where it had originally been stolen. A bloated man with badly dyed red-blond hair sat behind the wheel, next to him the 1.90 m (6 ft. 3 in.) tall Holger Meins, and huddled on the two jump seats in the rear compartment sat Jean-Carl Raspe. The most important minds of the Red Army Faction of the time, squashed together in the Zuffenhausen-built Targa had a satirical air to it—a consequence, not least, of Baader's penchant for heroic film scenes.

The car was parked facing oncoming traffic when the three terrorists made their way to the garage in which an even more exotic car than the 911 S was waiting: an Iso Rivolta, of which there were only 700 in the world at the time. A resident had observed how the three young men always wore gloves when opening and closing the garage—and that in spring. He notified the police and they laid in wait. The three RAF members didn't have a chance when the 60 policemen moved in. As his biographer Klaus Stern noted, Baader stood in front of the Iso Rivolta with a cigarette in his mouth and a pair of Ray Bans on his nose, waiting, as the neighbors alarmed by the gunshots observed, to be shot down—close to that object of desire that had seduced him into committing felonies from an early age. After a two-hour shootout, Baader was seriously injured and the other two were led away. The footage of the arrest shows a 29-year-old wreck who looks like he is in his mid-forties. His choice of cars would suggest that Baader was looking for this final showdown. They give the nihilistic terror, the megalomaniacal ideology, and the stupefying routine of life in the underground, a camp touch. They are the last wink of a Swabian pimp who drifted into terrorism on the back of the political upheavals of his time.

At the beginning of the 1970s a 911 was a very special car—and the highly motorized "S" was a real eye catcher, and not just for experts.

« Rebel energy: a 911 Turbo captured weaving through the streets of Paris.

In one of the numerous lovingly written biographies of Baader we are told that he actually wanted to go into film. In the late 1960s Russ Meyer's *Faster, Pussycat! Kill! Kill!* was featured at Swabian arthouse movie theaters, a film in which the heroine Varla, completely dressed in black and driving a black Porsche 356, lives out her anger at the world in an orgy of violence. The men in this film, as is often the case with Russ Meyer, are weak, seducible objects of desire that are used by the women in every respect. The gender roles are reversed, while the film's three heroines are introduced with a fast and merry car chase that establishes a central motif that runs throughout the film: the car as an erotically charged murder weapon. That Varla drives Russ Meyer's car was not just a cost-saving measure, it was also an expression of the identity between the heroine's pursuit of autonomy and that of the director. Asked what she wanted, she answered: "Everything—or at least as much as I can get."

The film ends with her death. Varla was a time traveler. Her dramatic makeup, the black hair, the pitch-black clothes, and black Porsche parody the morbidity of existentialism and the restlessness of the beatniks. Varla's hipsterdom has become unhinged: the aesthetic gesture of revolt, which remained a form of titillation for her cultural role models, has become naked violence. The settling of accounts with the rest of the world is now real. She makes her case for terror as a theatre of cruelty, and Russ Meyer, a policeman's son of German descent, stages it codly and mercilessly in his 1966 film. At this time the sports car, as it appeared in films such as *Vanishing Point* (1971), was a vehicle of flight and the outsider ethos, or in the case of the E-type Jaguar converted into a hearse in *Harold and Maude* (1971), a symptom of provocative decadence and contempt for the mainstream. Following the failed rebellion and awakening of the late 1960s, flight lost its deeper meaning and purpose. In the final scene of *Vanishing Point,* Kowalski, the film's Baader-like protagonist and outsider hero, races at full speed, pumped full of drugs, into a police roadblock, atomizing himself and his mechanical double in the final highpoint of an existential journey into oblivion that lends the film its narrative structure. In contrast to the intellectual's introverted gesture of self-destruction, Varla, Kowalski, and later Baader, offer a cinematic dramaturgy. Baader's decision to steal a bright yellow 911 S and re-spray it purple can be overlooked as a minor eccentricity. However, driving the wrong way down a one-way street in a well-to-do neighborhood of Frankfurt in the early hours of the morning, engine roaring—while the whole country is looking for him as public enemy number one—can only be interpreted as a form of existential roulette. It has little to do with revolution in the spirit of the leftwing classics. It is a feverish longing for absolute transgression. That Baader and his comrades—who more closely conformed to the image of revolutionaries—were arrested in a garage containing an even more exclusive sports car is symptomatic of a state of delirium. Baader, the car thief, like Jean-Paul Belmondo in Godard's *Breathless,* had lost control over himself, his life, and his band of unhinged followers with their high school accolades and Leninist idée fixe.

On the cover of the photo book Schlegelmilch dedicated to his favorite company, Porsche, there is a picture of a 964 Turbo glowing in the evening light, displaying its voluptuous curves half an hour before sunset. Light and shadow generate sensual, lascivious waves and valleys, which, without exercising too much fantasy, evoke the body landscape of a young, athletic woman. Thus the 911 touches on Andreas Baader's second great passion: the woman as an object of his own self-efficacy. In this respect, women, like Porsche and the country as a whole, were objects of abuse in this time of terror. Baader loved neither women, nor Porsche, nor the country. He wanted to plunder and possess them in order to subject them to his will. Nevertheless, his dreams and power fantasies remained decidedly conventional.

1974 1989

» The models: the 911 Turbo (front), 911 Coupe (back), and 911 Carrera Targa (right) lined up in 1976.

The G Model

The Golden Ratio

One year after Andreas Baader's arrest the classic 911 was replaced by the G model. This marked the beginning of a maturation process for the 911, which, after passing through three high-powered SC models, culminated in the high-class 911 Carrera. With its 231 hp and the corresponding road performance, this 911, in contrast to the S and RS models with their ostentatiously paraded athleticism, was completely without affectations.

This 911 extended and prolonged the commercial viability of the classic 911, subtly developing its formal language. The dimensions were almost identical and the interior remained virtually unchanged. While the G models produced in the first four years were serially produced variants of the classic 911 with basic motorization, in 1978, with the production of the first SC, the Carrera's wider bodywork became standard and the G model received that sensuous, highly elegant, and ideally proportioned appearance, which, especially in the last five years of the "Carrera" model, made it into the most handsome Porsche for many 911 fans. The 911 obtained its golden ratio. For friends of the air-cooled 911, who casually call themselves *Luftis*[1] (airies), the G model manifested the ideal of the 911. Only at the end, with the 1989 model, did the 16 inch Fuchs rims, 6 inch wide at the front and 8 inch wide at the back, become standard. "This further enhanced its appearance," reported Jörg Austen in his technical documentation of the 911.

[1] English-speaking fans of the air-cooled Porsches also take up the German term: *Luftgekühlt.*

S-CJ 8366
S·CJ 8261

GE · 10760

The Fuchs rims are as much a part of the 911 world as the boxer motor. As early as 1962 the supplier Otto Fuchs from the Sauerland region was commissioned to develop a low weight, solid, and—well—appealing, light alloy rim. It was conceived as an extra for the most athletic 911 and only became standard with the last year of the G model series. Originally the rim star was brightly polished and the background painted black, but with the G model the entire rim star was painted black. Rims are the sports car equivalent of shoes: a key accessory when it comes to cultivating an elegant appearance.

These Carreras are equivalent to the supermodels of our own era: Linda, Christy, and Cindy, whereby the Carrera bears the greatest resemblance to the classical beauty of Christy Turlington. François Truffaut's last film *Vivement dimanche!* (*Confidentially Yours*, 1983) begins with a sequence of a freshly washed black 911 SC with black Fuchs rims and beige leather seats. It is owned by the businessman Jacques Massoulier who was shot down close to his car. Truffaut films the car as if it were a woman, with the sunlight from above and the shadow from the side serving to emphasize its curves, while the headlight tubes project into the image like an oversized décolleté. The role of this beauty is played in the film by Fanny Ardant. And it is Truffaut that we have to thank for the relatively hedonist, anti-intellectual definition of the nouvelle vague film: it was about "letting beautiful women do beautiful things." And this also included driving exciting cars on a regular basis. The G model's cameo appearance was effectively a homage to its sophisticated elegance.

Hollywood also made liberal use of the G model's charms. In the thriller *No Man's Land*, appropriately named *Tatort 911* (Crime Scene 911) in German, the 911, above all the countless G models, played the lead role. This film was supposed to be a psychological study of two very different young men, a Porsche-mad policeman and the equally 911-obsessed son of a millionaire, who, together with his gang, specializes in the theft of 911s, preferably the G model. However, the figures remain pale and ill-defined, while director Peter Werner hardly misses a narrative pretext in the film's 106 minutes to set the 911 in scene, either cruising, driving at high speed, skidding, or, it goes without saying, in numerous car chases. Again, the G model plays the supermodel in this film: ennobling a relatively shallow plot with its polished surfaces and graceful movements.

The designer Thomas Elsner calls the model the "heart beat model." When he sees or even hears one "my pulse increases as if I had met a beautiful woman." Although he drove a Targa from the same period for many years, he can't get enough of these cars. On revisiting this model after years with a 996 or a 997, other 911 fans are shocked at the simplicity of even the 1989 models. Without power steering, and with a rock-hard clutch, driving such models is also physically demanding.

No connoisseur would dream of turning the radio on with the sound of this engine. It is the last singing 911, while its successor, the 964, roars and growls.

« The Carrera 3.2 Speedster (Turbolook) shows off its supermodel looks in 1989.

The windscreen wipers—like many of the buttons on the dashboard and the look and feel of the ventilation—originate from the Beetle. At high speeds the rear wiper becomes detached and the coupe's windscreen appears to extend straight up, while the two headlight tubes project boldly into the air. The front windscreen and décolleté produce an impressive barrage of noise and, for this time, a quite devastating drag coefficient of 0.4.

Sascha Keilwerth drives a 911 SC from 1978 that currently has 675,000 km (419,425 mi.) on the clock. His G model has over 360 hp and has already been lasered at a speed of 324 km/h (201 mph). For Keilwerth, who trained to be a car mechanic before he went on to become a graduate engineer and salesman, the G model is as much a classic 911 as the F model—to give the classic 911 its official name. These are cars for people "who eat their cornflakes without milk." On hearing that someone has bought a G model, he congratulates them on "the best car of their life." He loves the sound when he starts the air-cooled engine in the morning, "after a cup of oil," and its vibrations massage his back as the car slowly comes to life. Or on parking the car after the ride to the office, when the entire engine block clicks and crackles as the cooling cylinder heads readjust following the thermal stress.

A quarter of a century after its premier, the 231 hp Carrera engine still causes a stir with its harmonious, wiry performance characteristics. Following a muscular acceleration from 0–200 km/h (124 mph) the car has to be shifted into fifth gear in order to take it to the 250 km/h (155 mph) mark. The G50 gearbox works like a dream, and anyone who buys a well run-in model from this period may find themselves screaming with pleasure on the freeway at the wonderful driving experience provided by this last, raw, wild, classic 911. No connoisseur would dream of turning the radio on with the sound of this engine. It is the last singing 911, while its successor, the 964, an extraordinarily modern car in comparison, roars and growls.

The Turbo intensified the neurotic handling of the rear-engined car with a brutally abrupt turbo thrust that initially shocked even the most experienced Porsche and sports car drivers.

» The 911 Turbo's "flatnose" or *Flachbau* had to be handcrafted from the front fenders and so was a pricey feature—as well as a controversial one.

The 911 has frequently been upgraded, not in response to a fundamental desire for product optimization, but because Porsche was forced to react to the rigid safety requirements for sports cars in the all-important North American market. That is why the filigree brilliant chrome bumpers were exchanged for telescopic versions with bellows—which actually look better proportioned in combination with the Carrera's rear, which has grown in order to accommodate the increasing size of the boxer engine. The rims became bigger, the tires wider. The chrome, the automotive equivalent of stucco and parquet, disappeared. The comfortable chairs for the driver and front passenger were replaced by sporty "choir stalls" with the headrests integrated in the backs. Changing gear became noticeably lighter. The magazine *Auto Motor Sport* spoke of "a bold step into the modern world."

As always with Porsche, there were purists who accused the chief designer, Anatole Lapine, of having lost his touch for the sports car. Nevertheless, with his sense of elegance, Lapine was close to the spirit of Porsche: he despised the "pretentious" and loved luxury. That, over 30 years later, Lapine's design is considered a classic beauty underscores the fact that the right combination of innovation and tradition in the development of the 911 had been found. This was also due to the presence of Ferdinand Alexander Porsche, who acted as the supervisory board's custodian of tradition, as Lapine is fond of remembering.

Lapine, born in Riga, was trained at Daimler, contributed to the design of the Corvette at General Motors (back then he already drove a 356 Carrera from 1959), and designed the successor to the Porsche 911 at the end of the 1960s together with Ferdinand Piëch—who envisaged it as a three-seater sports car with four, eight, and twelve cylinders with the driver seated in the middle. It was due to replace the 911 in 1973; however, as a result of changes to Porsche's management board—as in the case of VW—nothing came of it. The Porsche family withdrew from operations. Porsche became a joint stock corporation and the family now exercised its influence through the supervisory board. When Lapine reworked the classic 911, this took place against a wider panorama of possibilities, so it is thanks to the designer's sensitive attention to detail that this G model was less the quantum leap longed for by Piëch than a critical reconstruction of the classic mythos in the spirit of minimalism. "In order to give something a timeless appearance one has to put a lot of work into it," explained Lapine to the *Stuttgarter Zeitung* newspaper in 1986. "How much effort do you think Marlene Dietrich had to expend in order to appear timeless?" Compared to its successor, the 964 model with its extendible spoiler, electronic driving aids, four-wheel drive, and bulbous front and rear bumpers, the Carrera looked like a renaissance sculpture. In 1989 *Men's Vogue* recommended buying tomorrow's classic before the new 911, with the silhouette of a pot-bellied pig, rolled into the Porsche showrooms.

The 911 became stronger and faster. The Carrera RS 3.0, of which only 110 were built, was equipped with 230 hp. Two years later the 911 Turbo was unveiled, catapulting the 911 world into a different dimension of road performance. The Turbo intensified the neurotic handling of the rear-engined car with a brutally abrupt turbo thrust that initially shocked even the most experienced Porsche and sports car drivers. Race engineer Peter Falk called the delayed turbo thrust on curvy tracks almost criminal, and at the very least "an acquired taste." For Walter Röhrl, who 30 years later would buy a 3.3 L Turbo, this car—essentially unmanageable for normal drivers—was a wonderful challenge.

The predecessor to the Turbo was unveiled at the Frankfurt Motor Show in 1973 in the middle of the oil crisis, causing a stir in the garb of a Carrera RS 3.0. Just over one year later the Turbo, almost ready for serial production, was presented at the Paris Motor Show. The rear section had been widened again, and the RS's ducktail replaced by a monstrous rear spoiler, which young Porsche families also used as a diaper-changing table. The chrome was replaced with matt black and a great deal of motor racing technology from the RSR and the Porsche 917. The timed 5.5 seconds from 0–100 km/h (62 mph) was a sensation at the time, and the top speed beyond the 250 km/h (155 mph) mark, more than impressive. However, the average consumption of 20.9 L was already out of step with the times. Nevertheless, the Turbo sold very well internationally, despite the initial doubts. In 1974 Turbo number 1 was presented to Louise Piëch as a birthday present. The thousandth Turbo came off the assembly line in 1976, just one year after the start of production.

The Swine's Car: Vol. 1

In Heinrich Böll,[2] the moral apostle of postwar German literature, the Porsche is driven by a swine. In the melodrama *The Lost Honor of Katharina Blum,* published in 1972, he settles accounts with the evil of this world in the shape of the popular newspaper called the *Zeitung.* The tabloid journalist Tötges, whose slimy manner is depicted in monstrous, Brechtian terms, drives a Porsche 911—the tin crown of a dissolute life and character. However, the somewhat heroic, romantic terrorist Götten also steals a Porsche 911 shortly before he meets and falls in love with Katharina Blum. It is a car for perpetrators, not for victims. It is an exclamation mark signaling testosterone-contaminated aggression—and a connecting element between the two men who bring about the ruin of the gentle creature Katharina Blum. If the 911 was hitherto a car for heroes and heroic individualism, the Porsche had now become a symbolic object and companion of the dangerous, evil, and even infamous.

Volker Schlöndorff and Margarethe von Trotta's[3] film adaptation of the anti-tabloid polemic begins with the scene where the terrorist steals a green Porsche 911 from an obviously drunk and rather disheveled representative of the moneyed classes in order to escape the policemen observing him. It is a rather blunt reference to Andreas Baader's stolen Porsche. A short while later—he has already met and fallen in love with Katharina Blum, the benevolent heroine—there is a short car chase in which the 911 shakes off the police's S Class: even before the kidnapping of the industrialist Hans Martin Schleyer, snatched from his chauffeur-driven car by the RAF in a hail of bullets, the limousine was already regarded in liberal and leftwing circles as a symbol of the hated Federal Republic's overweight ruling class of managers and ministers. In the film the S Class looks like an enemy car, while the good terrorist escapes his pursuers with cunning, courage, and skill thanks to his nimble 911 Targa.

Less than half an hour later in the film, after the arrest of Katharina Blum, the next 911 makes its appearance. It is brown, and its usually graceful rear has been disfigured by an inappropriately dimensioned rear spoiler, which, considering this G model's modest 165 hp, is rather overstated.

[2] Cologne-born writer awarded the Nobel Prize for Literature in 1972.

[3] Two of the leading lights of New German Cinema, a movement influenced by the French New Wave, which included directors such as Werner Herzog and Wim Wenders.

MERCEDES-
BENZ

This Porsche model didn't even exist at the time Böll wrote the text; however, Schlöndorff and von Trotta consciously selected a model that better conveyed the aura of the shady nouveau riche than the almost sculptural, peaceable bodywork of the classic 911. This is reserved for the terrorist, not the tabloid journalist. The "scandalmonger" and "muckraker" has also painted the rims of his 911 gold. The once elegant Porsche is thus transformed into a tin-plate, cinematic double of the dubious, all-in-all rather insufferable tabloid journalist Tötges, rolling through the image and text landscape virtually bursting with oversignification. Socially, the 911 is parked in the vicinity of the abhorrent. The only appeal this car has is as a terrorist's getaway vehicle; but even this 911 has been disfigured with the aggressively protruding extra headlights, which back then were only ordered by drivers who wanted to dazzle as many people as possible at night—an accessory also employed in this way the vulgar character assassinator and destroyer of truth. As a Porsche was an expensive car back then, as it still is, the fact that a simple reporter could afford such a sports car also said something about the immorality of capitalism. Furthermore, this type of Porsche caricature, together with its distortions, lends the owner's character—in addition to its abysmal depths—a completely unrestrained vanity, which, in this street ballad, he pays for with his life.

This is in stark contrast to the benevolent heroine who drives a green Beetle. Katharina, Greek for "the pure," is, as her surname

Blum betrays (*Blume* is German for 'flower'), very close to nature, and thus to the good. Heinrich Böll lets all the names speak. The terrorist Götten is close to the gods (German: *Götter*) and therefore powerful and good, but beyond human reach. The tabloid journalist is called Tötges because he kills (German: *töten*) people with his stories. That is why the Porsche owner is executed at the end of the film. The unfortunate Beetle driver ends up in prison. With Böll's novel and the Schlöndorff and von Trotta adaptation, the Porsche enters the age of its caricature.

There is a direct line that extends from Tötges to Helmut Dietl and Patrick Süskind's character Baby Schimmerlos,[4] the gossip columnist who, taking advantage of people's weaknesses as opposed to treating them with complete contempt, pursues his rather frivolous job in Munich, and naturally drives a Porsche 911. A white Targa in wide turbo-look, also with a rear spoiler and the additional headlights, which was only seen in Munich at the time in poseur circles. The rear spoiler as a synonym for the malicious became the garish makeup of a sports car that, until then, had enjoyed the undivided sympathies of the Germans, as surveys repeatedly confirmed. In the zeitgeist of the 1970s, and then the 1980s, it represented a problematic transgression of the egalitarian boundary that separates the accepted from the unacceptable. A 911 in war paint is as foreign to the educated middle-class moral majority who standardize and control the systems of discourse like ruthless tabloid journalism. It provokes hatred and contempt. And thanks to Böll, Grass, and Margarethe von Trotta the 911 becomes a bastion of reaction on wheels: an anti-Beetle or anti-Volvo.

The quintessentially German character of this relationship to an essentially German icon is exemplified by a narrative fragment from Max Frisch,[5] which he noted in his diary under the title "Sketch of an Accident." This tells the story of a holiday journey to the south undertaken by the doctor Victor with his beloved Marlies, which ends in a tragic accident and the death of the woman in the front passenger seat. Viktor is not to blame as he had the right of way, but even though he is exonerated by the police, this is no consolation. Unsettled by the nagging questions about his driving style during the trip to the Provence, Viktor drove faster and more resolutely than actually necessary. The woman refused to put on a seatbelt in order to compel him to slow down, remonstrating with him, "her eyes on the speedometer the whole time." On the freeway between Cannes and Saint Raphaël he drives 180 km/h (112 mph), although he had promised her he would only drive 140 km/h (87 mph). He interprets her fear as an expression of her lack of faith in him. He drives so slowly that they are overtaken by "every Volkswagen." The mood becomes oppressive. "She no longer sings, he no longer overtakes, they remain silent." And thus the pair of academics race into a crisis. Their love freezes with every kilometer. There is only one sentence concerning the car: "He drives a Porsche."

The Porsche 911 is a car for perpetrators, not for victims. It is an exclamation mark signaling testosterone-contaminated aggression.

« The shady side of life: in the 1972 novel *The Lost Honor of Katharina Blum* by Heinrich Böll, the 911 began to be portrayed as a vehicle with a dangerous and dubious side, rather than the car of revolutionaries and individualists as it had been in the 1960s.

At the end of the story they are driving towards a crossing in Montpellier when the co-driver draws Viktor's attention to a lorry. "He saw the lorry but he didn't brake; he had the right of way. It is even possible that he put his foot down in order to demonstrate his certainty. She screamed. The Gendarme from Montpellier said he was in the right." At best the Porsche driver cuts the figure of a mildly unappealing antihero, though the narrative perspective lends him the authority of the author. He is a melancholy sophisticate who loves driving fast, but whose life falls apart at the moment of the accident. Although he goes on to enjoy a career, rising to the position of head physician, and has a wife and children, he is unable to shake off the feeling of guilt associated with the accident. Porsche drivers are people like you and me, is Frisch's implicit message for his sophisticated audience. It is the opposite of a demonization. However, this would have been more in tune with the times, an antipathy born of a reaction to both the social tension in the wake of the student movement, and the shock following the first report of the Club of Rome from 1972, which, with unprecedented severity and radicalism, called into question the Western world's pursuit of growth and prosperity. The first post-modern apostles of abstinence recognized the signs of the times. Political progressives bid farewell to the concept of progress and executed an about turn in the spirit of the German philosopher Heidegger, away from technology and towards our roots in nature. The Porsche 911 was a provocation: a monument to optimism and the belief in progress, which over the course of its 10-year production period underwent a series of mercurial advances that were unthinkable at the time of its launch in 1963. A rigid moralism that fostered egalitarianism and a hostility towards the elites spread throughout Germany and the world.

[4] Gossip reporter from the 1986 TV series *Kir Royal: Aus dem Leben eines Klatschreporters*—a parody of a Munich newspaper, the *Abendzeitung* and the high society of the time.

[5] Swiss philosopher, architect, playwright, and author, whose diary entries—essays, reportage, political musings—often informed his works.

Rarely Minimal: The Rear Spoiler

In the 1970s the idea of harmonious, social cooperation began to fall apart. While the monetary union in 1990, which paved the way for German reunification, left everyone in Germany with the same 40 euros[6] and an illusion of complete equality, in the 1970s, society, with its pretensions and markets, was slowly but decisively drifting apart. This came at a time when Porsche realized that supposed niche products could generate impressive sales both domestically and abroad. Consequently the minimalist concept of the Porsche had to be abandoned step by step, or at the very least, its purism needed to be moderated. A break with tradition was unavoidable. The 911 Carrera RS's performance figures forced the engineers and bodywork constructors to take an unusual number of liberties with the 911's classic form. As this car had inherited large strands of its performance DNA from motor racing, ...

when serial production began in October 1972 Porsche saw no alternative but to equip the RS with a rear spoiler on the engine hood. With the assistance of the downforce, the potentially nervous rear-engined car, now equipped with 210 hp, was to be kept on the road, even at speeds of up to 245 km/h (152 mph). Out of respect for the classic form, Porsche engineers and designers restricted the aerodynamic stabilizer to the required minimum. As a consequence, the spoiler jutted from the classic silhouette like a duck's tail, a feature that was also be its future name.

The fastest German production car to date, originally approved for racing use only, was initially built in an edition of 500. However, Porsche had underestimated the interest in such a comparatively expensive super sports car. The advertising slogan "Only 500 men will drive it," proved to be a chauvinist misjudgment. Looking back, those responsible for the advertising at the time turned this misjudgment into an occasion for a foray in feminist propaganda. That over 1,500 units were eventually sold was incorrectly, and somewhat ironically, explained as a consequence of the large number of women who bought the RS. In truth, not a single woman ordered one. After its market launch in 1964, the 911 became a familiar if infrequent sight on German roads, while the extremely rare RS, despite its sales success, provided a further note of distinction. At traffic lights and parking lots car-mad children and fathers shamelessly gawped at the sports car without a trace of embarrassment.

For purists the spoiler was nothing short of sacrilege, whose reprehensibility was only lessened by the fact that it was introduced purely on functional grounds. Porsche's motor racing success was to find its way into the production car, and in the 1970s this was only possible with a spoiler. In 1973 Porsche presented the 260 hp Turbo, which was fitted with a significantly larger spoiler than the RS. The duck's tail became the turbo wing, which, beginning in 1977, was dimensioned to generate both the required downforce and cool the supercharged air for the turbo. In order to improve road grip the Turbo was given a wider track derived from the race-experienced RSR. The "crowning glory of a tried and tested concept," as the Porsche advertising described it, lent emphasis to an aggressive appearance that clearly announced the Turbo's technical superiority. A Turbo flying past in the fast lane with its dramatic rear was unmistakable. Other manufacturers such as BMW made pedagogical concessions to the general public. In 2002 the Munich-based manufacturers equipped their turbo with

[6] Referring to *Begrüßungsgeld*, specifically the 100 DM (around 40 euro) "welcome money" given to citizens of the GDR when Germany united in 1990.

MOTUL
72
2012

Krönung einer bewährten Konzeption

PORSCHE

turbo

Dieser Wagen vereinigt in vollendeter Harmonie Leistung mit Luxus. Seine überlegene Technik und sein funktioneller Komfort lassen keinen Wunsch mehr offen.

Dr. Ing. h. c. F. Porsche AG · Stuttgart-Zuffenhausen · Printed in Germany · Fricke & Co. · 2521.14

mirror-inverted turbo lettering on the front spoiler—a measure designed exclusively as a warning to the driver in the lead car, with a mere glance in the rearview mirror sufficient for them to immediately vacate the left-hand lane.

With the Turbo, Porsche set about optimizing the symbiosis between production and racing cars. The bulky 2 m (6 ft.) wide 911 Carrera RSR Turbo with its 500 hp engine entered the consciousness of car lovers at the same time as the 911 Turbo. The 5.5 seconds timed by the magazine *Auto Motor Sport* for its acceleration from 0–100 km/h (62 mph) was phenomenal compared to the British and Italian competition. The imports from the racing sector also re-established the hierarchy in the everyday world of civilian sports cars, while the Turbo placed increasing demands on 911 drivers. If the 911 with its propensity for rear drift was considered an acquired taste in terms of handling—even in its tame versions—then the Turbo with its whiplash-like turbo thrust was a sports car exclusively for experienced drivers. The machismo of the Turbo advertising spelled out what this car promised on sight: an adventure for real men. Thereby, Porsche was farsighted enough to bequeath the first Turbo to a woman: Louise Piëch, the mother of Ferdinand Piëch. The thousandth Turbo also went to a woman: Princess Antoinette zu Fürstenberg. Herbert von Karajan purchased one of the first serial Turbos produced in a lightweight version. The maestro, who could bring every orchestra and every masterpiece of classical music under his control with a wave of the baton, didn't doubt for an instant that he was also capable of controlling this car. Not everyone could be as certain. Every lapse in concentration, especially in the wet, was punished by the Turbo. The United States advertising slogan "Exclusive Explosive Expensive" served as a warning to customers. Anyone who underestimated the Turbo or overestimated their own driving skills ran the risk of losing control of this high-priced car.

Even the Porsche diehards who bitched about the turbo wing had an inkling that the Turbo's road handling and grip would suffer dangerously at high speeds in its absence. That is why the spoiler was accepted. As a rule it was the Porsche braggarts, who glued the bulky turbo wing to their simple 911s with their 165 hp, that were the subjects of derision. It was a violation of the 911 doctrine that stated one should not appear more than one is. Porsche granted its customers the freedom, only to realize that not everyone who aspired to a racy and imposing looking coupe was necessarily willing to pay for the corresponding performance. It was not just Heinrich Böll readers who regarded the souped-up 911s as cars for posers. Friends of the 911 also had an aversion to this type of brash showiness. However, the market demanded it, and many more monstrosities besides. Few customers took advantage of the *Werksturbolook*, WTL for short (factory turbo-look). Instead they bought flat-nosed conversion kits and monstrous

"Exclusive Explosive Expensive"

↳ U.S. advertising slogan for the Porsche Turbo.

« "Crowning an established concept" (↑) and "A superlative on wheels" (↓)—ads for the Porsche Turbo emphasizing its balance of performance and luxury, and engineering and comfort.

spoiler mountains from barbaric tuners and steel-plate beauticians. The author of this book still hasn't recovered from the shock that Porsche also offered the Turbo in a flatnose variant—the single most unacceptable disfiguration and break with the 911 spirit that even puts Porsche libertarians in a rage.

Luckily Porsche's relationship to the spoiler remained a distant one. The end of the G series heralded the age of the secret spoiler. The 964, launched in 1988, was equipped with a rear spoiler that extended automatically at 80 km/h (50 mph) and retracted at speeds below 30 km/h (19 mph). Unfortunately word got around among the police, who in the 1990s developed a preference for stopping new Carreras driving the city streets with extended spoilers. However, as it could also be operated manually, the extended spoiler was inadmissible as evidence. In the Porsche community the extendable spoiler proved a source of relief. It demonstrated that the 911's performance could be enhanced without it having to crawl through traffic-calmed zones with a corresponding battle-ready look. Since then every new series has been fitted with this construction, though the speed at which the spoiler is extended was increased to 120 km/h (75 mph) with the 996 series.

And in the case of the Porsche Panamera, even the 500 hp Turbo managed to escape the fate of an exclusive limousine with rear "antlers" disturbing a discrete bourgeois lifestyle. In interviews and podium events the Panamera's designer, Michael Mauer, confessed that he was no friend of spoilers, but that at speeds above 250 km/h (155 mph) he had no choice. This required a spoiler. From the perspective of the design pragmatist Professor Lutz Fügener, the spoiler shouldn't be over-dramatized. It was a necessity, and functionality had priority over any objections on grounds of taste. The 911 had genetic problems with respect to road handling due its rear engine, and that had to be compensated for with a spoiler. After decades in which the tuning subculture embellished its eccentric sheet metal fantasies with a preference for hysterical spoiler constructions, a cooler essentialism emerged in the first decade of the new millennium. The new three-part charter proclaimed: rims, chassis, finished. The only elegant exceptions, thanks to their heroic character, are the masterpieces from the Tokyo-based tuning stable "Rauh Welt Begriff" (Rough World Concept).

INI
nell

JAPANGO
HYDROXYCUT
fashiontv

» The RWB Rotana, a modification of the 993 Turbo at the Rauh Welt Begriff tuning stable outside Tokyo.

A Car for Heroes

» The maestro Herbert von Karajan with his silver coiffure getting into his 911 Turbo.

Herbert von Karajan was never a man for the quiet notes. With the displays of virility featured on his record covers, the Austrian conductor even succeeded in elevating classical music to the status of show business. Naturally this also included the corresponding motorization. It was not without a sense of pride that Karajan had himself photographed for the record of *Famous Overtures*—spanning Beethoven to Wagner—at the wheel of a silver Porsche, of which there was only one in the world. It was a 911 Turbo, and Karajan was the only person to own one with the lightweight chassis of a Carrera RSR—and that in striped Martini war paint and bold Turbo lettering. Even for the small circle of Porsche aficionados among his fans, this constituted a homage to the 911—with an added exclamation mark. In the picture the conductor and the vehicle look as if they are carved from the same noble wood. The silver of the Porsche, with its provocatively colorful lamination, harmonizes with the conductor genius' silver-gray shock of hair, while under his marble-like features one suspects a power of turbo-like intensity.

The photograph throws a hyper-realistic light on Karajan and his beloved plaything in keeping with the times, lending them both an air of artificiality with its bold color composition and rather crazy setting for a conductor. However, it is also authentic Karajan—he never made any bones about his love of fast cars and motorbikes, yachts and airplanes. His record company used each of these hobbies to stage shoots that radiated the sleek gloss of a manager calendar. The images enact a cool, technological ennoblement of the maestro, elevating him into a special class of international movers and shakers. Herbert von Karajan appears to be incessantly on the move, fleeing from orchestras and concerts, submitting to the intoxication of speed and the sounds hidden within it.

His pose with the 911 came at a time when Karajan was reinventing himself, when the technologization of the Karajan aesthetic became manifest in the recordings—and the soundscape was given a new chrome plating. The Berlin Philharmonic used to be a somber, Furtwängler-inspired[7] ensemble, with Karajan it made high-rev music. The aesthetic of brilliance was metallic, and in this respect fitted well to a conductor who aspired to lead his profession to world fame as its first pop star. However, for the Karajan expert Kai Luehrs-Kaiser, owning a private jet, with its added exclusivity, is an even more important distinguishing feature than owning a Porsche. At the same time, this mobile extravagance increased the pressure to raise the still relatively moderate fees at a breathtaking speed. This period also saw the emergence of Karajan's new hairstyle with its metallic-silver growth cut in a quasi-aerodynamic fashion as if the barber was forced to work in the slipstream. Although the Porsche was never really a playboy car, the over-potent sports car succeeded in dramatizing the conductor's playboy image. Together with the villas in St. Tropez and St. Moritz, Karajan also acquired a new audience among the layers of the middle-class who took delight in looking up at the beautiful and rich, full of awe. With his film star-like glamour, Karajan strove to attract a following beyond the music business.

For the hands that conducted the world's best orchestras, only the most exciting instruments would suffice for his hedonistic conquest of non-musical worlds. For Karajan the Porsche was also a musical instrument, as expressed in the witticism that the sound of a 911 can only be compared to a good Mozart concert. Although attributed to Karajan, there is no proof that he ever uttered it, and experts such as Luehrs-Kaiser dispute whether such an ignorant and brash one-liner could have originated from the maestro. He was not stupid enough for that. However, the saying that you can recognize a good driver by

[7] German conductor and composer who led the Berlin Philharmonic from 1922–45 and 1952–54. Remained in Germany during the Second World War and was adored by the Nazi elite.

the number of dead insects on the windscreen has been passed down to us as genuine Karajan. Karajan became a convert to Porsche at the end of the 1950s when he purchased a 550 A Spyder in 1959. On safety grounds, Richard von Frankenberg's former racing car was given a tamer motor from a 356 A Carrera. Karajan already owned a 356 Speedster, which he had purchased in 1955, and in 1961 a 718 coupe was added to the collection. His first 911—logically, one would like to think—was an S model, followed by the first Turbo in 1975 featuring a 3 L engine—with its, for the time, phemonenal 260 hp—and a red-blue Martini paintjob designed to evoke the successes of the Martini racing team. Karajan subsequently acquired two of the extremely rare 959s. An Indian red model with the delivery receipt number 0959 would be his last car before his death in July 1989. Karajan frequently visited Weissach in order to test racing cars and learn about the latest technical developments. He was also a notorious perfectionist as a Porsche driver, contacting the Salzburg Porsche center to inquire about the correct air pressure for his 911 tires.

The violinist Anne-Sophie Mutter inherited quite a few things from Karajan, her mentor, including a love of the Porsche 911. The story that she bought a 911 before she was 18, in anticipation of a pleasure that she was determined to enjoy at all costs, would become legendary. However, on becoming a mother, her automotive preferences changed. In order to be a good role model for her offspring, she bought a Chrysler Voyager instead of a sports car. Nevertheless, as she admitted in an interview, she would consider buying a Porsche again when the children were out of the house. Mutter also employed a sports car metaphor to illustrate her work with the London Philharmonic Orchestra. There are a lot of orchestras that have a velvety sound, but the London Philharmonic Orchestra—according to Anne-Sophie Mutter—"is more like a Porsche—dynamic and youthful, it can do anything. Its Mozart is fast, not in terms of the tempi but the reaction time. It is chamber music, but without making any compromises." A telling interpretation, not just of the London Philharmonic but also the 911 driving experience.

The 911's Near-Death Experience

The stories differ when it comes to the length of the line traced with the marker pen. However, they all agree that in early 1981, as the newly appointed CEO of Porsche—Peter W. Schutz—was sitting in the office of his head of development—Helmuth Bott—thinking about the future of the hard hit company, his attention was drawn to a chart on the wall depicting the development perspectives for the individual product lines, from the 944 and the 928 to the 911. Two of them projected far into the future, but the line for the Porsche 911 only reached to 1981. Schutz took a marker pen from the desk of his management board colleague and extended the line to the edge of the chart. At least that is how Schutz remembers it. There are rumors that Schutz extended the line over the edge of the chart to the end of the wall, others claim that he even extended the line around the corner to the end of the second wall. With this gesture Schutz made an important decision for the history of the sports car as well as the automobile manufacturer. There had to be an end to the talk of the demise of the Porsche 911. Instead this model was to be the company's savior. The long production run of the G model, 16 years in total, was an indication that in the late 1970s there was a consensus within the company that the 911 was reaching its end—if it hadn't been for the customers who kept on ordering the sports car with the nervous rear.

As the new CEO, appointed in January 1981, Peter Schutz, a Berlin-born American Jew, was determined to see more in the 911 than the long-serving helmsmen Bott and Fuhrmann, who, as engine developers, were so famous that power units were named after them. Nevertheless, both Bott and Fuhrmann had their doubts about the 911's future prospects. As engineers they saw an air-cooled rear-engine car, which viewed soberly, was neither a manifestation of the latest technology—even at the time of its launch—nor an irreplaceably charming vehicle. The two brilliant inventors failed to see anything positive in the 911's obvious shortcomings—which in the end meant they were incapable of comprehending the essence of the Porsche 911. Ultimately, it was precisely these glaring deficiencies, which Porsche-haters such as Jeremy Clarkson loved to make fun of, that gave this sports car its unique and lovable character.

The self doubt of Porsche's upper echelons in Zuffenhausen was fueled by a series of global political caesura in the history of industrial progress. The oil crisis rudely and quite unexpectedly ripped the Western world out of its cozy optimism, undermining the age's belief in mobility and progress that had remained unbroken until this time. In Germany it caught the car industry on the wrong foot. Porsche had just made the transition from a family-run company to a joint stock corporation under management control when the first oil crisis in the fall of 1973 resulted in a 70 percent increase in the price of oil. The dream of "faster, wider, lower" had become more expensive. The Porsche CEO, Ernst Fuhrmann, was convinced that, in future, cars, including sports cars, would have to be more economical, comfortable, and even a little more futuristic.

That is why he attributed great importance to the successor of the VW-Porsche 914. The development of this amenable sports car was completed by Porsche in 1975 after VW's CEO decided to abandon this model on the back of the oil crisis, canceling the joint venture with the Stuttgart-based company.

S CL 8

Porsche—also out of a sense of desperation—was braver and launched the 924 in 1976. With its mere 125 hp, it offered a respectable road performance at best—but certainly nothing impressive. As the weak-chested 924 was considerably less expensive than the 911, it opened up new markets for Porsche. However, this sensible, fast-looking entry-level model was not necessarily positive for Porsche's image.

The Porsche 928, which in retrospect looks like the oversized brother of the Porsche 924, had a completely different agenda. Between the 924 and the 928, the Porsche 911, with its completely different form and drive concept, looked like an unloved stepchild. When the 928 came onto the market one year after the 924, it was larger, more comfortable, and more generously motorized than the Porsche 911—with the exception of the Turbo. With its design language, the 1.83 m (6 ft.) wide and almost 4.5 m (14 ft. 9 in.) long coupe was reminiscent of an Italian gran turismo. It was designed by Anatole Lapine, who, with his cautious remodeling, transforming the classic 911 into the G model, had already proven the depth of his understanding of the Porsche tradition. Lapine saw his design as provocative and exciting, believing that it would prolong the car's youth. "Porsche forms must last for at least 15 years," he declared during the car's launch at the Geneva Motor Show in 1977. It was quite an accurate prediction. Production of the 928 was halted in 1995 after precisely 18 years. Lapine, who emigrated to the United States with his family in 1951 as a "stateless person," was conversant in the global language of car design, while remaining rootless. For Opel he designed the, for the time, stylistically influential GT, which close inspection is reminiscent of both the little Stingray Corvette and a rocket ready to take off to the future—with futuristic as opposed to phallic overtones. Together with the Citroën SM, the Porsche 928 was the ideal monument to a luxurious optimism that remained aloof from the oil crisis and Club of Rome reports.

The car was groundbreaking, but simply not a classic. Thanks to the transaxle concept, which positioned the engine at the front and the transmission at the rear, the Porsche 928 generated a highly undramatic driving experience compared to the passionately revved, nervously dancing 911. The 928 glided along the freeway, even at high speeds. As a rule the large displacement eight-cylinder engine purred and hummed contentedly, except when one hurled it round corners at high revs, which hardly any of the new customers were really interested in doing. Then the eight-cylinder engine would suddenly become loud and brazen. A sound that didn't fit to this vehicle. It was a sports car for cruising that delivered its power in a relaxed and cultivated fashion. Anyone driving a manual 928 couldn't fail to notice that the stick travel, due to the transaxle concept, was appreciably longer than the 911's crisp transmission. However, the 928 was best driven as an automatic. This made it even less sporty, but more comfortable.

> **"We have taken the harshness out of the sports car. It is no longer needed. We can drive in much greater safety and at far higher speeds now, without having to be harsh."**
>
> ↳ Ernst Fuhrmann, Porsche CEO 1972–1980.

« A back-to-basics 1976 version of the transaxle Porsche 924 exposing its front engine and rear gearbox.

In an interview with the magazine *Spiegel,* Fuhrmann proudly explained that, "we have taken the harshness out of the sports car. It is no longer needed. We can drive in much greater safety and at far higher speeds now, without having to be harsh." This assessment would prove to be a tragic error. Unfortunately Fuhrmann was not the type of manager and car engineer who secretly read Marshall McLuhan in the evenings. If he had been then he would have discovered that, as early as the 1960s, McLuhan had correctly diagnosed that the sports car could only have a future if, as a pure object of desire and instrument of pleasure, it was freed from as much utilitarian baggage as possible. Under Fuhrmann's chairmanship, and with a head of development like Helmuth Bott, the far-reaching functionalism, which had constituted Porsche's ideological core since its very founding, was given an excessively technological interpretation. Fuhrmann's notion of progress ignored the irrationality of the libidinous. Astringency and a whiff of excitement belong as much to a sports car as risk and challenge. In a world that was becoming increasingly perfect, or merely felt like it was becoming more perfect, the challenge of imperfection was a sensation to be savored. Furthermore, sports car drivers—from the first futurists to today—had the urge to continually prove themselves. To ignore this was to undermine the brand's core pleasure principle. In addition, Fuhrmann had overlooked the paradoxical irony of Porsche's own advertising. In the words of Ferry Porsche: "No one needs it. Everyone wants it."

Fuhrmann was too Protestant in his dispensing of the irrational, and lacked faith in the 911s potential for development. At virtually the same time as the oil crisis, the United States authorities began bombarding car manufacturers with increasingly strict noise, exhaust, and safety regulations. Here, too, the Porsche executives felt the 911 was not up to the challenge. "At 13 the 911 is old for a car," explained Fuhrmann in 1977 without much emotion. "We will continue to offer it. However, whether that is for two, four, or five years doesn't really matter." One could detect a sense of defeatism, though at the time Fuhrmann would have been better advised to devote his attentions to the stricken 928. It had quickly become common knowledge in the Porsche community that the GT's complex electronics were prone to failure and needed regular servicing. A short while later it became apparent that the planned improvements would effectively make production economically unviable. And when the 928 failed to make an impact in the racing scene, then the mood among even the most loyal customers hit a low point. Today they speak of the "Fuhrmann 928" and distance themselves from the 924, which tends to be regarded as a VW or Audi, if only because it was built in Neckarsulm.

For the middle class children in their townhouses, the card game Top Trumps, in its car version (*Autoquartett* in German), was a medium that helped to order and comprehend contemporary social reality. In violation of the Club of Rome's proscription, this card game was won by those cars that were the fastest, the strongest, had the most cylinders, the most impressive cubic capacity, or accelerated the quickest from 0–100. For these children having a Porsche in their hand was the equivalent to being dealt an ace. The VW-Porsche was disregarded as a type of inferior Porsche, while the mythical supercars such as the Ferrari Daytona or the De Tomaso Pantera, with their space-ship aesthetics, had something extraterrestrial about them and were not part of the common, everyday world of the card players.

As a vehicle for socialization, the car version of Top Trumps was invaluable. As adults, many of the children who grew up with the game in the late 1960s and early 1970s would form part of that hard core of sports car enthusiasts for whom progress could be measured with a basic set of parameters. These children had a simple belief in the future. Their fathers' (and mothers') cars, which as a rule were becoming faster and larger without drawing too much attention to themselves, were incarnations of both the wonder of social advancement and the spirit of engineering perfection. No one had to explain anything to these children about the idea of progress; it was the heart and soul of their Top Trumps game. Back then the future was a good, bright, and exciting place where things were quicker, prettier, and better than ever before.

However, the zeitgeist was not conducive to such optimism. In their capacity as adults, the overgrown, idealistic children of the Club of Rome warned of the limits of a growth whose narrow corridor threatened to strangle all such fantasies of the future, together with the belief in the curative power of technical ideas. The Club of Rome's report, in combination with the first oil crisis, traumatized the Western world. Instead of dreaming of flying into the future, living on the moon, or simply going on holiday in a UFO-like sports car, this hopeful gaze was now directed to the past. In a banal version of the Heideggerian notion of reversement, this turn was now interpreted as a renunciation of futurity. The modernization drive of the 68ers was exhausted, and, with the ecological movement spearheaded by the Green Party, so began the romanticization of country life and the primal, combined with hostility towards technology. Nature was opposed to culture, man lined up against technology. For the children whose worlds were more influenced by Top Trumps cars than the emancipatory projects of their parents, the time had come to make a decision: either remain faithful to their childhood fantasies or move with the times and slowly say goodbye to those smoldering, raucous, fuming dreams. At Documenta 6 Joseph Beuys presented *Honey Pump at the Workplace* as a metaphorical antithesis to the internal combustion engine and the exploitation mechanism of industrialization. In addition to installations, drawings, and performances, the exhibition also included design objects with an automotive focus, the inevitable upshot of which was that the car became embroiled in a discourse of extremities. In the case of Hans Hollein's car the stainless steel chassis was crowned by an operating table, and the ghastly vehicle was powered by a windscreen wiper motor. For the contemporary art mob the car, beyond the glorification of a Warhol, was a grotesque object, a death machine.

The engineers in Zuffenhausen had learned that there was no escaping the zeitgeist, but more than that they now understood that there were enough people in the world whose faith in technical progress was not to be shaken by such zeitgeist-opportunism. The success of the Carrera RS at the time of the oil crisis and the strong sales figures for the Porsche Turbo made it clear that adjusting to the present was something to be carried out in a spirit of self-confidence, not opportunism. The strict exhaust regulations in California drove Porsche's engineers to pursue increasingly sophisticated changes in order to produce faster but also cleaner sports cars. The French, who had lost their faith in the future of car building, rediscovered it in the building of trains. The TGV, "Train à Grande Vitesse," would soon fulfill those dreams of speed, which, in collaboration with Maserati, had eluded Citroën with their SM and Renault with their Alpine.

As if Hollywood had gotten wind of the mood of self-doubt in Stuttgart, the 911 was no longer featured as a companion for incorrigible individualists, as in *Le Départ* or *Le Mans,* but a murder weapon for secret agents from the Eastern Bloc. In the American action-comedy *Condorman* from 1981, a sort of James Bond parody, a pack of Porsche 911s hunt down the naive but lovable hero. The film's central scene features a Yugoslavian coastal town whose inhabitants are ripped out of their daily lives. Struck dumb, they stare in a state of shock until a baby cries and the church bells begin to chime, while in the distance the sound of five Porsche 911 Turbos can be heard, led by a bloodthirsty agent with a sliver false eye. It is the KGB pursuit squadron. Thus Hollywood stages the continuation of the Hitler-Stalin Pact. The Porsches, with their black tinted windows, operate like

» Limited editions: the much-maligned 928 coupe in 1977 (↑) and the 959 in 1986, which was produced in a run of only 292 (↓).

The VW-Porsche was disregarded as a type of inferior Porsche, while the mythical supercars such as the Ferrari Daytona or the De Tomaso Pantera, with their space-ship aesthetics, had something extraterrestrial about them.

» The 914 from around 1970–1972.

a pack of wolves. The leader Morovich drives a converted Turbo flatnose, while the hero of the film, a comic illustrator called Woody, escapes the five 911s in a Pontiac remix as a manifestation of the Anglo-Saxon will to freedom and individuality. On the inside it looks like a forefather of KITT, the Knight Rider's trusty steed, another instance of the trivialization of the muscle car that appeared at around the same time. The shots of the Porsches lend them an extremely threatening and aggressive appearance, even though the drivers are no match for the cunning blond-haired American. At the end of the almost 10 minute car chase, the American hero-mobile flies off the end of a pier into the sea where it turns into a speedboat. The driver of the Porsche sits cursing in his black monster.

In the Fuhrmann era Porsche was in danger of losing its soul, which is why the family intervened in the form of the supervisory board. Fuhrmann was removed as CEO and a short while later Schutz assumed responsibility for the company. In contrast to Fuhrmann, he knew little about cars and even less about Porsche; however, he had the right feeling when it came to the 911. Exactly 10 years after Fuhrmann it was Schutz's turn to give an interview to the magazine *Spiegel,* occasioned by the drastic fall in Porsche sales due to the high value of the dollar. On top of this, Porsche was no longer the undisputed ruler of the freeway's fast lane. At the end of the 1980s competitors entered the market with fast touring sedans such as the Mercedes 190 E 2.3-16, the M5, and even the Mercedes 300 E, which could put the 911 under serious pressure on the freeway. With the introduction of the cabriolet in 1982 Schutz had succeeded in increasing sales, especially in the United States, however the Carrera of the time was effectively under-motorized. In a sports car test the magazine *Auto Bild* made the sober judgment that: "The 911 is from yesterday."

As an emergency measure, Porsche borrowed from the super-Porsche developed by Helmuth Bott, the 959, which from 1986 was sold to Porsche fans worldwide in a limited edition of 292. With a top speed of 339 km/h (211 mph) the Porsche was the world's fastest production car approved for road use, a motorized personification of the Porsche engineers' virtuoso art of car building. Back then it cost 420,000 deutsche marks. For the forthcoming Porsche model, the 964, the developers adopted four-wheel drive, and a new chassis with helical springs as opposed to the outdated torsion spring suspension. In addition there was tiptronic, power assisted steering, and ABS. The 964 was a completely new car, although it was closer to the classic 911 than the 959. And as the limousine manufacturers agreed to limit the speed of their sporting over-achievers to 250 km/h, the 964's top speed of 260 km/h (162 mph) restored the hierarchy on the freeway—and in the children's Top Trumps game.

Ferry Porsche's doctrine of reduction extended to the last 3.2 L Carrera, connecting it in an unbroken line to the first 356 prototype, and naturally the Beetle and its countless forerunners. If it transpired that the 911 was to find its apotheosis in the Carrera 3.2, and thus in the words of the German philosopher Hegel had reached the first stage of perfection, then it should come as no surprise that in a country with a violent passion for metaphysics, there should be purists for whom the Carrera 3.2 constituted the core of their world view. They regard successive models as a schism and wouldn't dream of being seen driving them. The 911, as a sports car in an eternal state of becoming, generated an incomparably pedantic relationship to tradition. The first 911 is considered the holy grail of the 911 world and thus the *mètre des archives* of that passionate community that, over the course of the first 50 years, assumed an almost civil religious character. In a characteristically German, Heideggerian fashion, its development away from its origins was not just seen as progress, but as a loss to be bitterly mourned. The classic 911s increasing size, speed, and width was continually compared with its origins. Thus the deficiencies and inconsistencies of the classic 911 were reinterpreted as the character and essence of the sports car, and in the eyes of the traditionalists, the more perfect the car became, the less it appeared to do justice to the myth. Every change in its appearance was considered a plastic operation on something that was essentially perfect.

The Porsches' sense of their own history prepared the ground for such a dogmatic fundamentalism. Although Porsche as a company rose to success in the 1950s at a time of maximum corporate anonymity, from the beginning they placed considerable importance on the communication of the roots of their engineering craft and the contributions their family had made to the development of the automobile. This also included the Nazi era, a period that was largely suppressed and blanked out in Germany at the time. Thus they constructed a history out of the family saga that quickly lent the young company the aura of a longstanding tradition. And that at a time when it was only

in the garish films celebrating regional life, mountain village communities, or the historically coveted countryside that this idyll took on a nostalgic character. As a rule thinking about the past was avoided. Porsche had no understanding for this. Only a few years after its founding the sports car manufacturer began using its company history for advertising purposes. From Cisitalia and the first Volkswagen prototypes to the megalomaniacal, record-breaking "T 80" that Ferdinand Porsche designed for Daimler Benz—these were just some of the historical precedents employed in the brand communication in an effort to identify the 356 as the "sum total of all engineering experience." Exactly 10 years later, at the unveiling of the Porsche 911, this ancestral line was extended: from the Lohner-Porsche Chaise (1900) and the Mercedes-racing car for the Targa Florio (1924) to the Porsche 904 Carrera GTS, hardly a single one of the Porsche clan's designs was omitted. At a time when design, like pop culture, acted, thought, and designed in the spirit of an aggressive denial of history, Porsche proudly displayed its past. Porsche thought historically, while good design was only interested in the present, or even better, an exotic future. Thus the company was proto-postmodernist. If postmodernism was a culture of remembrance that refused to see tradition as something that had to be overcome at all costs (in accordance with modernist ideology), then Porsche employed this strategy long before architects and literary theorists made it the next great intellectual fashion. However, in contrast to the playful postmodernists who understood tradition—according to Wikipedia—as a collection of possibilities to be drawn on as desired in a display of virtuosity, Porsche's recourse to role models and roots was functional in character. The challenge was to explore the future potential of the old, whether it be the idea of the rear engine or air cooling, taking it to the absolute limit while respecting tradition. It was less about historicism than cultivating tradition in accordance with the latest technical developments. Furthermore, it lacked the almost compulsive irony common to postmodernism. Porsche was serious when it came to delving into the archives in order to gain a better understanding of its own future.

At the time this approach was unique to Porsche. The other car manufacturers were designing cars to look like space ships and futurism was the zeitgeist backdrop to the 1960s and 1970s. The design world was full of innumerable revolutionary ideas about the future of objects; however, hardly anyone was prepared to think about evolutionary development. The functionalism of the Ulm School and Braun's design was ridiculed. In this respect, Porsche, with its highly modern language of forms and anomalous cultivation of tradition, risked being misunderstood by its contemporaries.

1988
1994

» As competition in the late 1980s grew, Porsche developed the 964, which returned to its four-wheel drive roots.

The 964

Four-Wheel Drive, ABS, Power Steering

In the second half of the 1980s Porsche entered a downward spiral that threatened to accelerate out of control. In the shock of 1987, the dollar fell from 3.60 to 1.80 deutsche marks, and as 87 percent of its cars were sold in the U.S. market, this was a fatal development for the company. On top of that there was the threat from Japan. In America the Acura, known in Germany as the Honda NSX, was the new most feared opponent, along with the cut price Nissan 300 ZX Turbo. The NSX came with an aluminum body, titanium double wishbone front axle, …

valve control, and much more besides. At the time the 911—phrased rather dramatically—was still plagued with heating problems and misted windows. The cars were worlds apart. The drag coefficient of a G model was 0.40—more than that of a 356. The Audi 100 with 0.30 was considerably better. The 911 had to be overhauled in a hurry. The designers made use of integrated bumpers and a smooth underbody to reduce the drag coefficient to below 0.32. As a consequence, the 964 with a top speed of 260 km/h (162 mph) was just as fast as a Turbo G with its extra 50 hp.

The chassis was completely redesigned. The four-wheel drive was borrowed from the 959, which in turn was derived from the rally 911s from the mid-1980s. The Carrera 4 with four-wheel drive was the overture to the 964 model series. Although the traction it provided was essential for rally sport success—or a necessity for such an exceptional, over-motorized coupe as the 959—for a number of Porsche purists four-wheel drive for a normal Carrera appeared to be an exaggeration, or worse still, a violation of its essence. Until this time, skidding and (controlled) rear drift were

S-P 1988

part of the driving pleasure. As a driver one could keenly sense the front passenger's sense of unease when slinging a G model around bends, especially if it was the passenger's first time in a 911. However, with four-wheel drive this experience was reserved for ice and snow, and the pleasure to be found in drift was replaced by a sense of astonishment at the powertrain electronics' capacity to handle lateral acceleration, even on wet ground. But, despite what a number of 911 purists may have thought, this development actually saw Porsche returning to its roots, rather than betraying them. It was Ferdinand Porsche who in 1900 designed the first four-wheel drive vehicle in the shape of his electro-Porsche, though the brand would later pay its penance, developing the mother of all rear drift sports cars, the Porsche 911.

Compared to the classic 911s and the G models, the 964 was a sports car with both a completely different handling and sound. The roaring and singing of the six-cylinder boxer was replaced by growling and snarling. The four-wheel drive, in combination with the ABS, made this 911 almost idiotproof, if it wasn't for the unbelievable performance figures displayed by a well run 964. Even without tuning, it had a top speed of 290 km/h (180 mph) on the speedometer, which made it a serious competitor on the freeway, even for its successor model. "Porsche horsepowers count double," is a popular saying among Porsche followers, an expression of the knowledge that every effort is made in Zuffenhausen to ensure that the horsepower figures in the brochure and the vehicle registration certificate are delivered, if not exceeded. As a consequence there were never any disappointments, at least not with respect to the 911s will to perform.

The development engineers and designers would have liked to have packed more innovation into the new 911, but resources were scarce during the crisis and the development time was short. A PDK double-clutch transmission had already been road tested in the 944 Turbo and the 928; however, it never found its way into the 964. This model also ushered in the end of a long tradition with respect to the production site with the opening of a new bodywork factory—while the G model was still being built in those halls once used by the Reuter company.

The rear spoiler, which extended at 80 km/h (50 mph), was a startling feature. It protected the silhouette from the disfigurement of wild spoiler outgrowths, and provided those overtaken by a new Carrera at 80 km/h with the spectacle of a power-packed metamorphosis—as well as supplying the engine with more cooling air. The extensive electronic control systems and their associated cable assemblies led to a rapid increase in the weight of the 911—taking it to almost 1.5 tons. Although it didn't look like it, the 964 was a fat 911, especially with the four-wheel drive. The design was an aerodynamically optimized variation on the classic concept. The old cockpit architecture was retained, as were the bulky torpedo tubes for the décolleté, while the swollen bumpers made the 911 look stouter. For the designer of the 911, Michael Mauer, the 964 with its more muscular road presence—thanks to the pronounced fenders—is his favorite.

The four-wheel drive, in combination with the ABS, made this 911 almost idiotproof.

« The 911 Carrera 3.6: an aerodynamically optimized version of the classic, with a startling rear spoiler that extended at 80 km/h (50 mph).

Porsche historian Dieter Landenberger criticized the fact that hardly any of the parts used in other Porsche models were used in the 964, which is why its production proved so expensive. For the Porsche driver and fan Sascha Keilwerth the build quality of the bodywork is an indication that Porsche wasn't doing so well at the time. "The bodywork rusts at the fenders, and over the years the wind deflector and bumpers lose their form. The rear lights lose their plastic and color and even become brittle." Nevertheless, with almost 64,000 units sold the 964 can be considered a success. The marketing campaign with the popular Porsche Carrera Cup launched in 1990, as well as the unbelievable variety, also played their role.

In the past there was at maximum only a handful of 911 variants; however, with the 964 came the beginning of a comprehensive differentiation of the product palette. Customers could choose between the Carrera 4, 2, Turbo, Turbo S, Speedster, Turbo-Look, and RS, not to mention the special models such as the RS American, the lowrider, and the "Jubi," the thirtieth anniversary model and broad-shouldered tribute to the 911. The anniversary model was essentially a 964 Carrera 4 with the bodywork of a Turbo, i.e. its wide fenders and side sections. The numerals 911 were embroidered into the backrests of the foldable rear seats, while in the center of the hat shelf Porsche added a leather-covered bracket with two aluminum plaques. The plaque visible from the outside through the rear windscreen displayed the individual serial number of the special limited edition. The plaque facing inwards carried the inscription *30 Jahre 911* (30 Years 911) written in mirror writing so that the driver—as the homepage of the Jubi enthusiasts informs us—is reminded that he is driving a Jubi every time he looks in the rearview mirror. With the Jubi the 911's self-musealization reached its preliminary climax. The inside plaque transformed it into an exhibit from the history of technology, which, when in doubt, could be displayed in its "white cube"—the garage—or in the touring exhibitions of the

"This is the 911 for the next 25 years"

↳ Heinz Branitzki, Porsche CEO 1988–1990.

» The "Jubi," celebrating 30 years of the 911, set against a vibrant background, similar to that used in the Jung von Matt advertising campaign for Porsche.

Jubi conventions, or on Sunday drives. Museums as storage and presentation sites for material witnesses possess a static authority that the Jubi enjoyed wherever it parked, i.e. exhibited itself. With this plaque, which was also prominently displayed on the 2013 anniversary poster for the Jubi, this Porsche transcended the mundane world of the car as vehicle and disposable product. This anniversary vehicle gave an added impetus to the canonization of the 911 in all its historical manifestations. The sports car as a cultural artifact began to assume the aura of a historical document on the one side, and a sculpture on the other.

With the Jubi as ready-made museum, and later with its own museum, Porsche had understood that for a cultural nation such as Germany, the institution of the museum was an extremely popular medium for knowledge production and mediation. As institutions for collecting, preserving, and exhibiting, museums have great symbolic power—as well as being culturally contested. They constitute "key sites of culture" as concrete, visible manifestations of the abstract idea of history and representation. Porsche preferred to write its own history, rather than leave it to others. That is another reason why the museum in Zuffenhausen, and the highly professional archive with its passionate director, is at least as productive in generating Porsche's exegeses and promoting historical dissertations as the developers with their modernization of the 911 sports car concept. The engineers' vision of the future is based on the cultivation of the past in museum and archive. "The origin always remains the future," intoned Martin Heidegger in 1953. Incidentally, his publisher Günther Neske was a passionate Porsche driver, and there are persistent rumors that Heidegger was fond of riding in his Porsche. Here the Heidegger research is still in its infancy, but what a coup it would be if it could be proven that the theory of reversement was conceived in the front passenger seat of a sports car notorious for its rear drift.

An additional factor that contributed to the 964's success was the new advertising campaign from the young advertising agency Jung von Matt. When the two newcomers were invited to pitch their bid for the Porsche account, they succeeded in pulling off a coup in the spirit of the 911. The established agencies rolled into Zuffenhausen in double strength to make their presentations: complex, multimedia-based, ostentatious. In contrast Holger Jung and Jean-Remy von Matt arrived in a Porsche, stood up in front of the board of directors, and said: "There are two of us here today because only two people fit into a Porsche." With this sentence—as their competitor Amir Kassaei realized with a pang of jealously—they had won the account: "They had understood the essence of the company." This resulted in the campaign *So baut man Sportwagen* (This is how one builds sports cars). With its garish colors and somewhat overbearing slogans, it set out to give the brand an emotional overhaul after years and decades in which ruminative

mini-essays with small pictures were employed in an attempt to explain the charms of the 911. Cinematically the "re-birth of the cool" in Zuffenhausen was represented by the Turbo 3.6 that supercop Will Smith drove in *Bad Boys*.

The most unusual 964 was the genuinely terrifying "Panamericana" study, which was based on a C4. When Ferry saw his birthday present in 1989 his only words were: "Take it away." Anyone looking at this mutation today can easily understand the Porsche founder's irritation. The Dutch motorway police drove the 964 Targa—with the air-cooled 911 it was possible to drive longer distances in reverse. The 964 also brought with it many new colors: maritime blue, star ruby red, speed yellow etc., trendy colors that helped shape the style of the 1990s—as did the cup rims.

"This is the 911 for the next 25 years," declared the new CEO Heinz Branitzki on unveiling the 964. Although untenable in almost every respect, this prophesy announced that the period during which Porsche had thought about scrapping the 911 was now over. With the 964, the 911 became the eternal Porsche, and all the other models grouped themselves around this car. It had now officially become that car that it had long been in the minds of Porsche enthusiasts: the essence and passionate heart of the brand.

Moody's Porsche: The Hipster 911

This Porsche would become the object of desire for anti-nostalgic nostalgists. In contrast to the classic 911 and G model, it was fully galvanized and fitted with airbags, dispensed with chrome—the automotive equivalent of parquet—and had a modern, sober, unpretentious air. In 2007 a black 964 cabriolet would become the co-star in *Californication,* the controversial American TV series about a sex-addicted writer from New York. He is the charming, asocial bohemian whose most faithful companion is a 911. In a permanent state of disrepair, and generally unwashed, the car is like a mirror reflecting the hero's dark, dissolute, and yet touchingly natural and beautiful soul. On coming into money Moody buys himself a newer Porsche; however, it gets stolen and he ends up with his old Porsche, build year 1991. In the fourth series Moody's daughter crashes his convertible, so the forgiving father buys himself a similar model from a used-car salesman. While still on the lot, Moody smashes the right headlight to pieces—and the vehicle looks like his old car again.

Since this episode the Berlin author Moritz Rinke has been in search of a 964. According to Rinke, "Hank Moody has a certain way of slamming the door of his Porsche, letting his car get dirty, deliberately smashing a headlight when buying a new car. He doesn't inflate his Porsche, he owns it in a casual way as if he has become one with it in a completely natural fashion, without any commotion, as if it is completely natural that Hank Moody needs this car to live. He is very attached to it. Whenever he sits in the Porsche his worries dissolve. Of course he has sex in the Porsche, but he also sleeps alone in it as he doesn't have a real home. On one occasion he takes a ride with his daughter, and she is allowed to drive, a very tender scene, one of the most moving scenes in the series."

Hank Moody's way of driving the Porsche is an attempt to uncover the roots of the 911 ethos that have been buried under success and mass production. Essentially Moody wants to maltreat the 964 until it becomes transfigured into a type of classic 911. However, even before *Californication* the 964 had its unusual fans who recognized this 911's willful character. Heinz Gindullis, for example. Born in Nuremberg, Gindullis may not have invented Berlin-Mitte as the city's new party district, but he was certainly one of its co-inventors. Like so many young people with a talent for hedonism, he came to this once proud city after the fall of the wall. In its ruins the children of the middle classes from across Germany, and later the whole world, discovered a form of over-dimensioned history park and adventure playground. Heinz, who everyone calls Cookie, began his bar business in small, decrepit basements and empty storefronts, and quickly became one of the most active figures in Berlin's nightlife. At some point business was going so well that the 1.95 m (6 ft 5 in.) tall young man with the bald head was able fulfill a childhood dream: a Porsche 911. He had always played with toy Matchbox Porsches as a child. He was also the first person in his family with a driving license: his mother, father, and siblings didn't have one. Hence a Porsche also constituted an existential declaration of independence.

However, that in the year 2000 he would eventually buy an anthracite-colored 911 Carrera, build year 1992, happened as casually as the growth of his nightlife business. One of his DJs, stage name Zodiac, repaired and sold 911s professionally.

4FTY343

"I have got the car for you," he explained to Cookie, and parked a Porsche 993 in front of the club. Cookie was, however, deeply disappointed. The car was too polished, too well-behaved and cultivated. But Zodiac didn't become discouraged in his proselytization, and a short while later he rang again. Now he had really found the right Porsche, and delivered the 964 that Cookie has been driving ever since. Formulated somewhat romantically, it was love at first sight. The price was okay; however, the 26-year-old operator of what at the time were half-legal clubs and the first of Berlin-Mitte's hip bars, spent a long time considering whether he could afford the car. Not financially but in terms of image. His girlfriend at the time advised him against it. How could he, she asked him after the first test drive.

He had his doubts, especially as Berlin-Mitte at the time—at least when it came to cars and traffic—was in essence a precarious village in which social control watched over the observers of sub-cultural codes and their political correctness. After two weeks it was clear: I want this car. He bought it and has never looked back. After this purchase nightlife professionals always knew where Cookie was: a Porsche 911 was a rare thing in Mitte at the time and news of his acquisition spread like wildfire in the small bohemian scene. The new arrivals from Munich and Stuttgart were happy, the hipsters from East Germany frowned. While ordering a second latte in Café Bravo, Melanie, a good friend, asked Cookie rather derisively whether he would be able to buy a screw for his 911 with the profits from what she had just consumed. The anecdote says a lot about the spirit of provincialism with which the nightlife protagonists viewed that object of desire beyond their sneaker-turntable-mountain-bike world. A Porsche 911 was viewed with suspicion, even though it never came to any acts of vandalism.

Cookie succeeded in irritating both the Mitte pedants and the Porsche pedants. Long before the series *Californication* hit the screens, Cookie had discovered the charm of maximum neglect when it came to the maintenance of his Porsche 911. On one occasion he didn't wash the car for six months until people began to write funny things on it—greetings, initials, secret messages. Then the car had to go to the workshop for repairs and his friend Ralf, aka Zodiac, was horrified and had it cleaned. The Porsche had to be put through the car wash several times, recalled Cookie with a grin. However, the appearance of his 964 also undermined the pedantry of the Porsche purists in other respects. The front and rear bumpers were usually scratched before he had them re-sprayed in a ritual act. For Cookie the 911 is the ideal big city car. It is small, agile—"always quick off the mark, and the first away at the lights." He drives so dynamically that he ends up replacing the brakes more frequently than he would like. Nevertheless, he finds the Porsche too loud for the motorway—and that for someone who usually spends his nights in a hail of sound.

Egalitarian at the P1: Every Schmuck Drives a 911

In the late 1980s it was said of Munich, that party-loving city on the river Isar, that it had the most Porsche 911s of any city. "More than L.A." was the saying of the Porsche-driving pimps back then. And indeed there were plenty of places where the 911 appeared in such large, concentrated numbers that it acquired a carefree, commonplace air. The parking lot in front of the P1 was such a place. The P1 was a nightclub that at the end of the twentieth century put Munich at the top of the world's party spirit league table. A lewd, lascivious, loud, coarse, fantastic, exciting club that never had any aspirations of being underground. It was quite content to be simply the best joint to party in—no matter how.

During Munich's Oktoberfest, the P1 was frequented by the popper girls and boys in traditional Bavarian costumes, while during the week it was the haunt of numerous models and pumped-up law students, car dealers and hairdressers, football stars from FC Bayern Munich and TV starlets. The bouncers were legendary for their tough door policy and humor. Anyone who had made a name for themselves as a party professional or top pickup artist was always admitted. In the case of women, being "blond, sexy, and not dressed too complex" was a help.

It was a place of simple truths, and as such its forecourt of power was the parking lot, which by day belonged to the museum of contemporary art Haus der Kunst (originally built by the Nazis), and after 10:30 p.m., those good-mood priests whom it summoned to celebrate liturgy in the marble halls. On driving into the parking lot one was first summoned to make a contribution to the collection plate. Anyone donating a miserly two or three, and at the weekends five deutsche marks, was immediately directed to a parking space. Anyone making a generous offering, forking out 10 or 20 deutsche marks, was permitted to park their car—in the interest of truth, their Porsche 911—directly in front of the door. From time to time every 911 driver, regardless of how embarrassing the whole thing was, treated themselves to the routine of VIP parking. With the engine running at low revs, one rolled to the attendant standing by the top parking spots who indicated where one should park one's Carrera. A visitor from Mars or China observing the parking lot would have been convinced that the 911 was a type of cramped, loud Volkswagen, which in this country was customarily driven at night.

On leaving the P1 sometime during the night, the happy, raved-out Porsche driver was presented with his keys and proceeded across the parking lot, only to be confronted by a confusing array of over a dozen black or anthracite-colored 911s, which frequently resulted in them trying to open the door of the wrong car. A further source of amusement for the doormen in summer was provided by the parking lot attendants who occasionally got the keys mixed up, presenting the owner of a 964 Carrera 4 with the keys to a brand new 993 Turbo, who duly started to drive it away—until an acquaintance of the Turbo owner sounded the alarm. Ferraris were a rarity at P1. A blond woman from Lake Starnberg in a 348 TS was a topic of conversation among the pumped-up boys for weeks thanks to her nonchalant parking maneuver, and, in light of her virtuoso driving skills, incredibly tender age. Such a woman had to be a Fata Morgana.

The 911 was not a special car in front of the P1, in fact on some evenings it was the only car. It was not a car for making an impact, it was about being part of the scene—a beacon of hedonism and the dubious; of the pimp-like and athletic. It was not uncommon for party experts to drive home late Friday night

» Young people dressed in popper style admiring their object of desire.

only to load their skis into the passenger seat a few hours later and race off to the Alps. It was a Munich-mobile, the Volkswagen of a prosperous and pleasure-loving city that rarely felt a sense of embarrassment at its good mood, let alone apologized for it.

No one turned their heads to look at a 911 on the exclusive Maximilianstraße or in Munich's party district of Schwabing. No one apart from tourists. It was not uncommon for three 911s to be stood next to each other at the lights, which provoked a smirk at best, or merely a hearty yawn. In Munich during the late 1980s and 1990s the 911 entered the sphere of the commonplace. It was an inevitable process, not a painful one. It was the time when the Austrian fashion designer Helmut Lang opened his first shop in Germany (logically enough in Munich), and art directors and gallery owners from Hamburg and Berlin flew to Munich in search of respectable attire. It was Munich's summer and winter fairytale. The last high point before everything began to look like the living rooms of ex-FC Bayern Munich footballer Karl-Heinz Rummenigge and Giulia Siegel.[16]

In P1 no self-respecting woman was impressed by a blowhard who had leased his 911 at great financial hardship. In their own estimation—and they were not alone in this opinion—the best looking guys arrived on skateboard, by foot, or, less original, in a taxi. Women in a 911 were generally older than the young women who arrived on foot, with a taxi, or in their girlfriend's Golf IV.

The comedian Thomas Schröder, born in Kray, a district of Essen, invented a figure called Atze Schröder who reduced the P1-machismo to a petty-bourgeois stereotype from the industrial region of the Ruhr valley, where Germany

[16] Model, actress, TV presenter, and daughter of music producer and Eurovision Song Contest regular Ralph Siegel.

The 911 was not a car for making an impact; it was about being part of the scene—a beacon of hedonism and the dubious, of the pimp-like and athletic.

« Dressed to impress: poppers and their 911 coupe and 911 Targa parked at Lake Starnberg just outside Munich.

was far less wealthy, elegant, famous, or simply lacked self-confidence. Both the character and the artist deformed Porsche's claim to exclusivity, which was once the status symbol of the nobility, the established, and super-successful. The life maxim "Step on the gas as none of us are getting out of here alive anyway," established the counterpoint to that deep-rooted existentialist spirit that had inspired sports car drivers since the futurist Marinetti and James Dean. Driving a Porsche became a joke, as highlighted by stage characters such as Atze Schröder, who lent the Porsche myth a new facet: that of the egalitarian luxury product. With the Porsche Days convention in Dinslaken, this un-academic Porsche subculture, which rarely attracts the upper classes, established its own forum at the start of the twenty-first century—which appropriately is held on a harness racing track on May 1, International Worker's Day. The event in the city in the northwest of the Ruhr valley with its population of 70,000 attracts Atze Schröders from around the world. It is loud, joyous, and without the faintest trace of snobbery. The event is organized by Ingo Rübener, who has the following motto inscribed on the rear spoiler of his bright yellow 964 RS: *Immer in Eile Ingo der Geile* (Randy Ingo, always in a rush). In his words, the event unites the low-budget scene with proud owners who, logically enough, scrimped and saved to afford their 911. Here exclusivity is cashed in and exchanged for pure fanhood. Contrary to expectations, Porsche welcomes such events, using their rough charm to counteract the prejudice that Porsche is an upper-class monoculture. Driving a Porsche, but also driving a 911, has decoupled itself from the customer analysis that sees the classic Carrera buyer as a top earner with far-reaching financial possibilities: the Porsche fascination is serviced by both affordable used models and anarchic appropriations of the 911 as an object of pleasure. Hans, from the German road movie *Ein Freund von mir* (A friend of mine) is a mixture of Atze Schröder and the young Marc from *Le Départ*. The casual worker, played by Jürgen Vogel, initiates Karl, a highly qualified young insurance mathematician, into the fine art of living—whose summit is driving a Porsche 911 naked. In the film it is two meteorite-gray metallic Carrera 997s that the unsuccessful hedonist employs to infect the successful melancholic with his vital élan. The Porsche is no longer a getaway car to a different life, but merely the vehicle for those pleasures that a well motorized sports car can offer. If the hierarchy of pleasure in the 1960s and 1970s proceeded from the top down, the reverse is now the case. It is possible that the enthusiasts who have remained consciously "prole" in outlook have a better understanding of that luxury object than those tiers for whom the sports car was originally constructed. André Schäfer's affectionate documentary film *100 Porsches and Me* also captures the extent to which the social corridor of 911 owners and drivers has widened. The personification of this deluge-like leveling of distinctions is a blind doctor who even succeeds in leaving behind those biological limits usually associated with driving a sports car.

» Racing and rallies: where the 911 is pushed to its full potential.

1993
1996

» Motor-show star, as well as racer and police chaser: the 911 Targa has journeyed far.

The 993

The Fast Newcomer

The 964 was quickly overtaken by the competition, while its production proved too expensive. The faith that Branitzki, the unlucky CEO, placed in the 964 as the 911 for the next 25 years quickly proved illusory. The economic situation was catastrophic. When Harm Lagaay started at Porsche in 1989 he immediately began work on a successor. The most important technical innovation was the LSA rear axle.

LSA stands for *Leichtbau, Stabilität, Agilität* (lightweight, stable, agile). The new rear axle—as was so often the case with Porsche—was a direct import from motor racing and prevented spring deflection during acceleration. The 285 hp of the Carrera S represented the last evolutionary stage of the air-cooled and aspirated boxer motors. In fact, the engineers' specification sheets revealed that the 993 was actually designed with water cooling, but Porsche lacked the money to implement it. For the countless traditionalists this was a stroke of luck. That is why to this day the owners of the Carrera S remain at the top of the 993 community's hierarchy. For insiders such as Dieter Landenberger, the Carrera S or 4S is the most formally beautiful of the 993s.

Its handling was a further step in the direction of the power steering-related comfort that the 964 had already presaged in various ways. With this car one could eat up the miles on the motorway, from Berlin to Nice, without the ears, legs, or arms tiring. However, as an antidote to the threat of becoming too comfortable, Porsche returned to long distance motor racing with the 911 GT1.

The 993 also ushered in the era of Wiedeking's chairmanship with its lean production and Kaizen philosophy. "In the boom year 1986," recalls Wendelin Wiedeking, "Porsche sold more than 50,000 cars, almost two-thirds of them in the USA; in the model year 1993 it was just 11,500, and a total of only 300 in North America." Porsche was considered a potential takeover

911 targa

PORSCHE

candidate, and if it hadn't been for Ferry Porsche continually emphasizing that the family would never agree to the sale of the company, the line of prospective buyers would have been even longer. When Wiedeking was made CEO of Porsche in 1992, he set out to get the costs under control, sharpen the company profile, and develop products and markets. *Anders ist besser* (Different is better) was the title of his book of manager wisdom in which he explained his success strategy in rather popular "idiot's guide" terms. Even as the director for production and materials logistics, he broke with the corporate culture by relativizing the exclusive fixation on the product—although he didn't go so far as to call it into question. Up until Wiedeking's interventions, the quality of the product was the highest good, so much so that the company lost sight of the costs.

On top of that the suppliers were unreliable. "At the end of the 1980s more than 20 percent of all parts were delivered more than three days too late, a third of the deliveries were of the wrong quantity, and 10,000 parts from every million were defective," wrote Wiedeking. "In contrast at Toyota […] only around five parts from every million were unusable and 99 percent of all parts were delivered on time and in the right quantity."

The Porsches were too expensive: the production times had to be shortened, and along with them the costs. Wiedeking ordered his employees to read the MIT study on "The Second Revolution in the Car Industry." This was followed by a corporate evaluation, which came to shocking conclusions. "Nothing was in good order, not a single department." It suddenly became clear the extent to which Porsche was lagging behind the Japanese competition. This was perceived as a "real affront." However, in light of the 1992 recession, there was no other choice but to adopt a radically new course. Wiedeking had to cut 2,000 jobs, the management levels were reduced from six to four, and the entire workflow was remodeled. This took place just as the 993 entered production and continued throughout the model's entire lifespan. It was only with the 996 that the production conditions finally became inscribed in the product. This Porsche was to be the first globalized 911 and a turning point for the Porsche 911. Parallel to the restructuring of production, the company also positioned itself as the car industry's equivalent of the clever David. Having risen from its deathbed, the small brand's fragility was reinterpreted as a strength, which as in the Old Testament story, came with agility and the surprise attack. On top of this, Porsche also enjoyed the advantage of being underestimated by the competition at the time. Head of PR Anton Hunger groomed Wiedeking to become the brand's public face, and for the first time the marketing was conducted in a globally harmonized and integrated fashion. The coherence of the product, PR, and marketing brought success in its wake in the form of the 1995 turnaround. Porsche was once again the brand of the successful.

Father and Son: The Family Car

A Porsche is never one's exclusive property. Although the car provides a lifetime of pleasure, one is actually just preserving it for the next generation. A paraphrase of the philosophy of a Geneva-based watchmaker provides quite an accurate description of a 911 father's attitude to tradition. The Latin term *traditio* primarily refers to the passing on of real objects, as opposed to ideal values. However, both aspects come together in the 911 when the father's euphoria infects the son or daughter. In the case of a potentially irrational object such as a sports car, it is less about a convention that the father or the mother drum into the offspring than a shared passion and affection.

If the father regresses behind the wheel of his 911, then this can bear a strong similarity to his son's play instinct. On YouTube there is a clip—which you can access by entering the two search terms "Porsche" and "boy"—that shows a five- or six-year-old boy on the front passenger seat of an extremely sporty 911 as it turns into a main thoroughfare. Quietly—barely perceptible on first watching the clip—the boy slowly counts down: "Ready, steady, ... go!" At which the father with a black baseball cap accelerates so violently that he and his son are pushed back into the Recaro racing shells. The boy hoots with pleasure, while the father beams with pride at the fact his son is able to experience this acceleration in the midst of the city traffic as a pure, unadulterated pleasure. At the end of the 30-second transgression of the entire highway code the boy asks if he can have some cake before school. The father nods. "And chocolate?"—"That too," promises the father.

Every 911-mad father secretly, or less secretly, hopes that his children will share something of his passion. Happiness shared is happiness doubled. The clip shows an ideal scenario: father and son united in their passion, mutual absolute trust, and intimacy through joy and excitement. In the text accompanying the clip the father confesses, a little self-ironically, that he only drives so fast because of the "peer pressure" from his son. Porsche, like nearly all car manufacturers, has equipped their showrooms with play areas for such fathers and their children, so that the Saturday visits to these sacred sites of the 911 world are family-friendly in every respect. The children can draw in the Porsche coloring books or create havoc with the innumerable toy 911s, while the adjacent display cabinets offer toys for people of all ages, ranging from washable cuddly 911s, with precisely embroidered Carrera lettering and Porsche logos, to the snack box for the kindergarten and the yellow 911 cabriolet with electric motor and a top speed of 4 km/h (2.5 mph). In the 1980s Porsche even built an SC cabriolet on a scale of 1:2 equipped with a 2 hp Honda motor, which came supplied with an owners manual, parts catalog, and service manual—just like a "big" 911. Production was soon stopped on liability grounds, though. Today the over 2 m (6 ft. 7 in.) long millionaire's plaything is a much sought-after collectors item.

Porsche-mad fathers and godfathers can even begin with the conditioning of the innocent, infant mind in the labor ward. However, such unbridled commitment can sometimes produce the opposite effect, with the children becoming annoyed by their parent's excitement and monotone chatter about a cramped sports car that they don't always find that attractive.

Wenn ich mal groß bin...

...dann möchte ich auch einen großen Porsche. Er ist schick und schnell. Einfach Klasse.
Vati redet zwar viel von der perfekten Technik. Aber mir macht er einfach nur Spaß. Hoffentlich bin ich bald groß.
...dann wird er sich auch mehr für die technische Perfektion interessieren. Dann möchte er wissen, warum der Porsche sicherer, handlicher, wirtschaftlicher, umweltfreundlicher und langlebiger ist als er ahnt.
Wir informieren ihn ausführlich, wenn er einmal groß ist. Groß genug für einen

PORSCHE

mit Langzeitgarantie.

Oder fordern Sie jetzt schon unsere Broschüre: »Porsche-Ingenieure plaudern aus der Schule« an.
Dr. Ing. h. c. F. Porsche Aktiengesellschaft. 7 Stuttgart 40. Postfach 400640

Lucky 911-mad fathers receive a little compassion in return, though, and in a double sense: either as pity or empathy. If the parents succeed in turning the 911 into an accepted member of the family that is treated without any sense of pathos of pedantry, then there is a greater chance that the children will experience the roaring of the engine, the warmth of the boxer beating against the jump seats—as if specially designed for infants—as part of their home. A number of 911 fathers swear by the rear seat's soporific properties, its capacity to put a screaming baby to sleep within minutes of starting the boxer engine. Passionate discussions on which child seat fits into which 911 abound on the Porsche forums. Apparently no expense or effort is too great in the attempt to reconcile the appetite for cruising or high-speed travel with the children's safety needs—one of the reasons why the child seats for older Porsches are so incredibly expensive on eBay.

A precondition for the sports car as an idyll—where family members are seated in close quarters—is that each member of the family has the opportunity to share in the pleasure of this special car. For the son of a racing driver the Porsche's jump seats were often the only place where he could spend time with his father. The artist Donald von Frankenberg recalls with respect those journeys on the rear seat of the Porsche when his father's racing urge got the better of him, even in highway traffic. "I wasn't frightened at all," he wrote looking back. "I was an exception in this respect, maybe this was due to a kind of instinctive trust." Other passengers, the son recalled, were less keen on experiencing whether the curve of a highway exit could be taken at 130 or 150 km/h (81 or 93 mph). At the age of 10 he experienced such maneuvers on the back seat of the last 356 model, without a seat belt—and "always at full throttle." The tension between security and fear provided the ideal conditions for trauma. Donald also transferred this instinctive trust in his father to the Dutch Formula One driver Carel Godin de Beaufort, who stayed with the Frankenbergs whenever his Porsche was being serviced in Zuffenhausen. "He also drove as if he was in one big race!" recalls Frankenberg. Carel Godin de Beaufort was killed in his Porsche at the age of 30 while training for the German Grand Prix on the Nürburgring track.

When Donald got his driving license at the age of 17 his father handed him the keys to the 911, and the son, sweating with excitement, trundled through suburban Stuttgart. Then the father climbed into the passenger seat and directed the son to the freeway, escorting him until he hit the 180 km/h (112 mph) mark—and that in torrential rain. Donald von Frankenberg's shirt was soaked through with sweat. Years later he would find himself beside his father's grave, who, after numerous bad accidents and ultimately a fatal one, met his death on the freeway near Stuttgart at the age of 51.

"You can have a longer breakfast. You are back earlier for dinner. Could there be a better family car?"

↳ Porsche advertising slogan.

« "When I grow up, I want to have a big Porsche"—Porsche advertisement espousing the benefits of a lifelong relationship with your car with its *Langzeitgarantie* (long-term guarantee).

In the case of Dieter Landenberger, the director of the Porsche archive, his love for Porsche, and the 911 in particular, was less violent and traumatic. His mother drove a 924, though as a boy he frequently found himself a passenger in a 911. Sitting in the back right-hand corner, crouched in a fetal position in the hollow of the jump seat with a view of the speedometer, he rejoiced internally every time it broke the 200 km/h (124 mph) mark. "When I am older ... " was written in big letters over a picture of a boy playing with a white 911, while in the background a yellow G model stood parked in the parents' garage. This advert from the 1970s visualized an intergenerational contract, which, in a somewhat conventional fashion, was passed down from father to son. This cliché was exploded long ago. At the exclusive Mille Miglia old-timer rally one can see car-enthusiast families in which father, mother, sons, and daughters form a type of genetically linked racing team.

Happy and harmonic marriages are often subject to sharp disputes on the advisability of allowing the sons and daughters to ride in papa's 911, resulting in the issuing of strict instructions on the maximum speed and driving behavior in the curves. An advert for the 911 even employed this as the subject for its punch line: "You can have a longer breakfast. You are back earlier for dinner. Could there be a better family car?" Logically this advert could also be reduced to an invitation to drive recklessly, which is why the breezy advertising slogan was accompanied by a touching suggestion from Porsche, printed to the top right: "Porsche recommends: Drive carefully!" This was the cause of much laughter among the friends of rapid locomotion. The majority of Germans rejected this form of irony and advertising. The social acceptance of sports car drivers, and Porsche pilots in particular, was on the wane. In 1994 Porsche ended its collaboration with Jung von Matt. In the same year Germany's Green Party received over 10 percent of the votes in the elections for the European parliament. The educated middle classes had replaced humor with moralism.

The Green Porsche

In 1995 the head of development at the Association of German Car Manufacturers presented Porsche with a rather unusual request: to refrain from publishing the exhaust emission values for the 993 Turbo. In 1995, of all cars, the 408 hp, broad-cheeked, low-slung Porsche Turbo with a top speed of almost 300 km/h (186 mph) was the world's cleanest serial car. A VW Golf with 60 hp spewed out almost three times the amount of CO_2, and a Mercedes 600 SEC more than five times as much. This was achieved with the assistance of the twin catalyzers, which, as the *Spiegel* magazine eulogistically reported, clasped the drive unit in their "octopus tentacles," laboriously cleaning the exhaust fumes while being continually monitored by two Lambda probes.

Once again Porsche profited from the ecologically progressive legislation in its most important foreign market, the United States. As early as the mid-1990s it was becoming apparent that California was about to introduce even stricter exhaust specifications—which Porsche had already anticipated with the 993 Turbo. As a result, the development center in Weissach acquired a competence, which, as a high-tech service provider, it was able to sell to other car manufacturers. The impact of this coup was felt for some time, disguising the fact that a number of Porsches, even some 911s, were far from being role models when it came to consumption. In the Porsche forums 911 enthusiasts lamented the thirst for fuel of their 1986 Turbos (up to 26.5 L) , their 911 S or G models when speeding about town. However, these excesses tended to be the exception as opposed to the rule.

Even the Brit Jeremy Clarkson, renowned for his 911-skepticism, marveled at the low emission values in his good-humored short film on the 997 Turbo—compared to those of the Ferrari 430, the values were nothing short of exemplary. According to Clarkson, when driving in a highly polluted city, such as Los Angeles, Calcutta, or London, the air that the engine draws in is dirtier than that which comes out the exhaust pipe. He compared this Turbo to a huge vacuum cleaner, which, more appropriately, should have been called the Dyson Turbo.

The lightweight construction principle frequently aided Porsche in achieving respectable fuel consumption figures, even during times when this was not a criterion. The company's first brochure from 1949 even advertised low consumption figures, stating that at the highest cruising speed consumption was only 7.2 L per 100 km—though in retrospect Richard von Frankenberg considered this a little "naive." Nevertheless, from their inception the lightweight sports cars with their small displacement engines sported consumption figures that the competition with their eight cylinders and heavy bodies could only dream of. The Swabian frugality, the allergy against every form of dysfunctional extravagance, formed the gateway to an ecological consciousness long before it became fashionable. With its spartan accouterments, one could enjoy relaxed drives on the freeway, even in older 911s, while consuming as little as 10 L per 100 km. In the 1970s the 911 only used regular gasoline due to the lower compression ratio. In 1975 Porsche was the first car manufacturer to introduce hot-dip galvanized sheet metal as standard in order to provide the cars with long-term rust protection, while issuing them with guarantees that became progressively longer. In 1982 the world's first independently operated exhaust testing facility was opened in Weissach: the Messzentrum für Umweltschutz (MZU)—Measuring Center for Environmental Protection. With the 991 and the integrated start-stop technology, consumption has been improved again decisively, while this young 911 model also benefitted from the lightweight components and reduced diet.

PORSCHE

CABRIOLET

Die Karosserie bietet zwei Personen bequem Platz und weist hinter den Sitzen einen geräumigen Kofferraum auf, der ebensogut auch für Notsitze von zwei Kindern verwendet werden kann.

Wer auf Reisen den freien, offenen Ausblick auf die Schönheit unserer Bergwelt und Alpenseen, auf die Sehenswürdigkeiten unserer Städte und Dörfer genießen will, dem bietet das

Sport-Cabriolet Typ 356

die Erfüllung seiner Wünsche.

Beiden, im Fahrgestell gleichen Fahrzeugtypen gemeinsam ist eine besondere Sparsamkeit im Betriebsstoffverbrauch. Bei höchster Reisegeschwindigkeit erreicht der Kraftstoffverbrauch nur 7,2 Liter/100 km und kann bei gemäßigter Fahrweise noch erheblich gesenkt werden.

Perhaps even more important is the message that this car with its start-stop technology conveys to its smoldering, bellowing neighbors at each set of lights—that this sports car also wants to make a contribution to improving the global climate. The start-stop technology reduces consumption in the city, but above all it raises the prestige of the 911 driver who can sport the deluxe edition of "green conspicuous consumption" as a badge of distinction. With the unveiling of the 918 Spyder the greening of Porsche continued, making it the most photographed, discussed ,and romanticized car at the 2010 Geneva Motor Show. In addition to its eight-cylinder, 500 hp engine, this supercar in the tradition of the Carrera GT was also equipped with two electric motors adding an extra 218 hp. At low speeds this hybrid racing car had a consumption of just 3 L. This prototype with its extremely elaborate construction was a raging antithesis to the ecological Calvinism that had penetrated deep into the life of the middle classes, as confirmed by analyses of the Green Party electorate. Thus this prototype was not just perceived as a technological adventure, but as a thought experiment designed to shake the foundations of those convictions that called for a Protestant ethic of renunciation, as opposed to "ecological correctness." That the 918 Spyder also sported excellent CO_2 emission values, as low as just 70 g/km, silenced a number of cultural pessimists. Parts of the concept were utilized for the 911 GT3 R Hybrid racing car, which was equipped with a monstrous flywheel accumulator located on the co-drivers seat that was charged during braking and released its energy to the two electric motors on the front axle as required. During the 24-hour race on the Nürburgring, a GT3 R Hybrid held the lead for some time before it was forced to retire due to a technical defect.

A close study of Porsche company history reveals that this prototype was actually part of a tradition stretching back over one 100 years. Ferdinand Porsche's first coup was an electric car, which, when unveiled at the memorable Exposition Universelle in Paris in 1900, proved a sensation. At this landmark event celebrating the turn of the century and the dawn of the electric age, Porsche established itself as a pioneer in the use of electricity for modern mobility concepts. However, then as now, the disadvantages of an electric car proved to be the extreme weight of the batteries, the limited range, and the long charging time. This was recognized as early as 1900. Marshall McLuhan's rather brash prognosis that the sports car was the future of the automobile—which as a mere object of utility would be consigned to the past—received a new impetus. Ferry Porsche saw the ecological challenges, first and foremost, as an opportunity. "In my opinion the sports car is essentially a trailblazer for new developments, a role that it also played in the past," and would continue to do so when it came to ecological challenges. As consumption is dependent on weight and air resistance, the "sports car has the advantage." On top of this, Ferry Porsche saw developments aimed at the motor racing sector as an opportunity to both optimize performance

The more beautiful and expensive a vehicle, the more consciously it is used.

« The first Porsche brochure, printed in 1949, highlighted the 356's *besondere Sparsamkeit im Betriebsstoffverbrauch* (exceptionally economic fuel consumption).

and increase the efficiency of the engines—for example with the turbo. This would result in cars with "extremely low consumption figures." Without any outside guidance or exhortations from the side of politics, Porsche was implementary in developing "green technology." This matched the company's self-understanding.

Anyone scouring the internet for used Ferraris, Lamborghinis, or even 911s will find an amazing number with low mileage. The Porsche 911 is less a vehicle for everyday motoring than an indulgence: too good to use in the snow or rain, on salted streets, or even on a dull day with a gray sky and hazy sun. Comparing the Porsche to the everyday commuter carts for the non-millionaires is like comparing organic meat from the health food store with supermarket sausages. An advertisement spot from Mercedes features our modern customer savoring the aesthetic delights of the limousine in its garage, only to ride away on a bicycle. The more beautiful and expensive a vehicle, then the more consciously it is used. With this praxis owners of oldtimers and rare sports cars constitute the advanced guard of future car use. Less, but better. The LOHAS (Lifestyles of Health and Sustainability) demographic[1] have recognized that the best place for a Porsche during the jammed rush hour is the garage, and that the subway or urban rail link is the quicker form of transport. However, anyone who has to go into the office at the weekends, or maintains the absurd working hours typical for a workaholic, will have a great deal of fun with a Porsche 911.

What is completely taboo for Porsche lovers is using the car for the proverbial trip to the local bakers. This would result in the car's destruction in a relatively short space of time. As already mentioned, the 9 L of engine oil—in the interest of the car's well-being, especially older 911s—have to be driven warm before revving up the boxer. This love for the car goes hand in hand with a solicitous approach to its maintenance, and thus to an increased lifetime for a Porsche, which is decisive for the ecological balance. From the start Porsche refused to submit to the logic of the disposable product, and of all the Porsches it is the 911, in contrast to the less expensive and considerably thirstier Cayennes or 928s, that

[1] Composed of companies, consumers, and organizations that have an eye on the environment, social responsibility, and health.

has remained remarkably constant in value, much to the shock of many young 911 enthusiasts. Even those fit for the scrap heap, dug out from damp barns in the American Midwest and subsequently shipped to Europe, command high prices. In the anniversary year 2013 they cost as much as what a well-preserved model of the same build year would have asked 15 years ago. In the language of the bank advisor: a Porsche 911, with the exception of the 996, is a blue chip among used cars. If one believes the experts from the innumerable old-timer and young-timer magazines, then this price trend knows only one direction: bullishly upwards. From 1.1 to 1.7 million vehicles are scrapped every year in Germany—placing a considerable strain on the economy. Every year the EU produces nine million tons of automotive waste. Not so with the Porsches: over 70 percent of all the sports cars ever produced in Zuffenhausen are still extant, while an even higher percentage of Porsche 911s are still "alive." This transforms the sports car into an ecological showpiece, a fact that Porsche is very proud of. A genuine Porsche driver sees himself as a responsible consumer. He is no friend of speed limits, but neither is he a reckless fast lane tailgater. It is completely sufficient to know what the car is capable of—he doesn't need to put it continually to the test. He leaves this to the stressed-out sales reps and managerial staff in their Southern German station wagons.

Consumers decide over the ecological constitution of the globalized world—assuming they are equipped with the necessary minimum of prosperity and knowledge. Under capitalism the consumer continually and comprehensively shapes the world

Those consumer goods that have the potential quality and substance to be passed down to the next generation—and not just survive to the end of their lifetime—are the valuable ones.

« Shades of green: a Carrera RS driving though the Pyrenees combines driving pleasure with a long-lasting product in terms of design and construction.

with their demand. The credo of the liberal LOHAS originates from the patron saint of neoliberalism, Adam Smith, who postulated that the purpose of all production is consumption. Up until now, an ecologically conscious lifestyle has gone hand in hand with sermons on guilt, atonement and a significant loss of pleasure. However, it is precisely the luxury factor that provides the ideal preconditions for sustainable use. Those consumer goods that have the potential quality and substance to be passed down to the next generation—and not just survive to the end of their lifetime—are the valuable ones. The longer a product's lifetime, then the better the ecological balance. An appreciation for aesthetics and luxury must be strengthened "so that growth functions by means of beauty not quantity," as the former general secretary of the Club of Rome, the Hamburg-born Uwe Möller, observed in 2002. If the rich Western countries want to serve as role models, then they should spend their money on consumer goods with long-term value. On top of which, a repair culture would create new jobs.

Along with durability, it is aesthetics and the identification with the product that prove decisive in determining how long one keeps it. One should only buy things that can be passed on. This results in an intergenerational contract and a sense of connection with one's forefathers that extends beyond common values and origins to evoke a highly material, shared everyday world. A grandfather's chest of drawers, grandma's pictures, and mother's Porsche 911 make memories real.

In contrast to the expiry date of low-priced products, manufacturers of luxury goods are committed to extending product lifetimes. This is why Porsche, among other things, not only introduced a comprehensive guarantee system, but also secured the supply of spare parts for the owners of older Porsches. Furthermore, every Porsche owner can take their heirloom, no matter how shabby, to the company's classic workshop in Freiberg on the river Neckar for repairs—just as one can send every Hermès accessory to Paris. Luxury means not being thrown away.

If the 911 is to become a sports car for eternity, then its metamorphosis into an ecologically acceptable product will also have to proceed unabated. The writer Ralf Bönt has developed a green entelechy, an ecological apotheosis of the 911. "As it is not going away," remarked the trained car mechanic, "we will see a 911 with a curb weight of a few hundred kilos, discreet electromagnetic collectors in the roof and hoods, four electric motors at the wheel bearings, perfect weight distribution thanks to the batteries, and zero emissions over short distances. And maybe even with just the right amount of performance, as opposed to absurdly bloated stats. We are entering the age of intelligent driving."

1997
2006

» Water, water everywhere with the 996: the water-cooled Carrera 3.4 coupe glides along wet roads.

The 996

The Heretic

Porsche sensed that the 996 would send shock waves through a world view defined by clear lines and concepts. Under the heading "Design," the brochure for the new 911 included a therapeutic dialogue (or is it a fragment from Samuel Beckett?) intended to pacify the stalwarts.

Is that a 911?
Yes.
But it looks somewhat different.
Yes.
Does it drive like a 911?
Yes?
Or differently?
Yes.
Why has Porsche done this?
So that the 911 will still be a classic in 30 years time.

Thus Porsche found itself embroiled in a philosophical-semantic debate about conservatism, in which the politician Franz Josef Strauss[1] emphasized that as a conservative it was not about looking to the past, but marching at the forefront of progress. This was more in tune with the sports car driver's attitude towards life. However, the nostalgic forces of continuity were traumatized by the 996's break with tradition. If this form of progress was the price for maintaining the salability of a classic, then this form of progress was to be rejected. The 911 aficionados even marshaled biological metaphors to support their argument. For the 993 owner Per Hinrichs, the 911's DNA was passed down intact from generation to generation, resulting in an orderly ancestral line. In contrast the 996 looked like a mutation produced by cosmic rays or a steel plate tumor. "While the 993 was still a sports car, tight, small, and suitably capricious," stated Hinrichs, "the 996 grew into a managerial limousine." On top of that the 996 was too much the teacher's pet for traditionalists, fulfilling emissions standards up to 2020. It was even equipped with ESC—christened

[1] CSU politician and ministerpresident of Bavaria from 1978 to 1988, who was forced to resign as defense minister after the so-called "Spiegel affair."

Carrera
S PR 996

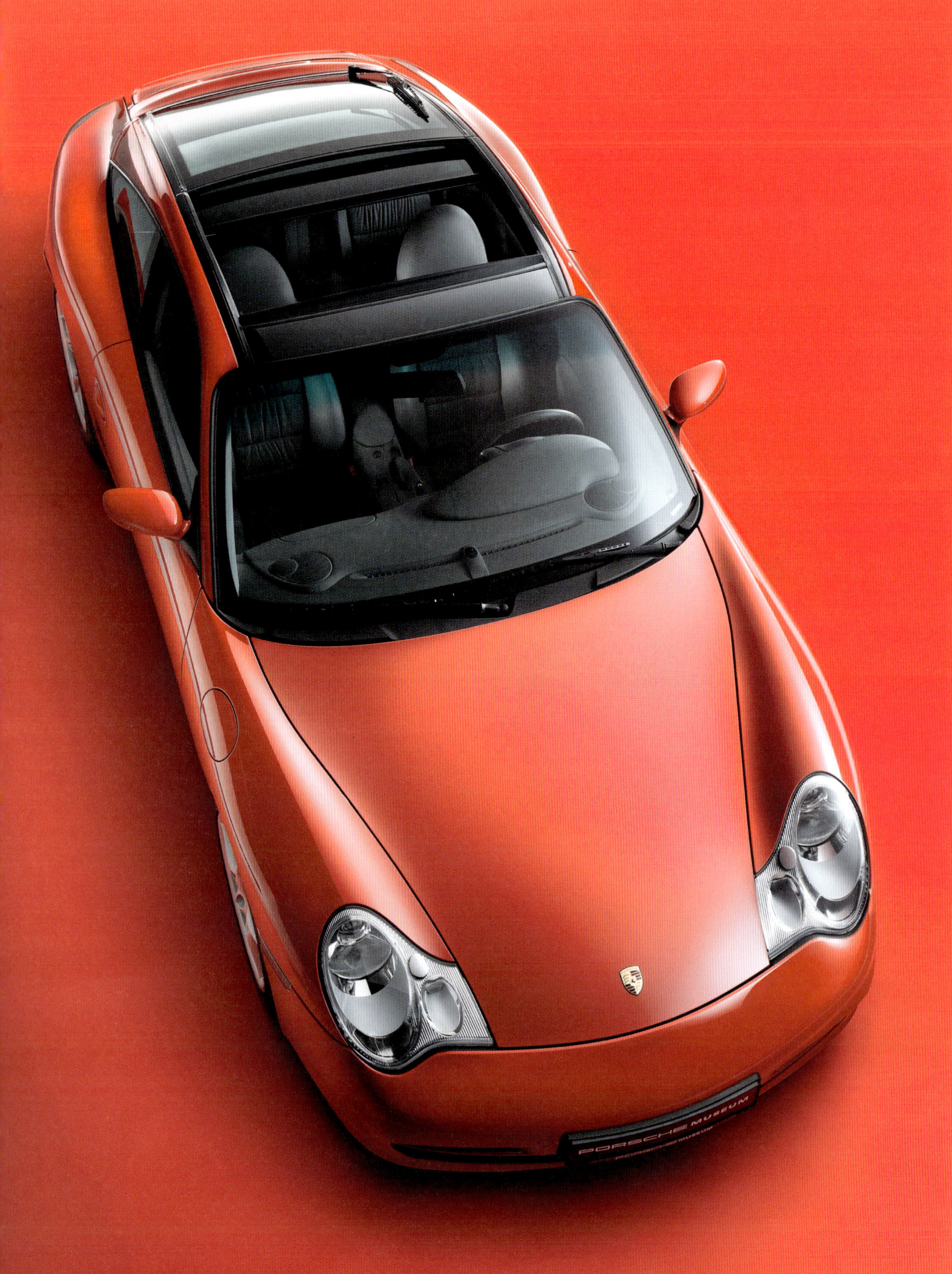
PORSCHE MUSEUM

PSM (Porsche Stability Management) in Zuffenhausen. "An electronic anti-skid brake for a rear wheel skidder." That was like putting training wheels on a Formula One car. And even the engine sound came under criticism. Hoarsely wheezing and with a high-pitched scream, the 996 with its extra 17 hp could overtake a 993. But that was irrelevant. Under wet conditions the 993 provided its drivers with every opportunity to become acquainted with the crash barrier—while the new 911 simply braked gently. There was no end to the list of objections. Even in the anniversary year 2013 it was only the British magazine *911 & Porsche World* that risked the prognosis that its time would come. "Inevitably good ones will start to rise in value. Get one now, we say." This notion still has little in common with German reality. However, since 2015 the prices for a coupe or cabriolet with a full service history and low mileage have been increasing. The 996 was always a good car, and today the first urban style guerrilleros are discovering its twisted charm. In 2012 the German Automobile Association (ADAC) reported that the 996 had the best breakdown statistics of any car of its build year. Anyone driving a 996 in times of the 991 is either unable to afford a different 911 or values its reliability above all else—a reliability that makes it the most solid car of its build year, as the ADAC breakdown statistics confirm time after time. A few rare style icons even see their 996 as a four-wheeled middle finger raised to the world of snobbery and the serial number fetishists. It is a vehicle of rebellion against the civil religion of 911 orthodoxy, a form of heroic heresy.

A few rare style icons even see their 996 as a four-wheeled middle finger raised to the world of snobbery and the serial number fetishists.

« Impeccably kitted out: a glass sunroof and other luxurious additions meant the 996 rattled the 911 traditionalists by seemingly becoming a "managerial limousine."
⇑ The plush interior of the 996 as seen in the Carrera 3.4 cabriolet.

The Big Break 1: Water

On March 31, 1998, the last air-cooled 911 was assembled in Zuffenhausen. According to rumors circulating in the Porsche community, its engine was built on March 27. If this is true then this day marks two sad events for Porsche traditionalists. This particular Friday also marks the death of Ferry Porsche, the inventor of the Porsche sports car, at the age of 88—which lends the end of the *luftgekühlt* 911 the character of a mythical break. It is hard to explain to outsiders the special importance of a cooling technique for a six-cylinder boxer engine. If one speaks to 911 followers and fanatics then it has a lot to do with the honoring of traditions that are being eroded everywhere—not just in the car industry—by technological developments, the zeitgeist, and social changes. 911 followers are traditionalists without necessarily being conservative.

The 911 is living proof that a seasoned product is able to measure itself against current performance criteria, rather than claim special rights for itself as the guard of honor of its own history. The 911 is, in the best case, both: a new and a tried and tested car, a product of its history and a step into the future, something both proven and unprecedented.

However, Porsche's adherence to air cooling was not just for reasons of tradition. Volkswagen paid two-thirds of Porsche's racing budget under the condition that the Zuffenhausen-based company only use air-cooled engines in its pursuit of victory. In the mid-1960s the VW Beetle fell victim to the same air-cooled monoculture that had its origins in Ferdinand Porsche's initial designs from the 1930s. Porsche's triumphs were intended to prove how powerful and forward-looking a supposedly outdated technology could be. However, in his memoirs Ferdinand Piëch was at pains to point out the Porsches' undogmatic approach to air cooling—both Ferdinand Porsche and his son Ferry. The air cooling hype was a by-product of history that assumed the character of a myth by virtue of the "wartime capability of the *Kübelwagen* [offroad vehicle]," which was reinterpreted as the car's guiding principle from the 356 to the Porsche 911. "The customers (the fans so to speak)," remarked Piëch, "made it into a world outlook; we technicians tended to be neutral." There were reasons for this neutrality. Air cooling resulted in a slightly lower performance; however, air-cooled cars were lighter. And it was precisely this ideal of a light, compact sports car that profoundly shaped the vital core of the Porsche customer's world. Even the engineering virtuoso Piëch had a weakness for it. During his studies he took a special interest in lightweight construction systems from the aviation industry, while Porsche's use of complicated auxiliary constructions to compensate for the drawbacks of air cooling held the same attraction for him as tricky equations for a mathematician.

The first time a *Wasserkraftwerk* (water power plant) drove a Porsche 911, the departure had to be precisely explained and mythologized—in the same breath—for the benefit of the

» The water-cooled 911 engine of a Carrera 3.4 built in 1998—the heart of the heresy and symbol of a new era.

traditionalists and Porsche loyalists. The company magazine *Christophorus* published a special issue, which in retrospect looks like a written apology for the break with tradition perpetrated by Porsche. In his editorial for the special issue, Anton Hunger, Wendelin Wiedeking's close confidant and chief press officer, pointed out that water cooling had already been employed in the Porsche 959 and a number of racing cars—and consequently the new was actually old. The magazine article itself began by emphasizing that the new Porsche 911 Carrera was powered by a six-cylinder boxer, as this motor with its flat construction was ideally suited to the rear engine concept. Furthermore, the countervailing motion of its pistons promoted smooth running. As there were no free inertial forces, this resulted in "good mechanical behavior" that lent the engine stability, even at high revolution speeds. Following a long introduction the author finally came to the point. In order to increase performance, lower fuel consumption, and lower emission values, four-valve technology was essential—and this was only possible with water cooling. In a Porsche advertising film Hunger expressed things more directly: experts immediately accepted water cooling because they knew that there was no way around it for a modern sports car; the nostalgics required a little more enlightenment (because they had no idea). Naturally Hunger didn't say this, but anyone with any sense could see that this was what he meant. In a comprehensive test the sports car experts from *Sport Auto* magazine, with their resistance to all forms of gimmickry, compared the bloated 996 with the Porsche 993—which had now attained the status of a cult car. The 996 proved superior to the air-cooled Porsche in every respect: when accelerating from 0–200 km/h (142 mph) and (in particular) when braking from 200 km/h–0. In the foreword to the comprehensive 15-page report, the author emphasized that this test ignored the issue of Porsche's traditionalism, simply letting the technical data speak for itself. On the Nürburgring the 996 was 11 seconds faster than the 993; on the Hockenheimring course, 2.4 seconds. Only in the slalom and the avoidance test did the compacter 993 prove more agile—not forgetting its ability to perform a 360 degree pirouette, a maneuver that the 996 was effectively incapable of. "The new Carrera has actually suffered a loss of charisma," was the conclusion, "however, irrespective of any subjective feelings, what we are dealing with here is a sports car that sets new standards in terms of dynamic road performance." Porsche's test driver Bob Wollek concurred: "For me this car is the best 911 there has ever been." Walter Röhrl had an even simpler rule: "Is there a faster 911 on the Nürburgring's northern loop: yes or no?" The answer was quite simple. In Latin, one word is used to denote breathing, a current of air, and the soul: *anima*. In this sense the air-cooled 911 is the ensouled 911. The 911s that followed first had to prove that they had a soul. They were under general suspicion. For the air-cooled devotees, joked Porsche superfan Ingo Rübener, the motto was still: "Water? No thank you!"

The Big Break 2: Form

As if water cooling wasn't enough of a test, the break with the drive concept was underlined by a new, radical-looking formal language. This 911 was to be perceived as something completely new, even at the risk of alienating some old friends. The community of 911 purists, which now had taken on the character of a religious congregation, saw with shock that the heresy of the 964 with its pot-bellied aesthetic and bulbous bumpers was only the beginning. Following the somewhat restorative approach of the 993, the 996 was in many respects a completely new car that self-confidently broke with many traditions. The most obvious was the change to the front section. The fried egg look of the headlights with the integrated indicators and fog lights generated violent reactions.

Although he had worked in Weissach since 1971, internalizing the Porsche DNA, Dutch car designer Harm Lagaay consciously broke with the round headlights, which for 35 years had formed part of the Porsche 911's core brand identity. Lagaay's irreverent design brought the tuners into play, with Strosek selling headlight covers designed to lend the 996 a somewhat more classical appearance. However, in reality this cosmetic treatment around the eyes simply made the disfigurement even more monstrous. The 911 now looked as if it was wearing dark glasses, like those worn by the German singer Heino.[2] The 996's amateur makeover gave it a grotesque appearance.

With the exception of the window landscape above shoulder height, Lagaay changed almost everything that was near and dear to Porsche customers. The wheelbase grew and the car became longer and wider—and more comfortable. The form of Lagaay's new 911 was a virtuoso interplay of convex and concave lines. The 911's gun barrels, which had served as its eyes into the world, were leveled out in the redesign and assimilated into the fenders—without being lent any particular dynamism. The 911's contours flowed. For macho followers of the 911 the gun barrels were their beloved's breasts, and the 996's décolleté was mortifyingly un-erotic, almost androgynous and boyish.

The hips had swollen along with the rest of the car, giving the 996 the appearance of a huge bubble. At around the same time the German philosopher Peter Sloterdijk published his *Spheres* trilogy, which began with *Bubbles*. The iMacs from Apple looked like bubbles, as did Nike training shoes and jackets from Comme des Garçons. Shortly before the new millennium design acquired a cosmic imprecision, banishing edges and corners with its soft, white excrescence.

[2] Born Heinz Georg Kramm, *Schlager-* and *Volksmusiksänger* Heino is known for his trademark combination of blond hair and black glasses—alongside being one of the most successful German musicians of all time.

» The 996, with its "fried egg" headlights, may not have been to everyone's taste, but it became the company's best-selling model.

In architecture the biomorphism of the metabolists enjoyed a renaissance, while the 996 adopted the form of a small embryo.

Along with the 911, the customers also increased in girth. The manager grown chubby on success could now switch from the Mercedes SL to the Porsche without a loss of comfort. The Austrian rightwing populist Jörg Haider was just such a 996 enthusiast, driving both a dark blue Targa and a medium blue cabriolet that he was fond of being photographed in. At the very least these pictures were a signal—even for the least politically correct of observers—that something was amiss with this 911.

The 996 had a better chassis and stiffer bodywork, but one didn't see any of this. A number of 911 fans bid farewell to their favorite sports car at this point. The Stuttgart-based architect and engineer Werner Sobek, for instance, who had his first encounter with a Porsche as a 5-year-old in provincial Swabia. That was in 1958, and he was hooked. In 1991, at the age of 38—sensible as he was—he purchased his first 911. The first time he started the motor he could only find one word to describe it: "Brilliant." His 993 would be the last 911 he would drive. He had had it a long time—until a friend crashed it. For Sobek the 911 embodied both the Ulm School of Design

The 996 was the most successful 911 of all time—if one just looked at the sales figures. While the classic 911 sold exactly 80,100 units in 10 years, the Porsche 996 sold over 175,000 units in eight.

« The design studio in Weissach, Germany, in 1997, where a dynamic wall drawing immortalizes the Carrera 3.4 coupe.

and bauhaus—but also the Werkbund (German Association of Craftsmen) movement with its pursuit of the perfect integration of artisanal and industrial production techniques, technical function, and design. Buying a 996 was out of the question. "The budget version with the fried egg headlights was an absolute no-go in terms of design," recalls the otherwise sober-minded architect in a fit of passion. "You can't do something like that." For Sobek, "that"—in addition to the outer shell—referred to the five round elements in the instrument panel, which at a stroke were now layered on top of each other, cutting into each other. "These are gimmicks that have nothing in common with timeless design." The happy years with Porsche were over. Sobek first bought a Maserati 3200 GT, then an Aston Martin Vantage.

The 911 had lost its face, and as if that wasn't bad enough, it took on a mean look—and to add insult to injury, the 911 also had to share this look with its cheaper younger brother, the Boxster, which was launched one year before the 996. For 911 followers the Boxster was a "lady's car," and that of all cars this pretty little roadster should bear such a striking resemblance to the mother of all Porsches represented a serious blow to the vanity of the 911 community. Even the instrument panels, a further heresy, were similar. In the Boxster the once striking landscape of five circular instruments, crowned by the large rev counter in the center, was compressed—a design adopted almost unchanged in the 996. The new dashboard looked demonstratively post-modern and a little squashed—as if one had put a Braun stereo in the steel press in order to reduce it to the size of a toaster. It was an anti-classicist gesture designed to highlight the revolutionary character of the 996 within the 911's ancestral line—prominently positioned in the interior, right in front of the driver's eyes.

The traditionalists' fears that lines of tradition could break, with the new replacing the tried and tested and destroying historical continuity, were confirmed. But Porsche could not have survived with traditionalists alone. Although the soft-focus design had made the 996 a less special car, it opened it up to new layers of consumers who were looking for something a little smoother and more comfortable. Of all cars it was the "false" 911 that would turn out to be the bestselling model to date. Years later Lagaay mockingly remarked that if the "fried egg" had been sold 320,000 times then the canteen couldn't have been that bad. In order to achieve this phenomenal score, Lagaay added together the figures for the 996 and the Boxster. However, in essence it was correct. The 996 was the most successful 911 of all time—if one just looked at the sales figures. While the classic 911 sold exactly 80,100 units in 10 years, the Porsche 996 sold over 175,000 units in eight.

The Big Break 3: The Globalized 911

The Porsche 996 was developed and produced, from beginning to end, under the reign of Wendelin Wiedeking. He hired experts from Japan to make the production process faster, simpler, and more efficient—while simultaneously tapping into the employees' innovation potential. After Wiedeking had introduced the production line to Porsche, bringing Zuffenhausen into the modern industrial age, the assembly time for a Porsche Carrera was shortened from 120 to 76 hours. Wiedeking's approach was rough and ready. He vociferously threatened redundancies, shouted at employees and management colleagues, and—according to certain sources—adopted a rude tone. In his book, Stefan Aust [3] describes how Wiedeking walked through the factory halls with an angle grinder, personally cutting up any unused metal shelves he encountered.

Wiedeking himself describes how the Japanese kaizen master Chihiro Nakao forced him to cut back all the shelves to a height of 1.3 m (4 ft. 3 in.) before the eyes of his employees, putting an end to the space-consuming storage of materials. The purpose of lean production was to make buffer stock superfluous. Wiedeking and his Japanese advisors, as the—in the words of Wiedeking—"high priests of the unvarnished truth," threatened to carry out further radical interventions in future should they discover boxes blocking the pathways again.

When the production of the 996 began a year after the Boxster's premier, lean production had become second nature to the Porsche employees. Nearly everyone welcomed the improvement in quality, the more efficient work organization, and the end to the squandering of money and labor time. However, this Japanese gift of impatience towards every form of inefficiency had also infected the product. The Porsche 996 became the 911 of the globalized age. Its lack of character in a number of areas—more than a mere accusation—was also the result of an economicized attitude towards those details that gave the car its identity. In the process Wiedeking crossed an invisible line in his modernization efforts. That the 996 and the Boxster looked remarkably similar from the front was less an oversight than a statement. Globalization as the great leveler of identities had now overrun the car manufacturer in Stuttgart. It is surely not a coincidence that the anti-globalization movement Attac[4] was founded at the same time in France. In the West it became clear what a violent impact the post-Cold War, globalized economy would have on those things most prized and familiar. The deformations took some getting used to. Even though the usual 911 driver rarely expressed any criticism of capitalism, they sensed that such an exotic creature as the Porsche 911 with its high development costs would only be able to survive under conditions of intense competition if its sales markets grew. Originally the advertising for the 911 was photographed in the factory courtyard at Zuffenhausen, with secretaries as photo models. Later the sales headquarters in Ludwigsburg, and the test track in Weissach and or its development center were used as a backdrop in a proud and cost-conscious utilization of the genius loci. This began to change with the 964, and by the time of the 996 the advertisements employed such ideal stage sets as endless desert roads (straight) or crooked coastlines (curvy). The 911 was no longer primarily Swabian—it was now destined to become a citizen of the world capable of anything—apart from speaking the

[3] *Die Porsche Saga: Eine Familiengeschichte des Automobils* (The Porsche Saga: A Family History of the Automobile) by Thomas Ammann and Stefan Aust. Published 2012.

[4] International movement opposing neo-liberal globalization.

In Hollywood the 911 became a status symbol for people in danger of suffocating in the alienation of their glorious careers.

« Global freedom: the 911 is equally at home zipping through the California hills as it is cruising city streets.

local dialect. Thus the 996 became the least Swabian of all 911s. Lagaay's successor, Michael Mauer, had studied in Pforzheim in the state of Baden-Württemberg, and although he originally came from the state of Hesse, his 2011 design for the 991, delivered in standard German, had a Swabian accent.

The target groups had to be expanded. Porsche's head of marketing, Gerd Mäuser, admitted that the 996's customers would be somewhat older and consist of 10 percent more women. The 996, especially the variant with tiptronic, could be comfortably driven by every man and woman without qualification. With its 300 hp motor, the 996 was a fast mover. However, it appeared to be more at home cruising around the city at 60 km/h (37 mph) in fifth gear. It was a Californian 911, a statement that illustrated how comfortable one could make things for oneself with the 911 concept.

In Hollywood this 911 became a status symbol for people in danger of suffocating in the alienation of their glorious careers. In the film *The Kid* Bruce Willis plays a slick image consultant who has escaped his past as a fat, clumsy child. As a sign of his success, he drives a Porsche 996 Carrera cabriolet—an automotive double of his rather stereotypical cosmopolitanism—the model with the very fried-egg-like fried egg eyes, which a short while later would at least be given a little contouring. This relationship between the successful, rootless individual and the eminently idiosyncratic says a lot about the break that this 911 embodies. The car has offered up its edges and corners, its own ancestral registry. In the film, the mythical alter ego drove a 356 cabriolet in the past. This old man, also played by Bruce Willis, is a pure character, the essence of idiosyncrasy and non-conformity, while the 996 driver only finds himself during the course of the film. He falls in love with his colleague, who also drives a Swabian car, which—as she is full of soul, integrity, and charm—is a Mercedes 300 SE cabriolet from the late 1960s. If this film had been successful enough to warrant a sequel, then in the next film Willis would have either driven an old Porsche or a 997, the 911 that returned to its roots.

The Outcome of the Heresy: Yet More Tradition

For the community of 911 traditionalists, the heresy had the character of a transgression that was subject to a staggered set of punishments, just as in the Catholic Church. The purists excommunicated the 996 drivers from the community of faith—they were no longer welcome at a number of 911 conventions. In order to be readmitted into the congregation it was necessary to renounce the heresy and, once again, buy a classic air-cooled 911 with its familiar visage.

It was remarkable how quickly Porsche itself reacted to the disquiet in the Porsche community in an attempt to prevent a schism. As early as 2002 the front section was remodeled and from then on could be immediately distinguished from that of the Boxster. With the introduction of the 997 in 2006, the classic 911 face was reconstructed, while the car's hips were made visible and palpable again. The orthodoxy of the 911 world in its most ritualized and dogmatic form may only be the life content and mission of a few thousand enthusiasts scattered around the globe; but nevertheless, its radical core with its purist doctrine is also secretly shared by the hundreds of thousands of profane 911 owners—and more or less openly supported by the Porsche company. The Porsche had become a mass product, and also looked like one. That was dangerous—and looking back one can say that no Porsche had strayed so far from the pure teachings of the 911 church than the 996. It remains a foreign body in the history of this sports car and also a turning point. So much so that the first remix of the 996's headlights can be seen as a form of penance for the transgression and violation of the true teachings performed on behalf of the entire community of the faithful. Porsche pledged improvement.

In this respect, the 996 dialectically strengthened the 911's core identity. With the Porsche loyalists' fried egg rebellion, it became clear that this sports car, regardless of what the production figures said, personified the brand's sacred core. Every other model profited, in a parasitic fashion, from the metaphysical power of a product that appeared to have bestowed eternal life upon itself. Just as the culture industry's puffed up superstars, with their lifestyles of total alienation devoid of any authentic relationship to life, cultivate their most loyal fan clubs and hysterical fans as the keepers of their own grail, so Porsche pursued a similar strategy with events, a comprehensive classic program, and, since 2009, a modern museum that pays special tribute to this company's unique history.

GT3
BB GT 712

Happiness in Estrangement

The 996 and its mass dissemination has robbed the 911 of its last trace of exoticism, and its face, even in smaller towns, now has a proud workaday look, while the pleasure at the sight of a 911 has shrunk to moderate proportions. Nevertheless, even the thousandth turn of the ignition key to the left of the steering wheel on a sunny, rainy, or misty morning announces a good start to the day, regardless of what comes next—provided the 911 remains an object of desire, even for those drivers satiated by prosperity and consumerism. The upshot of this is that a Porsche has to be sold as soon as the excitement is gone, or less drastically, consigned to the garage to restore its allure in anticipation of the return of the driver's passion.

The morning commuter traffic disgorges its upmarket segment of brightly polished company cars and their proud owners, basking in the display of automotive luxury as symbols of their own position in the hierarchy. The singular individuals sit reading newspapers or making their first telephone calls in the rear compartments of a limousines, while being effortlessly chauffeured to the gates of their domain. Between them are the car lovers: men in rare old-timers, women in loud Italian cabriolets, and somewhere among them, the Porsche 911 drivers, who—as a rule—have no interest in looking particularly original or connoisseur-like, with the exception of perhaps the drivers of classic 911s and the extremely elegant G model.

Anyone who rolls into work in a 911 is intent on honing their living technique. No time is to be lost in the morning; every moment is precious when it comes to having a relaxed breakfast with the family. And it is not just the comfortable mid-sized or luxury class company cars that give employees and managing partners the sense that they have entered their professional worlds as soon as they leave the house. The ergonomics of the seats, the functionality of the instruments, and the interfaces to the telephone and information technologies are a prelude to operating as a link within an exploitation chain. The colors of the limousines and station wagons match the dark suits and ties, the freshly ironed costumes. Instead of an "I" it is an "it" that holds the wheel—the civilized, well-mannered hustle and bustle of economic activity that is already warming up on the road to the office. A Porsche advert from the 1990s took a sideswipe at those executives in their adipose Mercedes S class limousines cruising to the next board meeting. It was incomprehensible how anyone could roll into the office in the morning with two tons of excess weight. Those under pressure begin their battle for survival at the first set of lights after their apartment, unleashing their aggression at the rest of the world on every stretch of asphalt conducive to acceleration.

Raging and gliding: both are possible in a Porsche. However, the appropriate behavior was best expressed by the instructions, printed in red, which Porsche stuck into its company cars for the edification of its employees: "You are driving a company car and thus represent the Dr. Ing. h. c. F. Porsche AG. Please drive in an appropriately defensive manner." Since Heinrich Böll and Volker Schlöndorff cast the Porsche 911 as a blackguard's car, the Porsche driver's basic stylistic imperative has become increasingly applied to everyday driving situations. The difference between 911-driving Porsche devotees and blowhards in search of a personality boost is frequently to be found in the latter's ruthlessness when it comes to exploiting their sports car's potential to spread shock and fear among their fellow men.

Of course crawlers, procrastinators, brakers, and blockers can turn even the most civilized Porsche driver into a speeder. However, the idiot accusation is more readily applied to a 911. Anyone rampaging in a 911 confirms latent prejudices about Porsche drivers who are frequently accused of using the sports car as compensation for a lack of stature or character. The sports car is a vehicle that can quickly cover distances between A and B. Thus the 911 owner also communicates that every second of his life is precious to him, that he intends to enjoy life to the full. It would simply be a waste to spend the journey to the office in a highly modern, air-conditioned, and spacious car. Ideally it is about the attempt to find pleasure in life, even in the everyday working routine. In the United States the saying is: "With a 911 you don't let the traffic fuck you—you fuck the traffic." Sascha Keilwerth, the Porsche mechanic, racing driver, and aficionado has translated it into a more civilized form in German, which translates back as: "With the 911 you have a car with which you can ride the traffic, and not the traffic you." Ultimately, on arriving at the office each morning, a 911 devotee such as Keilwerth has "the feeling of standing at the very top of the victory podium, the winner of a rally through the everyday world." For the liberal FDP politician Christian Lindner, one of the few self-confessed Porsche drivers among top politicians, "the 911 is not a car for the everyday, but for every day." The sports car ripens with age like wine. According to Lindner, "We see its quirks and impracticalities as an expression of character"—a strategy also employed in anticipation of these qualities being projected onto the driver himself.

In the USA the saying is: "With a 911 you don't let the traffic fuck you—you fuck the traffic."

« Whether it is the car of rebels or new-money conformists, the 911 always garners a second glance.

A closed circuit of references. It doesn't long to be anywhere else. It is exactly there where it wants to be. Naturally there are thousands if not hundreds of thousands of Porsche 911 drivers who don't feel any of this because they primarily use this car—like a Rolex, the blond girlfriend (or the blond husband), and the skiing holiday—as a means to bolster status and self confidence. Like all identity-definers a Porsche 911 lends itself to masquerading and self-aggrandizement on the stage of social life. Thus the 911 also becomes an instrument of suppression, an accessory to the victims of a frenzied competition for recognition for whom the joy of victory and the sense of deliverance is increasingly short lived. That is why the rules of micro-fashion now apply to the Porsche 911 and its drivers: every detail counts. Where is the break, how does one measure the pain of the interminable competition that adds Rolex to Porsche to dark blue suit (or costume) to loud telephone conversations at the lights? And what is that Sansibar [5] sticker doing on the tail of that freshly washed Carrera? Has the car of the rebel, the loner, and the outsider now become the steel plate uniform of new money conformism?

In the Pixar cartoon *Cars* Sally Carrera is a complex, broken character. The pretty woman is personified by a 996 Carrera, build year 2002, who in Los Angeles once lived that superficially attractive and fast-paced life common to its high-flying denizens—without being happy for a single moment. That is why she left the sunshine state of California and took to Route 66 in search of herself. Following a breakdown she becomes stuck in Radiator Springs, where she succumbs to the small town's rough charm. She decides to stay and open a motel. Sally Porsche is an echo of that Barbie Porsche, supplied in white and pink, which was designed to lead young girls at play into the conventionality of gender roles and beauty ideals. The Barbie Porsche was a 964 cabriolet, which on eBay was also sold in a pimped version in matt silver. That Hank Moody drove exactly the same model as a means to escape the moral straightjacket of the WASP outlook, put an end to pop culture's connoting of the 911 as an ornament for conservative pedants—an outlook that the Barbie toy still propagated with its posters and adverts. Sally Carrera once dreamed this Barbie dream and experienced its emotional limitations. The happy end in *Cars* is romantic in a dual sense. The hero Lightning McQueen falls in love with Sally, choosing the most attractive proposition in Radiator Springs. That Sally has a tattoo on her rear, immediately below the spoiler, underlines the fact that she is a young woman. Her tattoo, known in German slang as *Arschgeweih* (butt antlers), in English "tramp stamp," also makes it clear that Sally is at home in the provincial town. Her urbanity is acquired. This tattoo can also be interpreted as a mark of her alienation. In Radiator Springs she rediscovers herself, putting the little town back on the road to success with her unusual qualities, her charm, and intelligence. Sally Carrera overcomes her self-alienation, reconciling her inner drive with reality.

[5] High-class restaurant on Sylt, an island off Northern Germany. Bumper stickers flaunted a visit to Sansibar.

The Virtue of Impatience

When Sally Carrera married a racing driver, two manifestations of restlessness were combined—an appropriate union in an age in which globalized capitalism compresses work and stress becomes an everyday phenomenon. However, on the other side, speed lovers were now confronted with a hostile culture. In 1986 the slow-food movement was founded in the land of Alfas, Ferraris, and Maseratis, and in 1999 the homeland of the futurists also saw the birth of the Cittàslow[6] movement. Deceleration was implanted into the clamorous everyday world as a hedonistic project. Pleasure required time. This also complemented the cultural valorization of old- and young-timers where driving pleasure, not speed, was paramount. Nevertheless, sports cars, including old ones, remained symbols and agendas of acceleration and impatience, monuments cautioning against wasting time and space.

In an aging society, which thanks to its prosperity knows how to enjoy the blessings of deceleration, the impatient individual performs an important function. He terminates the go slow pact and its well tempered human dynamics with an unruly impatience towards every form of time wasting. He is intolerant of the well-balanced types—softened by yoga and the esoteric writings of Coelho—who insist on living out their dissenting attitude towards these hectic times on our streets. In combination with his bad manners, the impatient individual fulfills a disruptive function in traffic, preventing the harmonious and obstructing the comfortable.

Although the Porsche with its natural-looking, biomorphous authority has little need of over-accentuated displays of aggression, a rapidly driven 911 belongs to the highway's unruly chapter. It is constructed to spread disquiet and leave its drivers in peace as far as possible. It has something unsettling about it. This urgency isn't generated by the hasty pursuit of a rendezvous beyond the vehicle and its driver. Instead, it is an existential restlessness with a physical aversion to time wasting. Driving fast is a call to change society, a plea that proves all the more effective and infectious, the more elegant and tactful the overtaking, braking, or acceleration maneuver. Rushing should not be a manic state, but a form of locomotion judged solely on its efficiency. It goes without saying that pedestrians, cyclists, or uncertain drivers should be given every opportunity to cross the street or take a turning. The fast driving ethos stipulates that one should never impede the locomotive impulse of other road users. Consideration for others is a form of respect for their dynamic claims on a shared world.

The chivalry of the fast lane is dying out. Cruising speeds of 200 km/h (124 mph) and more are now the province of an increasingly tiny cohort of motorists—and that despite the fact that small cars and family vans are now capable of top speeds beyond what in the 1970s was still considered the "sound barrier." As late as the 1990s BMW 5s, Golf GTIs with 16 valves, and the large displacement Mercedes E class jostled in the fast lane, making best use of what the engineers had provided these increasingly sporty, everyday cars. However, the zeitgeist was rapidly changing, though it was not the increasing energy costs, but the feeling that speeding was somehow out of step with the times that proved decisive—a fate that would later befall smoking. On top of this there was greater traffic density on the freeways, which was also slower and more congested, largely due to the lorries traveling to and from Eastern Europe.

[6] Italian organization dedicated to keeping cities "slow"—providing a slower-paced life for citizens with an eye on sustainability, the environment, and local food production.

» Accelerated awareness: a 917 driver feeling the need for speed lines up at the start line.

1973 TARGA FLORIO WINNER
1. Müller / van Lennep Martini-Porsche Carrera RSR
2. Munari / Andruet Lancia Stratos
3. Kinnunen / Haldi Martini-Porsche Carrera RSR
4. McBoden / Moreschi Chevron
5. Nicodemi / Moser Lola
6. Steckkönig / Pucci Martini-Porsche Carrera RSR
Shell
Bosch / Bilstein / Dunlop
MARTINI INTERNATIONAL CLUB
MARTINI
MARTINI
RACING
PORSCHE
STUTTGART
PORSCHE
Dr.-Ing. h.c. F. Porsche A.G. Stuttgart-Zuffenhausen · MARTINI & ROSSI AG Bad Kreuznach · Entwurf Atelier Strenger · Foto Dr. Biesenberger · Printed in Germany · Poster Nr. 2

At the time when the first 911s began to populate the freeways and inner cities, Richard von Frankenberg called on Porsche drivers to act as role models for other motorists. "I don't just mean a role model in terms of (manual) driving skills or the ability to assess a situation correctly, I also mean with respect to helpfulness, politeness, giving hand signals etc." But the justification for this was unashamedly presumptuous. "Thanks to our powerful machines, we are in a better position to make up the 10 seconds lost than other drivers." This sense of superiority was further emphasized before driving fast was elevated to a kind of ideal standard. "It is up to us, the drivers of sporty cars, to show the mild mannered, homely citizens that the speed of a car is always paired with the politeness of its owner." According to Frankenberg's article, the homely citizens believe that it is driving fast that disturbs the flow of traffic, when in fact it is exactly the opposite. "In the majority of cases disruption is caused by someone crawling rather than driving, thus gathering a column of cars behind them with their indecision: should I, shouldn't I, right or left, or maybe in the middle … " He concluded that the sports car driver is more attentive and courteous than drivers of " 'run of the mill' cars." In a declamatory essay on motor racing Frankenberg was even more explicit. Sports car drivers are so excited by their vehicles that the adrenaline increases their concentration. Contrary to police reports, many accidents are not a consequence of excessive speed or taking a bend too quickly, but of a lack of concentration and attention in the seconds before the accident: "a lack of focus on driving as the single most interesting activity once one has climbed into one's car … " Regardless of the accuracy of Frankenberg's basic idea, it constituted a provocation to the egalitarian logic of the politically correct community of drivers. To the proponents of rational traffic concepts, this romanticization of sports car driving must have appeared like a grotesque legacy of futurism with its implicit death wish. Nevertheless, the passionate doctrine of fast driving still has its adherents among today's Porsche drivers—though without the condescending air that is no longer considered contemporary.

"It is up to us, the drivers of sporty cars, to show the mild mannered, homely citizens that the speed of a car is always paired with the politeness of its owner."

↳ Richard von Frankenberg, racing driver and journalist.

« Porsche's race victories were used to great advantage in its advertising, as well as being intertwined with the brand. The Targa was given its moniker after the Targa Florio endurance race in 1965.

For Walter Röhrl, who has tested and co-developed cars for Porsche for decades, this rather snooty division of the world into sports car drivers and beginners is not an option. In his opinion, sports car drivers bear a special responsibility in everyday driving situations. In a classic work the rally legend appealed to sports car enthusiasts, adopting an informal tone: "Ideally you should also put yourself in the position of the drivers of the two cars in front of you and the one at your rear." Sporting in the sense of "fair" as opposed to "fast." "Driving sportily means driving consciously, with attention, concentration, anticipation, actively," recommended Röhrl. It is permitted to view the car as a sports accessory, but not as a weapon, as this would "lend our complexes a dangerous power over ourselves and others." The German rock singer Udo Lindenberg,[7] a manic 911 driver, has a clearly defined sports car ethic. He crawls through the city, much to the annoyance of those driving behind him, because, as he says, he doesn't want to "hurt any of these kittens and hedgehogs, disturb a single hair." On the freeway he tears up the asphalt, for what it's worth: "Bombing along like 'Enterprise'—Scotty, beam me up, and go! Together with Dr. Valium, 300 km/h [186 mph] with my terrestrial space capsule to take a peek at Timmendorfer beach."[8] In Udo's universe there is only fast or slow, nothing in between.

Motor sport enthusiasts see sports car drivers as, in some respects, the close relatives of racing drivers. From this they derive a special ethic of responsibility, imposing standards with respect to driving style. In the Porsche clubs this conditioning is further strengthened by the brand ethos that has always been at pains to distinguish athleticism from agressivity. As a consequence, unlike the cars of some exclusive manufacturers, Porsche sports cars, even on the freeway, are respected as opposed to feared. This was the case in the past, and remains so today. Ideally the Porsche radiated a natural authority, even in the fast lane, which highly motorized station wagons and mid-sized limousines had to fight for using coercion and flashing headlights in a relatively abrasive fashion. To this day there is virtually no other vehicle on the freeway that enjoys such a natural right of free passage as the 911.

Motor racing has shaped the identity of all Porsches, and that of the 911 in particular. The sports car—in all possible variations and racing versions—has recorded a total of over 20,000 motor sport victories, which makes it the world's most frequently produced racing car. In this respect, the Porsche driver's impatience is the secular form of the racing driver's religion—always to be the first over the finishing line. Ferry

[7] Hat-wearing rocker famous for songs such as *Bunte Republik Deutschland* and *Coole Socke*.

[8] Udo Lindenberg wrote the well-known song *Hinterm Horizont* on this high-society beach.

» Rally, racing, and all-round conscientious driver Walter Röhrl in a Carrera 3.8 coupe Supercup in 1994.

RECARO

The Bergspyder is fragile and bold, powerful and vulnerable, wild and poetic.

« German racing driver Rolf Stommelen in the super-light Porsche 909 Bergspyder in Mont Ventoux, France, 1968. The car weighed in at just 375 kg and the paint was so thin it rubbed off with cleaning.

Porsche's decision to use motor racing, instead of expensive marketing and advertising campaigns, as the image factor not only changed the self-image of the employees, but it also increased the competitive pressure on the product. Porsche had to win both on the freeway and the racetrack. The word "sport" in sports car resounded loudly and insistently. That is why the walls of both workshops and fans' bedrooms were lined with those detailed, tabulated victory posters that listed which 911s in which concentration were successful on which famous racetracks. The posters were the bank statements of motor racing fame, and a guarantee that the essence of the 911 as a piece of sports equipment had not been lost, regardless of how comfortable it had become over the years. Motor sport contributed to brand management and customer care. In the United States in particular, the mechanics from Zuffenhausen that were placed at the disposal of exclusive customers were more efficient at selling the product than the customary traveling salesmen could ever have been. "Win on Sunday—sell on Monday" was the motto of the sports car trade. Every Porsche victory resulted in dozens of potential customers in the showrooms. On top of this, motor racing stimulated further basic research into performance and durability. The Porsche 909 Bergspyder was a product of such unbridled research at the limits of the physically possible. This sports car, with which Porsche won the 1968 European Hill Climb Championships symbolized the essence of the Porsche doctrine: the racing car had a dry weight of 375 kg (827 lb.) and a plastic body mounted on an aluminum lattice. The paint was applied so thinly that it came off during cleaning. The brake discs of the qualifying winner were made from beryllium and were more expensive than the rest of the car put together—as the mastermind of the Bergspyder, Ferdinand Piëch, recalls. The racing car was so incredibly light that even experienced drivers had difficulty controlling it in the threshold region.

"That is what comes out when you boil down a 911," remarks Dieter Landenberger, not without a sense of admiration, when leading visitors to this museum exhibit. Indeed, this racing car is the fulfillment of Ferdinand Porsche and his son Ferry's dream of an ultra-lightweight vehicle—and in particular, that of

"Now almost any car can drive fast. What is decisive is not how fast it drives, but how it drives fast."

↳ **Jerry Seinfeld, comedian, writer, and producer.**

» The Nürburgring racetrack lined with Porsches in 2015. The Nordschleife—a route through the Eifel forest named the *Grüne Hölle* (green hell)—was a previous location for the German Grand Prix.

the grandson Ferdinand Piëch, who pursued this project with unflagging intensity. In order to understand Porsche as a brand and a myth it is worthwhile perusing and immersing oneself in the Bergspyder. This racing car is fragile and bold, powerful and vulnerable, wild and poetic. It is an extreme vehicle, uncompromisingly committed to the ideal of weightlessness. It doesn't contain a single gram of steel. It brought to an end an essentially naive era of car manufacturing, gazing far into the future with materials such as titanium, magnesium, and beryllium. Thanks to its weight, the 275 hp eight-cylinder engine can accelerate the car from 0–100 km/h (62 mph) in 2.4 seconds. An unbelievable value to this day.

When the classic 911 was entered in the 1965 Monte Carlo Rally, this was originally intended as nothing more than a test exercise to see how it would hold up under extreme conditions. The drivers Herbert Linge and Peter Falk were under instructions to deliver the pre-serial production coupe to Monaco in one piece for a photo shoot in front of the local Prince's Palace. During the rally the duo's sporting ambitions became so inflated that they earned fifth place in the overall rankings, and—it is said—a fit of rage from Ferry Porsche who was furious that his humble instructions to carefully guide the brand new 911 across the finishing line in one piece had been ignored. The rear engine was ideal for rally sport (before the age of the Audi Quattro), as the boxer's power, thanks to the weight of the engine, was effectively transferred to the road. In 1968, 1969, and 1970 a pre-serial production 911 won the Monte Carlo Rally. In 1978 this was repeated with a 911 Carrera.

From the beginning Porsche customers used their vehicles for motor racing, sometimes recklessly. To this day motor sport clubs are an important arena for Porsche AG and a meeting place for the Porsche family and community. In the past Porsche owners drove their sports cars to the racetrack, applied a few racing decals, completed a race, and then drove home with a trophy. James Dean was such an amateur sportsman. In the twenty-first century such practices have virtually disappeared from motor racing. However, in 2009 a racing team drove their serial, road-licensed GT3 RS along the freeway to the 24-hour race at the Nürburgring, won thirteenth place in the overall rankings, and subsequently cruised home along the freeway. Apart from changing the brakes, all the mechanics had to do was refuel, change the tires, and clean the windscreens. It demonstrated that even a production car from Zuffenhausen was capable of holding its own with the fastest racing cars of the time in a grueling long-distance race.

Ideally, a sports car unites two concepts: that of the racing car, with which one can achieve victory in motor sport, and that of the road vehicle, with which one can accelerate one's everyday life. A sports car can gravitate to one or the other pole. In the case of the 911, the buyer's choices range from the comfortable standard Carrera to the extremely venomous GT2 RS, depending on which of the pillars of identity he places most importance on. For the engineers this means they always have to consider both, something that has been trained at Porsche from the beginning—as company history has amply proved.

Therefore it comes as no surprise that the 911 was and is a popular private car among racing drivers (Jo Siffert, Niki Lauda, Mark Webber). In the film *Le Mans*, Steve McQueen relaxes in his civilian 911 before engaging in his death-defying pursuit of fast lap times in a Porsche. In the moving, almost two-hour-long documentary *Senna*, about perhaps the greatest Formula One driver of all time, the 911 makes a short cameo appearance at the end of the film. As if in slow motion, Senna—who drove his Formula One monsters to the limits of the physically possible—rolls along a main street in his silver G model Carrera cabriolet. The 911 served one of the most daring drivers in the history of Formula One as a relaxing spa. For the millionaire's son such a car was also a birthright, an appropriate accompaniment to his beach-near, jet-ski-riding, women-beguiling private life. The film ends with these out-of-focus private recordings of Senna in a 911. One had seldom seen him drive so slowly, on or in a car. He crawls along and beams. The Porsche is the vehicle of his passion, a refuge from the all too pronounced death drive of the racing world.

Nevertheless, it is perhaps the 911 driver who exercises more caution when accelerating that understands his vehicle best. Jerry Seinfeld has a dispassionate relationship to speed. Although he is reported to have driven at 320 km/h, in other words around 200 mph, at the unveiling of the Carrera GT at a former Russian military airport—and also drove at speed on German freeways—Seinfeld did not define the pleasure of driving a sports car in terms of speed: "For me, its top speed is not one of the Porsche's top ten kicks. The handling and the design are more important. Now almost any car can drive fast. What is decisive is not how fast it drives, but how it drives fast."

R8
Audi Sport
R8
HYUNDAI

2004 2013

The 997

Neoclassicism

With the 997 began the 911's neoclassical phase. The 997, which looked like a re-contoured 996 with a facelift, placated the traditionalists. Furthermore, the 997 looked like a leaner 996 with a six pack, which once again displayed the athleticism and muscular sensuality of the classic 911. The community was quickly reconciled. Porsche had understood that the development of the 911 must be carried out more cautiously if it was to avoid alienating the stalwarts. In a short space of time, quicker than with any 911 before it, the hype around the 997 soon elevated it to the status of a potential classic.

Shortly after the production of the 997 was halted, a lively discussion on the classic appeal of this 911 began in the fan community. Doddie, a regular reader of the PFF, a leading internet forum for Porsche enthusiasts, was certain that the 997 was on the road to becoming the most popular classic Porsche. The new 991 was too perfect—who exactly was driving who with this car, asked Doddie. In contrast, in a few years time his 997 from 2007—the 911 driver thinks historically, always and for evermore—will be seen as a representative of one of the best water-cooled 911 series, produced when Porsche was still independent, before it had been swallowed by VW. With VW's acquisition of Porsche, the fans turned a shareholder rebellion into a mark of distinction. In this remarkable thread Doddie quotes Mies van der Rohe's aphorism that less is more and calls on his readers to take good care of their 997s, especially the first "pre-facelift" model: "Enjoy the advantages of your car on the way to becoming a genuine classic of Porsche history." And because even passionate 911 fans, despite

S AY 911

长钰商务酒店
ICBC
中国工商银行
53833266
TEC
Carrera
STEC
向前30米

In a short space of time, quicker than with any 911 before it, the hype around the 997 soon elevated it to the status of a potential classic.

« The 997: a global status symbol and a success with the traditionalists as well as commercially. This Carrera 3.6 coupe courts stares in Shanghai, 2009.

all their enthusiasm, are intent on remaining objective, he lists 14 reasons why the 997 has the makings of a classic. The arguments range from the small, shapely, narrow rearview mirrors and the friendly grinning facial expression without dazzling running light strips to the smooth circular headlights, which, compared to the bloated insect eyes of the 991, were so much more handsomely proportioned.

Doddie's article garnered a great deal of support—as well as a number of melancholy responses from cultural pessimists familiar with the 997's production figures—which did not bode well for its classic status. A 356 driver named Helmut wished the 997 drivers all the best with their dreams of the car's classic status; however, for him as a purist, the 911's classic phase ended with the 964 as the last model with the torpedo tube headlights. Wolfgang 31248 from Münster chose a democratic definition, emphasizing that classicism is in the eye of the buyer and user. "Ultimately it is WE who generate the demand." The users of the Elferliste forum looked even further ahead: "All rear engine Porsches will become classics—at the latest when there are none of them left."

Thus the friends of the 911 share a definition classic introduced into literature and pop culture by the writer Rainald Goetz.[1] "In the best case the classic is like the best pop music: namely a hit," wrote Goetz. "Hits are so good that you never get bored with them; exactly the opposite: the better one knows them, the better one wants to get to know them." And further: "The primary characteristic, effectively the cardinal symptom of both a hit and a classic, is that it gives one courage, new strength, new nouveau, and new energy for the next attack." That this passage from Goetz's essay also talks about the "total full-throttle speed" of pop is more than appropriate.

[1] Prize-winning contemporary author whose work draws on German counter-culture. Once cut his forehead during a reading at the 1983 Ingeborg Bachmann Prize and allowed the blood to flow while he read.

turbo
turbo

Elitism in Harvestehude: The 911 Monoculture in Hamburg

At the beginning of the twenty-first century a Porsche 911 monoculture emerged in the prosperous districts of Hamburg, which in its rigidity generated elegant streetscapes that were unique even by international standards. Parked in front of the resplendent, white-painted, renovated jugendstil houses with their gray or anthracite window frames and doors stood the metallic black and anthracite Carreras, generally less than five years old. Range Rovers, Cayennes, or Mercedes E class station wagons dominated the ranks of the first cars. In the wealthy merchant city the Porsche 911 became the cashmere pullover among sports cars. With a lack of humor echoed in the choice of box tree and yew tree hedges for the front garden, the car classic became the favorite vehicle of Hamburg's prosperous families around the river Alster and in the district of Blankensee.

There is a rumor that this style choice was also inspired by Jil Sander, who as early as the 1980s saw her 911 Carrera as a minimalist statement directed against the dominance of the British sports saloons that could still be felt at that time.

The charm of the 911 was the relaxed approach it took to meeting the standard definition of a sports car—in contrast to the eccentricity of a Ferrari—while its sound and form, even on repeated viewing, still retained the capacity to activate emotions that other cars lacked. Not even the homogenous sidewalks in Hamburg, Munich, Dusseldorf, or Kampen, which sometimes resembled a customer parking lot at a Porsche center, were capable of diffusing the 911's unique character. For J. Philip Rathgen, car journalist, style expert, and native of the Hanseatic city of Hamburg, this victory had less to do with the classic Carrera of the 1980s than the 996 with its fried egg headlights. Finally, with the 997, the omnipresence of the 911 in a number Hamburg's streets, above all to the west and north of the river Alster, grew explosively. At one point there were as many 911s as Minis and Range Rovers, frequently accompanied by the dog breeds Rhodesian ridgeback or Weimaraner. The 911 key, which a number of years ago had assumed the car's form, was prominently displayed on the tables of the fashionable Italian restaurants. The clientele consisted of incredible numbers of small, haggard men, explained Rathgen. And naturally numerous women: Rathgen's circle was populated by countless women with a PR agency or a boutique in Uhlenhorst[2] who also exercised understatement in their choice of sports car. These women had been wearing white jeans and riding boots since 2009, and, seated next to the small, haggard men, were prone to stand out with their over-dimensioned bags that would have taken up all the space on the front passenger seat. The Porsche often went hand in hand with the Hermès belt with the "H" and, as a rule, a sporty Rolex watch.

[2] Idyllic, high-class area in Northern Hamburg.

» German actress Iris Berben in a Carrera 2 3.6 cabriolet with tiptronic transmission in Hamburg, 1995.

This rigid canon of elegance is a heritage of both Hanseatic, upper class distinction, with its long mercantile tradition, and an extension of the popper aesthetic that emerged at the end of the 1970s as a counter-dissidence to punk in an attempt to distill subcultural traces from the mainstream. In this sense the 911 was a continuation of the Vespa scooter with more resources and more horsepower. The canonization of status symbols and recipes for elegance spawned imitators among the social climbers and new money people. Thanks to the accessibility of the look, Hamburg's urban landscape became homogenous in the extreme. Naturally this also incited rebellion and opposition, which extended to the defilement of 911s that were scratched, dented, or even set alight. For over two decades it has tended to be Hamburg's made-up, self-made women, as opposed to the trophy wives, who have seen the 911 as an appropriate expression of their success "without going completely crazy," as Rathgen expressed it. The form appeals to the icy women: the 911 as an automotive god who is worshipped by all but refuses to be the subject of idolatry. Another factor in the 911's popularity in Hamburg is the fact that it was never a car for the hood, it was never popular in St. Pauli.[3] It was too conservative for pimps.

For over two decades it has tended to be Hamburg's made-up, self-made women, as opposed to the trophy wives, who have seen the 911 as an appropriate expression of their success.

« The 911 was an attractive accessory for the self-made woman as much as the self-made man, working well with the Hermès belt and sporty Rolex watch.

However, for the descendants of the wealthy traders and their business partners, the car's solidity was an important argument. Just as they viewed themselves as respectable merchants, so the Porsche was seen as the product (to express it in a somewhat rotary club fashion) of Germany's "decent" small- and medium sized business sector.

In the midst of Hamburg's style obsession, which can only be compared to that of London, Paris, or Milan, the 911 became the only constant in the fashion-dominated lives of the cultivated society ladies from Harvestehude.[4] The 911's message is as simple as it is Hanseatic: if you want success, don't change the recipe. That is the source of Porsche's greatness, a role model for the enterprising Hanseaten. In 1982, a city that until then had been governed exclusively by the Social Democratic Party almost elected a mayor from the conservative CDU in the person of the cosmopolitan bourgeois and driver of a black Porsche 911 Walther Leisler Kiep. In terms of color—like so much in Hamburg—it began with the dark blue and black of a maritime captain's uniform, then came anthracite, and finally, among the innumerable advertising executives, the obligatory and supposedly modern white and matt paint jobs, preferably in military green. With the discontinuation of the 997 series, brown metallic paint jobs have now established themselves as the new black in the universe of taste.

Outwardly, Udo Lindenberg followed the Hanseatic fashion for black 911s, but he did it, as in all things, with an anarchistic poeticism. As a herald of both the unconventional and the popular, the rock musician and artist who has lived in Hamburg since 1968 developed a passion for the Porsche 911 early in his career. With his first big earnings from the hit "Andrea Doria" he bought his first "shit-brown" 911 in 1973. This is the car he drove to pick up his mother Hermine, an event captured in photos that picture a proud man with long hair and a receding hairline, and an even prouder mother with neck scarf and blow-dried hairdo holding on to the A-pillar as she climbs into the passenger seat. 40 years later this sports car is still his "fast racing car, Formula 1, space capsule, Udonaut." In a charming article in the lovingly produced *Porsche Klassik* magazine, Lindenberg talks about his Porsche-Panic-Family, his "Black Panthers," the Panamera, the Cayenne, the 911s, with and without turbo, from the G model to the latest 991—all in black. "Looks tasty; the eye listens too," he explains as he starts up the engine of a G model Turbo.

[3] Party district where the Beatles played, as well as the home of the Reeperbahn (red-light district) and cult, left-wing football team, FC St. Pauli.

[4] Picturesque *Villenviertel* or "mansion quarter" of Hamburg bordering the Alster lake.

The Fashion Icon

In 2008, during the period when Hamburg was being transformed into a metropolitan 911 convention thanks to the proliferation of 997s, the MoMu fashion museum in Antwerp played host to an exhibition of the work of the young Belgian designer Veronique Branquinho. It also saw the unveiling of her old classic 911 that she had completely covered with English salt and pepper tweed—a fabric covering reminiscent of the felt used by the German conceptual artist Joseph Beuys to lend objects a melancholy gravity and metaphysical capacity for storing warmth. Branquinho made the 911 heavier and more enigmatic, and simultaneously more elegant and feminine. With the Protestant astringency typical of the Antwerp school of design, she intensified the bodywork's minimalist design. At the end of the 1990s Branquinho did for women's fashion what Helmut Lang did for men's fashion: she provided a contemporary interpretation of comparatively strict role models.

The woman in Branquinho's shows was autonomous, proud, and had succumbed to a sophisticated concept of beauty. The creative elites who wore Branquinho liked the twist within the twist. Everything was designed to look simple, but on closer inspection was not. The 911 in tweed, both inside and outside, lovingly interpreted its striving for perfection. The single color fabric heightened the rigor, making it appear even more austere and conceptual. However, in order to prevent the Porsche being decelerated to the point where it became a statue, the fashion designer projected the nihilistic road movie *Vanishing Point* onto the wall behind the 911 installation. In a magazine project, conducted a year before the exhibition, the designer, with unusual car expertise, curated the cultural history of her favorite cars, including all the Opel Manta models, Steve McQueen's Mustang from *Bullitt,* and exotic vehicles such as the Bitter coupe and the Citroën SM. An eye catcher was the Porsche 911 G model in black with black Fuchs rims, although it featured rear windscreen wipers that were much contested by collectors. On the preceding double page, Branquinho presented her favorite record cover, which appeared to exercise a similar influence as her car preferences. Portrayed as the "Queen of the Road" in a fur coat, the urbane, autonomous woman was seated in a Porsche 911, visible from the black leather lining of the driver's door. That she was in black appears inevitable. The photo is strongly reminiscent of a scene from the Anglo-French co-production *The Marseille Contract* from 1974, in which the beautiful daughter of a mafia boss in a yellow 911 S Targa becomes embroiled in a car chase with an Alfa Montreal, which in the lousy action film is re-choreographed into an erotic ballet. The classic 911's rear drift is transformed into a fertility dance, which the icy heroine with the big dark sunglasses, black leather jacket, and dark leather gloves performs virtually without moving. The emancipated woman wins the race and applauds the gentleman—who is also dressed as if he had just stumbled out of a fashion magazine—as he

» Veronique Branquinho's tweed-covered classic 911 alongside her fashion collection at Antwerp's MoMu fashion museum in 2008.

In the capital cities of elegance from Hamburg and Milan to Paris, the colorful aspect of the Porsche myth had little impact.

» At the end of the rainbow: the 1960s and 70s visibly left their mark on Porsche's paintwork shades—and the bolder shades, with their quirky names (like aubergine, Irish green, and Gulf blue), are highly sought after today.

crosses the Finishing line in second place. Veronique Branquinho was only one year old when the film was released at the cinemas.

The Porsche as a fashion and design icon is reduced to its austere, almost rigoristic modernism, which appears to have as little historical foundation as the idea of the bauhaus design school as the epitome of white modernity. Just as the apartment blocks in the city of Dessau (the home of bauhaus) and many other residential landscapes from the classical modernist period were often extremely colorful (see the Papageiensiedlung—Parrot Estate—in Berlin), Porsche, in the context of its defined forms, was experimental when it came to materials and colors. For the director of the Porsche archive, Dieter Landenberger, the houndstooth seat covers in the classic 911 are "more sixties" than any of the Porsche's other style elements. In the late 1960s and early 1970s Porsche paid its tribute to the zeitgeist with bold, adventurous colors such as viper green, Indian red, or blood orange, designed, in an almost programmatic action, to banish the everyday gray from the German middle classes. The Carrera RS was delivered in white, while the lettering on the sides and rims was finished in blue, red, and green tones. In the capital cities of elegance from Hamburg and Milan to Paris, the colorful aspect of the Porsche myth had little impact.

In 1974, when Porsche became the first manufacturer to replace chrome with matt black, this high-tech reductionism quickly established a precedent, and other premium manufacturers followed suit. The matt, technical look not only went well with the watches, pipes, and bags that Ferdinand Alexander Porsche designed for his label Porsche-Design, it also complemented that somewhat restrained distinction that the German and European upper classes cultivated out of fear of social envy. While the garish colors of the 911 old-timers are now much sought after, the majority of Porsche customers preferred a more limited paintwork canon for their "daily drivers." Even though Porsche's extras program, alongside the many serial options, provided customers with every possible freedom, the mainstream of 911 customers remained beholden to convention.

PORSCHE
PORSCHE
PORSCHE
PORSCHE
GOODYEAR

The Swine's Car: Vol. 2

Daniel Deserno is an extremely disagreeable individual. He is not just a reckless gambler on the financial markets in his professional capacity as an investment banker, but he also indulges in wild goings on with a host of women, preferably slim, together with his beloved Porsches. As in a street ballad, Bodo Kirchhoff adopts a fundamentalist approach in his novel *Erinnerung an meinen Porsche* (Memories of my Porsche), and like Heinrich Böll in his time, the tale would not be complete without the villains getting their just desserts. The womanizer is castrated with the aid of an Alessi designer corkscrew, an intervention that also robs him of the feeling in his legs. He can neither walk, penetrate, nor drive his Porsche, whereby the Porsche, with the suffix GT, is also employed as a synonym for his once functioning sexual organ (German: *Geschlechsteil*—GT).

"Porsche was and is the greatest," explained Kirchhoff. "If creation has celebrated a triumph anywhere—apart from bringing forth those capable of winning the Tour de France without doping—then it is with this car." This quote from the first quarter of the novel immediately positions the Porsche at the rather distasteful peak of social Darwinism. The hero raves about his Turbos. The latest with two intercoolers makes a sound "like the hissing of a woman who comes even though she is still angry at you." For sexists, who unlike Hank Moody are virtually without charm, the Porsche is part of foreplay or sometimes the ideal masturbation aid. On the maiden journey of his Turbo cabriolet, the first-person narrator "tightly fixed the chrome gear stick to my own personal Porsche with a red ribbon left over from Christmas in order to experience every gear change, and during the shifting up and down of gears on a route in Hintertaunus, I even succeeded in coming at full speed."

With this wild fantasy, Kirchhoff undermines the popular prejudice of the impotent little man who buys a Porsche as compensation for his inadequacies—while presenting such a despicable portrait of the copulating erotomaniac in his Porsche that the peace-loving dispassion of the sexually impotent almost seems preferable. For the 39-year-old banker the Porsche becomes a telegram addressed to the outside world that announces how much money he earns, how horny he is, and how much he wants to be admired by his environment, by other people.

A glance at the novel's publication date explains the work's somewhat bitter note. The text appeared in 2009, making it—as

PORSCHE

the critics noted with interest—a quick fire reaction to the financial crisis, just as Böll's writing was a reaction to Germany in the time of the RAF terror (or should one say the terror of the tabloid newspaper *Bildzeitung*?). In an interview about his novel in the *Spiegel* magazine, the author presented himself as an economics expert. As a boy, selling ice cream in the rich American suburbs, Kirchhoff already sensed that this prosperity had feet of clay. Such sentiments are expressed without the least trace of irony. A social critique that sees the spoiler on the protagonist's Porsche as an indication of his depravity will inevitably resort to moral arguments.

If the leftwing, ecologically correct daily newspaper *taz* were to organize a congress in Berlin, then a Porsche driver would be invited to sit on its lifestyle panel as a public spectacle and object of pity. In Kirchhoff's novel, as in Böll's and the corresponding film adaptations, a restrictive speed limit is imposed on the flow of ideas. Kirchhoff understands little about Porsche itself. Personally he drives a used jaguar with little removable wooden trays, as he confesses in the interview. He wrote his novel in Frankfurt with a view of the high-rise banks, and from his apartment he could see the bankers racing across the bridge over the river Main in the morning in their Porsches. He believes these sports cars to be the bankers' little company cars. Significantly, the cover of the paperback edition features the picture of a Boxster with a smashed up rear, though it is actually irrelevant which Porsche this novel could be referring to—beyond the hero's mutilated genitals. The *Frankfurter Rundschau* newspaper rejoiced: "Bodo Kirchhoff gives the Porsches of this world their just desserts." This must suffice.

In retrospect, the popular prejudices against 911 drivers reinforced in the novel can be seen as a distant echo of those high risk stock market activities that the Porsche CEO at the time, Wiedeking, fell prey to. In 2005 the ambitious and assertive car manager began an innocent-looking series of VW share acquisitions, which thanks to the flourishing business before the financial crisis even raised the possibility of a takeover of VW by Porsche. In May 2008 the supervisory board gave its approval for the takeover of VW. Then came the financial crisis, the collapse of share prices, the economic downturn, and the panic of Porsche's managers who had run up 10 billion euros in debt in order to acquire Volkswagen. Despite fresh capital from Qatar, the sports car manufacturer was once again faced with economic ruin. In July 2009 Wiedeking was sacked with a juicy pay-off of 50 million euros. David had been defeated by Goliath, not least—contrary to the Old Testament story—because David had underestimated Goliath and overestimated himself. Success had clouded the senses. On a meta-level, the 911 driver, who as a rule chose the role of the "high-flyer" in his professional life, was provided with a lesson in how quickly a life in the fast lane can come unstuck.

The First Time

There are few 911 owners who can remember the precise moment when the sports car's silhouette or that of its predecessor first impacted their life. As a rule—as the dozens of interviews conducted in preparation for this book corroborate—this occurred in early childhood. For many boys (and girls) there was no turning back. Porsche advertising repeatedly references this magic moment, placing the memory of this childhood longing at the heart of its romanticization of those moments of happiness that the 911 continually provides, even for grown-up customers.

In an advert from 2005, little William, he must be around 12 years old, is sitting in a geography lesson with a look of mild disinterest when a slate-gray metallic Porsche 911 drives past the school. William gazes at the roaring 911 driving past him in slow motion as if bewitched, eagerly devouring it with his eyes. William's pencil falls to the ground, catching the teacher's attention as she sees that he is not following the lesson. She reprimands the boy, and the class laugh. Later, as he is sitting in the library—as a punishment?—he draws a Porsche 997. At the sound of the school bell William hurries to his bicycle, racing through a well kept, prosperous, middle-class district to the next Porsche center. On arriving he asks about the new "nine eleven," and the friendly salesman invites him to take a seat in the silver Porsche. William devoutly savors the pleasure, and, on getting out of the car, asks the salesman for his business card, announcing that he will come back again in 20 years time. In this Porsche ad, the *puer senex,* the man-boy, is already in possession of that knowledge that will soon make him into a Porsche customer. He knows who he is and what he wants. He appears to be immune to the laughter of his schoolmates and refuses to acknowledge the teacher's authority. He is not frightened by the pointer she swings in her hand; far more disturbing is the fact that this supervisory body is capable of ripping him out of his dreams, and is permitted to do so.

In another American Porsche film the son, who is roughly the same age as William, confronts the father with his old dreams. The boy, who lives in a modernist villa high above the city, is rummaging through the garage in search of a new inner tube to mend the flat tire on his BMX bike when he discovers a box of old photos featuring a classic red 911. Papa's first Porsche. And next to it in the garage, a new 997. The father finds his son studying the pictures and explains how, as a young man, he found the 911 in a barn, dusty and decrepit, before painstakingly restoring it. The next morning the father finds a box of craft supplies on the roof of the new 997 for building a classic model 911. The boy has scribbled "Don't forget" on a Post-it attached to the present. The boy reminds the father of the boy in him from the time he first discovered his passion. The son represents the keeper of the flame. There is also a German advertisement from Porsche that addressed the theme of the 911 as a childhood sweetheart—an epic failure—entitled "Class Reunion". Boring stuff.

LB-P 420

PORSCHE
S-04326

It is an incomparable experience, rhapsodizes the Porsche owner, when one acquires one's first Porsche and that original euphoria is still fresh; when the 911 fan who has just entered adulthood empties his savings account to buy an inexpensive, used entry model that promises—with respect to mileage and condition—a carefree life. When, after numerous viewings and test drives, the picture clears and one knows which 911 it will be, the trip to the bank becomes an unforgettable experience with weak knees, trembling hands, and a shaky voice. The older lady at the bank counter inquires if everything is okay. And as it is more than okay, the young man answers: yes, super. With the money in the old satchel, which also served as a faithful companion during his student days, the young man looks forward excitedly to the evening appointment when the disappointingly thin paper envelope with—lets say—20,000 deutsche marks will be exchanged for a white Porsche 911 with 165 hp, build year 1977. The sales contract is signed, the vehicle registration documents exchanged, and then the keys, too. A brief handshake and then the young man—who has the feeling that his entire childhood and youth has been leading up to this moment—walks to the white 911, unmistakable among the miscellaneous selection of parked cars. He opens the door and sits down. He is nauseous, he beams, he can't believe it. It feels like a miracle; he is frightened of waking up to discover it was only a dream. He sticks the key into the ignition to the left. He summons all his strength and turns it. The six-cylinder boxer springs to life with a roar, the engine howling with every downward thrust on the gas pedal. This is now yours! The 911. The car is put into first gear, carefully maneuvered out of the parking space, and then, all too quickly, the most beautiful hundred meters in a car are over.

The first time is a never to be repeated experience. Driving is still wonderful, but never as earth shaking as the first time. This sounds pathetic, and it is. Porsche fans divide their friends into two categories, those who can understand such an absurd feeling for an expensive heap of steel and technology, and the rest, to whom they conceal their love for a sports car under a mantle of self-irony and detachment. These fans would never betray their 911, as long as it still triggers these feelings—which are experienced all the more intensely when it comes to looking for a new model.

This reactivates the primordial longing and memory of that first quest—without completely recapturing its excitement. With every further 911, the process becomes more rational and routine, although the falling in love moment remains, not least because a Porsche, even as a used sports car, is an expensive pleasure. The genuinely rich can't really appreciate that sense of happiness experienced when a Porsche, purchased with hard-earned savings, becomes the fulfillment of a larger-than-life dream. For the parvenu, the social climber, and the ambitious the Porsche is a symbol of having arrived in that world, which since his earliest

A Ferrari is a lover, but a 911 is like a wife. The idea of eternal fidelity, engendered by the 911's long production runs, also promotes ideas of monogamy among its users.

« The moment where the love affair with Porsche begins. In this case, the object of desire is a 912 1.6 coupe from 1965.

childhood, he has naively imagined to be a happy and beautiful place. One which, in contrast to the barren world of his parents, is about fun, happiness, and the audacity of transgression—not the ambition that deforms people's characters in the process of assimilation, as opposed to setting them free.

The first time is unique. However, if one really looks inside oneself, every time is a different first time. For over 40 years Udo Lindenberg has succeeded in conserving the Eros of the maiden voyage. "Every time you climb in it as if it was the first time, like on stage. And each time you lift off, like under the concert spotlights. A pleasure, a kick, which from the very first encounter is a new, unique experience each time." According to the popular wisdom of the Porsche driver, a Ferrari is a lover, but a 911 is like a wife. The idea of eternal fidelity, engendered by the 911's long production runs, also promotes ideas of monogamy among its users. In 2013 the 911 also celebrated a type of golden wedding anniversary with its most seasoned customers. The erotic fantasy that the first time—though it is not possible to recapture its virginal excitement—can be kept alive by magical means over years and decades, lends an aspect of the product's solidity to this loyalty built on enthusiasm. In the fast paced modern age with its lack of commitment, as signaled by the "anything goes" mentality, the vow of fidelity as a consequence of a fulfilled first time is the exception as opposed to the rule. Thus all additional journeys remain emotionally coupled to the excitement of that first event. Formulated a little more narcissistically, remaining faithful to the 911 throughout the continuum from love at first sight to shared happiness in old age also requires a high degree of self-fidelity. The 911 as the image of its owner combines the permanence of the object and its seductive power with the permanence of the erotic imperative and the desire to be seduced. That is why this book remains an incomprehensible labor of love for some less horsepower obsessed readers. It is the cultural history of a romance.

The Sculpture

Something is not quite right, thought Erwin Wurm as he stood at the lights in Vienna in his new 997 Turbo. A white Turbo, as new as his own, had pulled up beside him, driven by a "grilled prole," a man with a thick gold chain and a sun studio tan. "My god, what an ugly car," exclaimed the world famous artist, before realizing that he was actually sitting in the same model, albeit painted in a more discrete color. He drove home immediately and called the Porsche dealer to inform him that he would be returning the Turbo.

As a replacement he bought a 997 4S Cabrio, which he subsequently sold in 2011. Since then he has driven an Aston Martin for speed and a Range Rover for safety. "Somehow I have ended up with the English cars, no idea how that could happen. A whim!" Wurm thinks for a moment. "At some point I suppose I felt as if I could be mistaken for a dentist from Dusseldorf in a 911." Erwin Wurm is responsible for perhaps the most exciting and substantial artistic intervention ever unleashed on a 911: the *Fat Car.* Even as a young boy, he was fascinated by the 911. "Back then," recalls the artist who first saw the light of day in 1954, "there were very few Porsches around. Today Vienna is full of them." Following his first success on the art market he bought an old blue 911 with two previous owners, which—as the media is fond of reporting—he parked in a prominent position in the courtyard of the University of Applied Arts in Vienna where he began teaching as a professor in 2002. Unable to afford a new Porsche, Wurm employed a used Carrera cabriolet as the foundation for his first *Fat Car,* which he paid for by selling models of the sculpture. "I am an artist, I live from selling my work," he commented with a smirk. Even though—and precisely because—he found the 911's form so wonderful, it was not the car's sculptural qualities that proved decisive, but the potential he saw for its deconstruction. "The intention was to destroy the 911's form by making it fat." That the 911, compared to other sports cars, was relatively slim and delicate was an advantage. "There was no point in fattening up a car that is already fat. That is why I didn't take a Turbo or a 4S with a broad rear," Wurm emphasized. Ideally he would have like to have used James Dean's 550 Spyder, but this idea was unaffordable.

As a social signal the Porsche was perceived as a "phat car," a "fat-cat car as one used to say in the 1970s." In a world in which people define themselves through their material possessions as an unmistakable sign of their financial means, the Porsche was a "statement of prosperity and sporting prowess."

As a product from central Europe, which one could identify with, the Porsche as a signifier was both exceptional and unassuming. An exotic car such as a Lamborghini would have taken the interpretation of the sculpture in a completely different direction. The *Fat Cars* were a great success for the Austrian artist. Advertising agencies worldwide stole the idea of the *Fat Cars* until Wurm responded with litigation. He never heard anything from Porsche itself, which was offensively disinterested in his work. However, much to his surprise, when he eventually decided to contact Porsche he received a brusque rebuttal.

To all intents and purposes, Porsche was and is taboo for writers. Albert Ostermaier, the Porsche-driving recipient of the Brecht, Kleist, and Toller literary prizes, is convinced of this. "It is okay for painters, actors, directors—such cars are exciting in this context—but not for writers or poets—that is a betrayal; a betrayal of art, of truth, of everything that is holy to the culture section of the highbrow press—and which only applies to others anyway. The poet is reduced to the image from Spitzweg's painting,

» The result of Tobias Rehberger's drawings—recognizable as the classic *Elfer*. The German artist sketched a 911 from memory and asked specialist mechanics in Thailand to build it.

> "I would put the classic 911 in the living room as a sculpture. It is more than a car, it is a metaphysical state, as if Picasso had designed it in one stroke."
>
> ↳ Albert Ostermaier, writer.

» Erwin Wurm's *Fat Car* from 2005: another take on the 911's multifaceted personality.

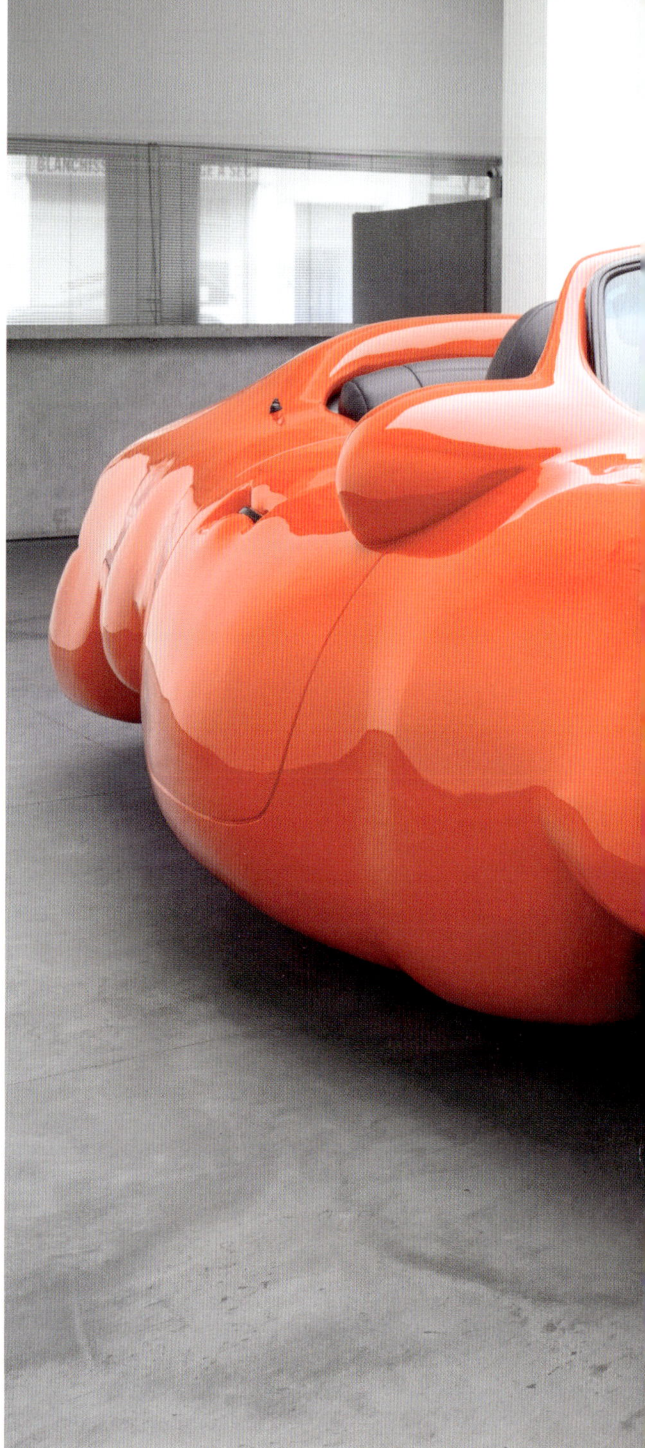

of the impoverished bard lying in bed holding an opened umbrella[5]—and if at all, is only allowed to race in spirit. Having said this, Porsche and poesy is a wonderful alliteration, and taboos are there to be broken. However, I first had to free myself from all outside influences before I could buy my first Porsche without feeling the need to hide behind sunglasses. A few days later I was at the cinema and had to laugh when I heard the legendary words 'Men in crisis buy Porsche.' Porsche helped me overcome the crisis, it gave me the confidence to do what I wanted to do and not worry about what people would say."

Ostermaier doesn't state what kind of crisis it was. At any rate, the Porsche helped. Like Cookie and Rinke, Ostermaier is tall and quite handsome—not just in women's eyes. And intellectually he is no slouch either. He grew up in a family that had driven BMW for generations. As a boy he never played with cars. The only air-cooled runarounds Ostermaier was interested in during his childhood were the FC Bayern Munich players Uli Hoeneß and Karl-Heinz "Kalle" Rummenigge.[6] The most important part of the car was the tail where he could attach his FC Bayern sticker. "My mother," recalls the native of Lake Starnberg, "always drove the fastest BMW, and as a child 'on the road,' being flung from one side of the car to the other in the washing basket, speed quickly assumed a comforting quality for me. I developed a feeling for it—and how insufferably difficult it is with people that are too slow. Out of loyalty to BMW I had to ignore Porsche. However, this didn't last because anyone born with a feeling for beauty, anyone for whom the golden ratio and average speed is not a contradiction, is bound to succumb to Porsche at some point, like the first love which proves so unsettling to one's parents ... "

[5] *The Poor Poet* (1839) by Carl Spitzweg, German romantic painter. Exemplifies the starving artist.

[6] Hoeneß was later president of FC Bayern Munich. He was investigated and found guilty of tax evasion for millions of euros. Rummenigge is the current executive board chairman of the team.

[7] The first version of a text, to which later ones can be compared. Similarly the classic 911 is the *Urelfer*.

For Ostermaier the classic 911 is the "urtext[7] that never loses its validity, its truth." It is more like an object than a vehicle—a radical idea. "I would put the classic 911 in the living room as a sculpture. It is more than a car, it is a metaphysical state, as if Picasso had designed it in one stroke." He has little patience for the Porsche purists who scent decline in the modernizations. "A Porsche is always faster than our aesthetic sense." And if the classic 911 is the urtext, then we have to "continually re-translate it:

some things go missing in the process; others are gained. Decline assumes that one has already risen to a great height. And this is undoubtedly the case with Porsche, which repeatedly rises anew." Neither the air- nor the water-cooled is the genuine 911, but the "heart-cooled." But words are essentially inadequate to describe this car. "The sensuality and seduction is in the unspoken. The most powerful Porsche engine is fantasy; words such as 'rear' are an insult." And the sound of the six-cylinder boxer? "Like the right hand of a boxer just before it hits the opponents glass jaw." Ostermaier poeticizes his happiness with the 911. "The most beautiful 911 is that of your dreams; the 911 of memory which is only landscape, rhythm, music, a mere instant and exchange of glances; the 911 racing through Paris as it awakens, or standing alone on an escarpment over the Atlantic finding its second wind." Ostermaier, leftist, football fan, confidant of FC Bayern, and quintessential son of Munich, drives a black 997.

Minimize it to the Max: Seinfeld's Traditionalism

Jerry Seinfeld is a traditionalist. "I have never driven a Tesla because I love internal combustion engines and spark plugs," explained the comedian. The rest of Hollywood may drive hybrid compact cars and battery-driven sports cars, but Seinfeld remains faithful to his Porsches. Born in Brooklyn in 1954, Seinfeld wrote television history. With the series *Seinfeld* that ran on the NBC channel from 1989 to 1998 he earned more money than any other comedian before him, up to 100 million dollars per year—which he frequently invested in products from Zuffenhausen.

He has a parking garage for his collection, and at Santa Monica Airport near Los Angeles, a kind of car hangar. His financial means make him one of the most unusual collectors, though his pedantry and fanaticism are typical. In the summer of 2011 he acquired a GT3 RS 4.0, one of a limited edition of 600. He even had the car signed under the trunk lid by Hans Mezger, the head of Porsche's motor sport division at the time. Like many of his Porsches it is black—and atypical for a GT3 RS—without any racing decals. For Seinfeld, black is the color for a car "which you love so much you don't want to add anything to it."

Despite a roll cage, bucket seats, and a spoiler that could also be used as a surfboard, Seinfeld likes his road-approved racing cars "minimalist." This is a matter of principle: "I love essentializing cars—that means reducing them to their essence," explained Seinfeld. "I completely remodeled a Speedster from 1958, detaching the bumpers, removing the top to leave a small plastic windscreen where the regular windscreen is usually situated." The Speedster is a highly individual construction, but it remains a really dainty car, "like a black jelly bean." This type of minimalism is unusual, especially in the United States with its love of show. It is a perceptual trap. "People don't know what they are looking at," reported Seinfeld, "but they recognize it is something very special—a pure form. Brash, new, garishly painted cars automatically attract attention. Such a brutally simple car like my black Speedster is a counter-design, an alternative to a culture that is frequently too loud, too puffed up and strained. The majority of high-end sports cars remind Seinfeld of Halloween costumes: monstrous masks for their drivers, as if designed for the Cirque du Soleil. In contrast a Porsche feels "like a warm, round stone in one's hand. It feels good to the touch," emphasizes Seinfeld. "I start loving these things as soon as I feel like they are becoming a part of me—in contrast to all those objects that are designed to ennoble or enhance my status. A Porsche is very humanistic."

If one compares the really fast Porsches such as the 911 Turbo S to a Ferrari 458, then these cars appear sober, laid-back, and in an idiosyncratic fashion, minimalist. "And only someone who wants this should drive a Porsche," states Seinfeld. "Anyone driving this sports car is looking for the minimum, not the maximum." For Seinfeld this means functionalism in its most concise form, as opposed to modernist folklore. "I am an adherent of Mies van der Rohe's maxim which stated that a fascinating simplicity is something precious, and is very difficult to achieve. This exciting simplicity is something I also look for when writing comedy. That is the essence of my aesthetics, as expressed by Braun or Apple. 'Less is more' has become a popular saying, though I don't think there are many people who actually understand what this means. Ferry Porsche put it more simply: good design calms."

2011 and Onward

» The seventh generation of the 911, the 991, is faithful to the past while showcasing engine development and efficiency.

The 991

The First Time, for the Seventh Time: A New 911

In the middle of the green heartland, in the yard of Porsche's development and design center, hidden by earthworks and high steel gates, stands an object whose liturgical birthday would be celebrated a short while later in September 2011 at the Frankfurt Motor Show. It is the new Porsche 911. A 48-year-old car, the seventh generation of a sports car that had decided never to grow old.

Like no other car, the 911 cultivates its ancestral line as proof of its own immortality. Above all, the 911 guarantees its own future by being faithful to its past.

It is a sunny day in early summer as the designer Michael Mauer carefully, not to say solemnly, lifts the tarpaulin from the one-to-one model. Behind him—for comparison—the current model from the 997 series, still on sale at the time, is on display, while another tarpaulin conceals the original of the new series. When the veil was finally lifted, even the nerd who had studied every photograph of disguised prototypes on the internet, analyzed every computer simulation, repeatedly devoured every video of the sinister test vehicles with their mask of decals, was seized by a kind of shudder. That this series, christened 991, appeared almost identical to its predecessor from the front was a mere prelude to a game of deception. The previously unseen looked like a mistake, a provocation, because of its disfigurement of the familiar (and beloved).

PORSCHE
S GO 544

» The generation gap: the 901 (front) and the 991 (back) have almost five decades between them but the family resemblance is still clear.

The car looked wider and stockier, the headlights were spaced further apart; all in all, with its clear, bright gaze and sinuous fenders, the car looked like a studious triathlete.

» The 991 GT3 RS—about the closest you can get to a race car in road-legal form. The 4-liter engine spits out 500 hp and the new carbon-fiber louvers are not just aesthetic but the result of race aerodynamics.

The highly reflective designer, the fifth to occupy the post since Ferdinand Alexander Porsche, sensed the uncertainty of the 911 fanatic, giving an irritated response to the objection that the rear of this car represented a cultural revolution as opposed to a gentle development. No, this is not how it was meant. In his opinion, the 911's success was due to a careful but rigorous development of the design, and naturally the technology, too. That is why he had to maintain a respect for its history, while simultaneously questioning everything. And the longer the history of the 911, then the greater the respect for the icon and the desire to challenge it. At some point a symbolic regicide is inevitable. Naturally, the nice man didn't go as far as to say this. For its friends, the 911, with the exception of the 996, was always the perfect car. Now there was a new perfect car, and the followers of the Porsche desperately struggled to find room for it in his head and heart. The car looked wider and stockier, the headlights were spaced further apart; all in all, with its clear, bright gaze and sinuous fenders, the car looked like a studious triathlete.

Mauer, who considers the 964 and 963 the successful development of the classic 911 and G model, sensed that uncertainty—which he had long since overcome and processed—in the Porsche enthusiast's questioning look.

In a technology-oriented presentation prior to the exclusive unveiling of the new 911, he explained the essence of the Porsche in terms of the relationship between height and width, the modeling of the fenders, and Porsche's predilection for fastbacks. A few months later at a podium event with intractable architects and designers—every one a 911 fan—Mauer repeated his sober analysis. The topography above the hood is typical Porsche, while its expression in the 911 is product identity.

The rear is its new element—the ridge that runs from one side to the other, lending the 911 precision and the appearance of width. Thanks to the crouched look and the ridge, the "butt looks broader," though it is exactly the same width as its predecessor. The effect is strengthened by the recessed rear window, the strong shoulders, and the narrow rear lights. In principle the 911 must have circular headlights, or at the worst elliptical, as in the case of the 991. Something that is immediately criticized by the architects on the podium: the headlights are five percent too large, the rear is reminiscent of an Aston Martin, and the kink has to be carefully considered.

Mauer doesn't get flustered easily. The vehicle's architecture defines its dimensions, which also betrays whether it is a sports car or not. The 20 in. wheels are a necessary consequence of the driving dynamics, as is the tuning aesthetics, while the extended wheelbase is dictated by the engineers. Length brings stability, as they say. The flyline, the sloping roof, is quintessential 911. Due to the vehicle's reduced height and longer wheelbase, the 991 has a completely different optical dynamic. After 13 years, the side mirrors are once again mounted on the doors. Every detail is thought through to the end by Mauer, who, in distinction to Ferdinand Alexander Porsche, is no longer the designer of a vehicle, but of all four Porsche series, plus the series that are planned for the future. All his ideas follow a master plan. The stylist as engineer calculates the effects—and yet still seeks to be understood by those for whom the 911 is always, and above all, an affair of the heart.

The 991 could escape its ecological critics if it wanted to, though it appeared to be looking forward to the confrontation. It is a monument to cheerful belligerence. The appropriate car for our age.

« Waiting in the dark for its owner, the 991 is tamer. It's a machine that's bigger, wider, lower, and faster than every model of its heritage—an evolution that's not forged by nature but by the pride and focused work of engineers.

Porsche's technology and development center is located outside the not-particularly-large city of Stuttgart, which a few weeks prior to the exclusive preview had elected a Green Party state government whose leading representatives had made it clear, even before assuming office, that they were not particularly fond of the masterpieces from Zuffenhausen.

Although the 991 was designed under the mild mannered minister-president of Baden-Württemberg Günther Oettinger, this model possesses an edginess that has the capacity to scandalize. In contrast to the cozy 996, the elegantly restrained G model, or the slender classic 911, the 991 has a combative athleticism. Its rear has an evil stare, as if it was capable of setting alight those arsonists who in 2011, especially in Berlin, ignited the automotive status symbols of the upper middle class. From the front it has the appearance of an intellectual, while at the rear it has donned the mask of the avenger. At the same time, it is a committed ecologist: thanks to the start-stop technology, consumption has been reduced, despite the increase in performance. The test reports worldwide were falling over themselves. Even Jeremy Clarkson's *Top Gear* magazine awarded top marks. The 991 could escape its ecological critics if it wanted to, though it appeared to be looking forward to the confrontation. It is a monument to cheerful belligerence. The appropriate car for our age.

Despite the optical gamble of the rear quarter and interior, for traditionalists the 991 represents a further stage in the restoration of the classic 911 ethos. The 991 is lighter, rougher, and more dangerous than its predecessor. That the name 911 is once again featured on the rear is a reaffirmation of the ancestral lineage extending back to the last SC model with its velvety, athletic 240 hp engine. On top of that, in 2014 the roll bar will be reintroduced for the Targa. Thus Porsche, now a VW subsidiary, has set about inoculating itself against the possible infection of the Wolfsburg corporate virus by paying tribute to its own history.

» A 911 Targa 4S waits at the historic Skovshoved filling station on the outskirts of Copenhagen, Denmark, that was built in 1938.

The Reality Machine

For those so inclined, the current 911 can be driven "pure"—just like a Porsche 30 years ago. Anyone turning off the electronic driving assistance is confronted with a 911 that aspires to be dangerous and challenging. Sceptics were worried that Volkswagen would appoint a bureaucrat and VW vassal to head Porsche, with the consequence that the Gallic-like Swabian sports car village would be swallowed up by the Roman-Wolfsburgian empire, losing its identity in the process. What does a conglomerate that produces the Jetta and Passat do with the emporium that dreamed up the GT2 RS? In 2010 Matthias Müller was appointed Porsche CEO. Müller's father was race director at the now defunct car manufacturer DKW, so the boy had motor racing in his blood. The head of Porsche's works council, Uwe Hück, a passionate election campaigner for the Social Democratic Party (SPD), found vocal expression for his sense of relief in words that others found hard to share, stating that the CEO Müller smelt like Porsche, was lower to the ground, and had wide tires.

He was Turbo. What Hück, who once fought at Wiedeking's side, was driving at was that the sports car's animality must be anchored in the CEO's personality. The comfort-loving years were a catastrophe for management, a period when decisions were put on the back burner. The years in which the 911 threatened to lose its edge damaged the independent existence of the sports car that had become the lifeblood of the brand.

Comfort distracts. Driving a sports car at speed requires immediate feedback from the steering wheel, chassis, and instruments, providing as much data as possible about hard reality. Following the takeover by VW, a number of experts felt that edginess and the sensuous would be the first victims of the new company synergy. But VW had learned something. When Volkswagen surveyed its brand family, the field sorted itself into sensible brands with a broad appeal, such as VW, Škoda, or Audi, and potentially eccentric brands such as Lamborghini or Porsche, which were purchased for the unique experiences they provide. It is about a kick that has virtually vanished from the digital world. It is about an archaic feeling of freedom. As a symbol of liberty, the sports car—that intoxicating confrontation with a loud, nervous, gasoline-scented reality—is on the retreat. A car as a promise of freedom is proving less and less beguiling to young people. The smartphone is more important.

If the entry into adult life used to be marked by the driving license, today becoming a part of the grown-up world tends to be associated with the first iPhone or tablet computer. This is especially the case for young people in big cities where the inclination to buy a car at a young age has fallen markedly. The car companies respond nervously, producing cars with names that sound like Apple products or equipped with useless interfaces. Others dress up their small cars like a computer mouse and upholster its seats in the bright colors of a screensaver. The thesis of the French philosopher Jean Baudrillard that things are disappearing, a thesis that enjoyed widespread popularity in the

SACHS
CLUTCHES · SHOCKS
Federation Insurance
Bob Garretson
86
Cup & Tourenwager
Trophy
apple computer

In a 911 all the senses were activated, including the *popometer*, an instrument prized by racing drivers for ascertaining road conditions and the vehicle's grip.

« The ties that bind racing and design: an Apple-sponsored racing 911, which remains the only race car that the tech company has ever supported.

1980s, now, at the beginning of the twenty-first century, sounds like a platitude. Things are disappearing, reality is becoming digitalized, and social networks establish all the connections between people previously served by road networks. Proximity becomes relative, and good old reality is now an option, not an obligation.

A number of car manufacturers have jumped on the bandwagon, eliminating reality from the driving experience to the point of unconsciousness.

In the case of the 911, up until the 996 the gas cap was situated on the left, on the driver's side, so that after gassing up, the inside of the sports car smelt of gasoline. In a 911 all the senses were activated, including the *popometer,*[1] an instrument prized by racing drivers for ascertaining road conditions and the vehicle's grip. Instead of being cushioned, the surface irregularities could be felt in the hands on the steering wheel and throughout the whole body pressed into the tight seats. Even though the 911 has become a little more comfortable and milder with every series since its launch in 1963, the 996 with its almost power steering-like comfort marks a terminal point in this development—compounded by that suspension tuning at the press of a button, which also has its origins in motor racing. With this system the driver of a 997 could choose whether they wanted it hard and racing car-like, or comfortable and GT-like. The character of the 911 could be changed at the press of a button, if one wanted.

In its own publicity material Porsche never sold the purity of this sense experience. In the 1950s and 1960s the 911's predecessor, the 356, was advertised as a comfortable car. The 356 C was described as "Well sprung with a lively suspension. In a Porsche you don't feel the road," promised the advertising text. The Porsche is neither too hard nor too soft. However, this promise was made

[1] Literal translation: butt-meter. Because the driver sits so far down in his vehicle, he must rely on this sensitive instrument to feel whether the car is in balance—as noted by Michael Schumacher and Sebastian Vettel, among others.

at a time when the consequences of the war in Germany and its shadows could be observed on every street corner. Luxury was pacification, and it was precisely in this spirit that the 356 promised a more comfortable journey compared to its direct competitors.

In 1967 the *Spiegel* magazine described the 911 as a "vehicle of happiness." The occasion for this article in the assault gun of democracy was a comprehensive study on the satisfaction of Porsche owners. This was accompanied by a mini social study on what at the time was still a small, elitist circle of Porsche drivers who viewed their vehicle as an elegant antithesis to the comfortable mass locomotion on the streets. Even back then, the Porsche driver—despite his taste for distinction—had no interest in being lumped together with the successful types at the wheel of a comfortable Mercedes. The 911 drivers wanted a fast, comparatively low risk piece of sports equipment that was also a pleasure to drive when forced to slowly maneuver it through the host of Sunday drivers and crawlers. At the time, the most important reason for buying a Porsche—which secretly remains the same to this day—was the top speed. Driving pleasure was also cited as a reason by approximately the same number of buyers. Back then Porsche owners drove their 911s (and 912s) an average of 25,054 km (15,568 mi.). This highlights the extent to which this challenging sports car was an everyday companion for those in demanding professions, as opposed to a third car and weekend vehicle, as is often the case today. At the end of the survey, when asked whether they would buy another 911, 70.6 percent of male Porsche drivers answered yes, 18.5 percent "maybe," and only 10.9 percent no. This was the same for women, or at least similar.

She was 26, newly separated, and filled with the feeling that her life had just begun. The decision to buy a new car slowly ripened in her. On scanning the possibilities and after numerous test drives, the Porsche 911 quickly crystallized as the only possible option—without a 911 among her circle of friends or family having served as a precedent. Neither her mother, father, nor anyone she knew had a history with a 911. It was the car in and of itself (black Carrera 4, coupe, build year 1989, black-black) that spoke to her: "I am the perfect car, consummate in form and function." Whether observing its silhouette, listening to its luscious engine sound, or experiencing its seemingly limitless power on accelerating, this car promised to be the perfect companion for the prospective scientist's undertaking: emancipation, traveling long distances at speed as a means to exploit the world to the full, and belligerence.

The 911 embodied autonomy, both financially and in a very concrete sense. She had the feeling that she could jump into this car at any time and drive wherever it took her. It was an invitation to start again, intensifying the feeling of being dependent on nothing and nobody, of "being one's own master." The 911 appeared to inhibit the feeling of loneliness, placing the pleasure and benefits of being on one's own in the foreground. What could be better than taking an aimless spin on the freeway, experiencing this car with all one's senses: smell, sound, speed. In dream interpretation the roadway/street frequently symbolizes one's own path of life and the car oneself. During these drives on the freeway this emotional symbolism could be experienced in its most pleasant form: the 911 promotes instinctive trust and a fighting spirit, holding out the prospect of a promising future, awakening a feeling of pleasant anticipation. Alongside the euphoria of departure, the vehicle also gave her a sense of safety and solidity at all times, which other sports cars could not. It didn't send her down the wrong track or invite her to indulge in ill-considered flights of overconfidence. No, quite the contrary, driving a 911 always grounds one, demanding that one concentrate on the essentials. And not least, its stable value said: "I keep my promise, I am not some short-lived adventure that you will regret, I am enduring." It was simply the perfect partner. The daughter from a family of Hanseatic merchants was won over by the argument that this sports car represented an unusually stable investment. A 911 displayed a similar resistance to inflation as the gold bars in a bank's safe deposit box, while guaranteeing a considerably greater fun yield. In 1972 an RS 2.7 cost just 34,900 deutsche marks, and is now worth over 600,000 euros. Today, even a used, relatively conventional 993 fetches its new price. The classic 911s are now worth five times what they were originally sold for. If one assumes that in each phase of life the 911 fulfills a different psychological function, i.e. has a different symbolism, then in such an early life phase it represents the promise one has made to oneself to give everything, to always aspire to the best, never to be satisfied with mediocrity, to always look for new challenges, and to remain free and independent. One could also say that driving a 911 in one's adolescence has educational potential, promoting motivation, courage, and trust in oneself.

Like in good therapy, an encounter with a 911 doesn't result in dependency but independence from the same: many 911 drivers have internalized the life feeling and promise developed with its assistance. It has become an inner object, eternally present and recallable and thus dispensable as a concrete object of the moment. That is why 911 drivers can be separated from their passion for years, only to return to her in a state of clam. In addition to certain constant elements (elegance, quality consciousness, and power) the 911, depending on the person's life phase, serves a range of different psychological functions. While it is an object of desire for the child, it stimulates the play instinct and fulfils childhood dreams for its adult owners. When balancing in the middle of life it functions as a symbol and reassurance of successful undertakings, while in old age it reactivates the feeling of freedom and vitality one experienced with it in the past. This makes it capable of performing the role of a lifelong companion, the first love to whom one returns to again and again. A never-ending story. An immortal car.

» An object to keep its owner firmly grounded, the 911 can be equipped for any eventuality.

The Individualistic Utopia

Individuation Through Mass Consumption

There comes a time when the 911 leads even the most sober, pleasure loving, and consistently rational driver to become what he never wanted to be. By the time of his fourth, fifth, or sixth 911, the once young, now gray-haired man, stands on the forecourt behind the exit to the carwash wiping the inside of the door dry with a kitchen towel, stroking the last damp corners of the rubber on the fenders, and removing every last drop of water, wherever it may be hiding. Although he has been driving a 911 for over 20 years, the new one, which may be an old model, has led him to the point where he gazes at his coupe with a pounding heart, unable to believe that there could be something so thrilling and graceful, combining poise and elegance in such an irresistible fashion, in this often so unsightly, coarse, and unrefined world.

In the evening, following a long drive on the freeway and a few sprints on the country road, he stands on the sidewalk listening to the clicking and crackling of the air-cooled boxer. Before entering the house, he breathes in the unique 911 scent, which has seeped into his shirt and suit, one last time—and looks forward to the next morning when this same smell, with its promise of a never ending mechanical age, will greet him again when he gets back into the car.

Naturally, there is some truth to the thesis of an intelligent young woman of good background who concludes that the 911, which she loves, is often driven by sterile, uptight "total jerks" (as she says); men who experience a flash of pride when a pretty woman peers into their Porsche. The new money milieu, with their polo shirts, oversized watches, and fancy sunglasses, abuse the highways for PowerPoint presentations of their valuables. A 911 is paraded like a trophy wife or a disproportionately large dog. In the symphony of overstatements, the subtle notes of the 911 go unheard.

However, no breath is wasted on these drivers, male or female. It is possible that they are in the majority when it comes to certain build years, but they are incapable of sullying Porsche's reputation. They don't really get in the way. The young woman loves these cars, which is why she takes an interest in their owners. However, the more banal the 911 owner, the more completely they are eclipsed by the car itself.

Genuine 911 fans see themselves as soul-guerillas fighting the icy world of those status fetishists who apply a newly purchased 911 like a layer of Teflon to reinforce their crumbling sense of personal worth. 911 fans are hooked on their passion. Their love for their sports car is as fresh as the day they first set eyes on it. They reminisce about the time when the first engineers in Zuffenhausen allowed an occasional customer to take the car for a test drive, in order—according to Richard von Frankenberg—"to see whether he is a good enough driver and can shift gears without grinding them." The Porsche was originally designed as a

» A long life—technically, aesthetically, and in the heart of its driver—is one of the 911's many selling points.

car "for those who know," a criterion that a Detroit techno label would later apply to its records. Not a car for everyone, but only for those who are actually worthy of it. Or in the words of the Swabian assembly workers: "I wouldn't sell him no car, he ain't earned it." The official word from Zuffenhausen sounded more friendly. "If one were to judge you according to your choice of car," speculated the foreword to the owners' manual for the first 911 in 1964, "then one would have to conclude that you belong, without a doubt, to a special class of motorist."

"If one were to judge you according to your choice of car, then one would have to conclude that you belong, without a doubt, to a special class of motorist."

↳ Foreword to the owners' manual for the first 911.

« Once assembly was complete, the mechanics stamped their names inside the engine case, making the process personal.

Shawn Stussy, the Californian surfboard, T-shirt, and jacket designer, was known for offering large sums of money to people who wore his things—but happened to be complete sleazebags. He was prepared to bribe them to give back the caps, hoodies, or baggy jeans. This fantasy of exclusivity resonates with the romantic dream of a consumer society in which there is virtually no alienation or dislocation between product and consumers. A world in which the producer's intention coincides with the customer's projection, something that functioned at Porsche up until the late 1970s due to the relatively small circle of customers. The Porsche mechanics from the early days were as much formed by the Porsche as it by them. They were one with their work in an inspiring sense. In 25 hours of manual labor they assembled a motor, and on completion stamped their initials into its crankcase. Porsches were uniquely manufactured objects for individualists. With the mass production of the assembly lines, and ultimately—thanks to Wiedeking—the Japanese kaizen, a connection in the old fashioned sense was lost. This is why it became all the more important for the brand and its "die hard" customers to overcompensate for this shift in production conditions with a maximum of emotionality. If the automobile is modernity's central technical object, as Peter Sloterdijk suspected, then this struggle for individuality is also a liberal humanist project, albeit somewhat elitist and unsuited to direct translation into the mass market for disposable vehicles. California is the birthplace of the R Gruppe (sic!) that combines the 911 cult with hot rod culture, thus fusing two minimalist bad-boy cultures and aesthetics. This group of 911 enthusiasts, whose main passion is for tuned classic 911s, sees itself as the anarchistic heart of the Porsche underground. In this collective, which carefully selects is members, driving a Porsche is exclusive and rebellious, as it was at the beginning with James Dean and the proto-feminist racing drivers. And the Californian group's spiritus rector and honorary member: Steve McQueen. The iconic appearance of the 911 has transcended its commodity form. At the turn of the century Tobias Rehberger, a Stuttgart-born artist, drew a few sketches of a 911 from memory and sent them to Thailand where mechanics specializing in producing fakes constructed a working 911. Despite the botched proportions and imprecise, brutalist details it is immediately recognizable as a 911, thanks to the torpedo tube, the flyline, and tapered rear. The iconic form of the 911 was treated with considerably more respect by the architect who used the flyline as the model for the Porsche Pavilion in the motor city of Wolfsburg. Both the sculpture and building are icons (sic!), which as extrapolations from the reference object underline its cultural fecundity. 911 enthusiasts have their own language. Their sociolect unites a community that, with its innumerable magazines and internet forums, is becoming more diverse every year. The ideal is a semantics that can be derived directly from the driving license or the 911's technical history: "I drive a 964 with multi-part rims, 030 fitted factory side." Or: "I drive a 3.2 Coupe with G50, Fuchs and WLS." WLS stands for *Werksleistungssteigerung* (factory performance upgrade), just as WTL means *Werksturbolook* (factory turbo-look), and G50 is a gearbox that was fitted as standard into the last version of the G model beginning in 1986. Often enough these fans are not that wealthy, their 911 is not part of a larger collection in a spacious garage complex. Instead, it is a piece of materialized excellence, an indulgence, a life dream. They care for their 911 like a member of the family, sending it into long hibernation with an opulent oil change, protecting it from cold and wet, and listening attentively every day to check whether the motor is coughing or stuttering. When the trip ends in bad weather, rainwater is removed from the door sills, if necessary with a brand new cashmere scarf. The air-cooled fanatic has long since become attuned to the minutest sounds of his 911's warming motor, which with a glance at the oil temperature dial should not be driven at more than 3,000 rpm. He knows how damaging high revs can be for the lifetime of a boxer. The speedometer in the center of the instrument panel has found its counterpart in the 911 driver's brain and auditory canal.

The high degree of individualization is one of the 911's unique selling points. Hardly any car is like the other. And anyone who is looking for something really special can assemble a car from the extras program that caters for the most extravagant color and material combinations. Since 1986 the extras program has traded under the title "Exclusive." Even the name implies a relatively conventional individualization praxis, which fits to Porsche's wealthy customer base—and especially its new money clients. However, it finds less favor with those purists who see the 911's true essence in a minimum of extravagance and a focus on essentials. One of the most beautiful individualizations, by virtue of its radical reductionism, is by Jil Sander. Like Jerry Seinfeld, she found herself on a journey to the center of the brand's core: to the kingdom of the absolute minimum.

Even though the 911 has long since become a mass phenomenon on the streets of Western metropolises, it still stands out from the voluminous models. The 911 protests against the uniformity of the limousines, SUVs, or station wagons. There are some German manufacturers who essentially produce just one car that is supplied in different sizes. A successful car design has become a rarity. Ugly bodies with squeaky engine noises and ridiculous colors overrun town and countryside. Frequently enough these unsightly cars are also occupied by undiscerning drivers whose distaste for this form of locomotion is apparent at every junction, with every movement of the steering wheel. The twitchy inefficiency of their efforts to navigate through the daily routine reflects the worthlessness of their tin boxes. They treat their cars badly, wearing out brakes and tires with hectic movements and senseless actions. They despise their cars—while secretly being mocked by them. Metropolitan traffic is a complex ballet whose rhythm and tempo has to be renegotiated every morning. Whoever lacks the necessary automotive musicality misses their cue and sabotages the formation dances and soli of the other participants. Mass traffic is a social praxis whose beauty is not taken seriously.

The protagonists of the ambitious middle classes who have made it their job to educate and decelerate all road users are nothing short of depressing. With pedantic self-righteousness they claim the top speed as their own, if necessary with coercion. These people, who Karl Heinz Bohrer so aptly compared to the Mainzelmännchen [2] cartoon figures, frequently find their control freak impulses coming unstuck on the laid back manner in which the drivers of muscular limousines and sports cars emancipate themselves from such schoolmasterly pedants with a light push of the gas pedal and a short-term suspension of the traffic laws. These compulsory driving lessons are exclusively motivated by the resentment of the parvenus. It is a very German and extremely embittered attempt to enforce equality on the roads.

Although it is now good manners to display a connoisseur-like appreciation for architecture, fashion, and design, such a valorization of beautiful cars with an exciting sound and graceful motion has fallen out of favor. The ecological verdict rules. On the other side, new sites such as the Meilenwerk service centers for classic cars or the museums of the large car manufacturers have emerged, offering

[2] Anton, Berti, Conni, Det, Edi, and Fritzchen. Diminutive animated figures created by Wolf Gerlach and used as ad bumpers on the TV channel ZDF since the 1960s. Also used on the satirical *heute-show* (today show).

a sophisticated reading of the car as a cultural object. In addition, there are the old-timer trade shows and fan club conventions that have the character of makeshift technical museums. In the process the Meilenwerk succeeds in enacting a "détournement" that is much marveled at by the museum theoreticians. The accommodation of old-timers in a split-level building, originally conceived of as a garage, has brought forth a self-organizing, rotating exhibition whose curator is a quartermaster. The owners of the old-timers ensure that their vehicles are always in top museum-quality condition, presenting the sometimes very rare objects to car lovers in their pure being, devoid of any pedagogical luggage. Nowhere are artifacts more freely associated and presented to such a heterogeneous public. Followers of the 911 are materialist conservatives. Values are not abstract but a form of concrete poetry. Values arise through use. The 911 as a blue chip car has a penchant for clarity and transparency, which political conservatism lacks. Like the idealist conservative, the materialist conservative sees himself as the antithesis of indifference and arbitrariness. In a reaction to the transitoriness of fashion he sets out in search of something that endures, the classical. The disdain with which Ferdinand Alexander Porsche uttered the word "fashion" also underlies the 911 community's skepticism towards any overzealous concessions to the zeitgeist. The materialist conservative is an advocate of evolution as opposed to revolution, whether it be the minor variety of fashion or full-blown social revolution.

There is no such thing as a typical 911 driver. They are united in their eccentricity.

« Self-styled "urban outlaw" and unlikely looking Porsche enthusiast Magnus Walker, whose 911 obsession began at the age of 10 when he visited the Earl's Court Motor Show in London.

The sensibilities of the followers of the 911 described in this book, including their neurotic apprehensions, have served, by means of tight feedback loops, to sensitize Porsche managers and engineers to the desires and fears of its customers. In the pre-digital era Porsche managers found themselves in constant chat with their customers. Thanks to the intensive customer support and the active participation in the Porsche clubs, the Porsche driver and customer remained the primary point of reference for product development. With the growth in production figures, maintaining direct contact with the extended family became increasingly difficult, which is why club sport events and club culture became all the more important as arenas for meeting those for whom a Porsche was an extension of their selves, rather than a consumer product. The American Porsche club has over 100,000 members—a world record that it shares with the Harley Davidson club. For a nation like the United States with its love of mobility and freedom, Harley Davidsons, like Porsches, are cult objects. Looked at soberly, the fact that of all cars it should be a German car, a rolling, roaring, statue of liberty that inflames the passions of the Americans, appears to be an irony of history. For the Americans the 911 is a very German car. In the countless interviews with Porsche club members the attribution "something German" recurs like a magic formula for precision and athleticism. For many Americans the Porsche reminds them of their European roots—allowing them to dream a different American dream to that told by the large displacement Corvettes, Mustangs, or Dodge Chargers.

There is no such thing as a typical 911 driver. They are united in their eccentricity. "It is simply wonderful when one finds something that one loves," explained Jerry Seinfeld, although he was unable to say which of his Porsches he loved the most. "Actually my favorite Porsche is the one I happen to be sitting in at the time." This is why all of Seinfeld's artifacts are ready to drive at any time, including his archetypal Porsche built in Gmünd in 1949. The traditionalism of the followers of the 911 also lends itself to a romantic interpretation. Everything that one loves should remain as it was at that moment when one fell in love with it. Fidelity to the object of veneration corresponds to the object's permanence. Love that is to endure requires an object that endures.

What kind of car is it that keeps even the most levelheaded person awake at night in anticipation of that moment next morning when they unlock it, pulling the door to with its unmistakable clack and reverberation, before finally turning the key in the ignition to the left of the steering wheel to be greeted by the roaring of the six cylinders in the rear—and drive away?

Why does it never cease to be so stunning?

The 991 Mk II

And You Don't Stop to Punk Rock

At the end, things come full circle. In California, where the future of the West was never afraid of moving forward in harmony with tradition, young and not-quite-so-young men and women have decided to live out the present as the savior of the past. "Luftgekühlt" is the name of the series of events staged by plucky Le Mans winner Patrick Long and his mate Howie Idelson, where all those style aficionados and petrol heads who drive an air-cooled, and specifically not a water-cooled Porsche, meet up. Water cooling is the trademark of present-day engineering prowess. The husky, throaty sound of the air-cooled model, produced until 1998, stands for the pleasure derived from the direct sense of speed and sliding, which the old Porsches, the 356s, but first and foremost, of course, the 911s so typified.

A manifest symbol of individualism, the 911 becomes the membership card of a club, in which tattooed, dreadlocked lone wolves with diverse roots gather to find their place in society through a shared love. Lit by the California sun, with the added attraction of svelte women and gym-honed men in their T-shirts, the car park becomes a salon of post-bourgeois delight. The cars are highly polished treasures or decrepit rust buckets; they are fast or slow, loud or quiet, tasteful or provocatively indecent. They are the chariots of those stalwarts who want nothing to do with the soulless tanks the automotive industry is churning out these days.

The first Luftgekühlt event took place in 2014. In the car park of Deus Ex Machina, a high-end, forward-thinking bike workshop. There were silkscreens, DJs, and a barbecue. Kids romped, grandfathers laughed, and by mistake it also morphed into a spontaneously assembled museum of Porsche history, featuring the most expensive of rarities. A year later the event was three times as big, and yet another year later, 10 times as big. The spirit, though, always remains the same. The hyper-individualism of the Californians, to a certain extent the essence of Anglo-Saxon anti-collectivism, has, of all things, made a fetish out of a Swabian cult object. Magnus Walker speaks in one of the videos that document the event of the "Church of Porsche," and of Porsche as a language that everyone there speaks. And as such there are Hollywood stars hanging out alongside car mechanics, writers alongside doctors, designers alongside wealthy wives.

It is also design meditation. One follower of style instinctively recognizes another by the wristwatches, shoes, and baseball caps they have seen many times before. The old Porsche world is the more beautiful. That has left its mark on the market. The prices for air-cooled 911s are climbing, climbing, climbing, and have long since left comparable competitors well behind. The cars are no longer being produced, and that makes them so valuable. After years of nouveau-riche ostentation, new vintage car markets in Asia are discovering the charm of the fragile, slender, and compared to new cars, decidedly tiny 911s. The 911 has become a blue chip. That is attracting more than a few investors in garage gold, and even more dreamers, who are suddenly remembering the now almost faded promises they made as youths and putting an old 911 in the garage as a stand-in for their lost innocence.

Porsche has responded. With the 911 R, the company rolled out a new model in 2016 that transposed all the virtues of the air-cooled autos into the present day: no turbo, no paddles on the steering wheel, and no excess weight. The R is reminiscent of the old R. Limited to 991 units, the R sold out after a mere 30 seconds, and three months later the price had gone up five-fold. The original R was a super-light piece of machinery. R stood for racing. And the mini-series, built from 1967 until 1969, was primarily true to form. With its 2-liter engine and 210 bhp, weighing in at just 820 kg (1,808 lb.), the R was the essence of that dream of lightness which Porsche always followed.

The R group is likewise an instance of Californian sub-culture—a lived world that breaks firmly with the European petty-bourgeois 911 mindset. It was only with the relaunched R that the Porsche manufacturers in Zuffenhausen came to realize that a grail of 911ism had survived in American exile; it was one that the company HQ had to bring back in whatever form in order to recharge its batteries, even though the 911 had long since become a sort of mass product. But one that was blessed with an aura and history that other automotive manufacturers had either never had, or that had long since been firmly eliminated.

So what is the 911 mainstream up to? The new 991 Mk II represents not only a model update; it also signifies something tantamount to a change in era. What's new? On the outside, not that much at all; at the rear, where the 911's engine has been for 52 years now, quite a lot. The downsizing trend is reaching legendary sports cars, and after Ferrari with the 488, Porsche with its 911 is now also delivering less cubic capacity, but more bhp and torque.

Instead of 3.8, it now boasts an almost modest 3.0-liter engine, as it last did, almost 40 years ago, with the air-cooled 911 SC. Yet neither acoustically nor performance-wise is the lack of engine size noticeable. On the contrary. Fuel consumption has been cut by almost 12 percent, and the performance readings are impressive. For the first time ever a member of the Carrera family can get from

0–100 km/h (62 mph) in less than four seconds. The downsizing presents Porsche with lesser challenges than its competitors. Unlike Ferrari, Porsche has years of experience with series production in the form of the turbo-charged six-cylinder boxer engine, and the 911 turbos have been regarded as benchmark agility fiends for over 40 years.

Even the stock 911 does not disappoint on the racetrack. It glides through bends easily and confidently, reaches speeds of up to 245 km/h (152 mph) on the straight, where the LMP1 vehicles (the Le Mans-winning Porsche race cars) can only get up to 290 (180 mph), and the way it steers, brakes, and sticks to the tarmac makes it a joy to drive. The spec sheet has 308 km/h (191 mph) as the 911's top speed. The fact that the high torque of 500 newton meters (369 foot-pounds) is already reached at a comfortable 1,700 revs means that when driving on a racetrack the car almost never falls beneath the high torque level. It thrusts from below and with a marvelous snarl pulls away at over 7,000 revs.

The importance of tires in the development of sports-car construction cannot be over-emphasized. To be honest, or so the head of the 911 model series August Achleitner explains in a mixture of clarity and calm so typical of engineers, it is the properties of the tires that set the limits to further advancing this classic sports car, particularly as regards how far the rear axle load can be taken. Adding wider tires at the front and rear and lowering the series car by 10 mm has improved road performance. Translated into the time it takes to complete a lap of the Nürburgring—nowadays regarded worldwide as the benchmark—this means: The Carrera S is eight seconds faster than its predecessor. An achievement that illustrates how this 991 Mk II is less an evolution and more a genuine leap in development.

The optional rear axle steering and the sportier GT steering wheel strengthen the link between the series model and motor racing, or rather sport superstars like the 918 Spyder. This does not come amiss in everyday driving either—for example, exploring the mountains around the Circuit de Catalunya after the morning spent on the racetrack. Nor does the 911 seem sportily overdressed in 20-km/h (12-mph) zones, in traffic-calmed village thoroughfares with bumps and plastic chicanes. The four-seater coupé is totally in its element on winding country roads, which you can maneuver round with absolute precision. Here the 420 bhp seems almost luxurious and lavish.

The leap taken by the new turbo generation of Turbos and Turbos S presented in early 2016 can only be guessed. With its predecessor the Turbo S already widely considered the best car in the world by the magazine Auto Motor und Sport, the 580 bhp Turbo S has now broken the three-second barrier for accelerating from 0–100 km/h (62 mph). The brochure gives a reading of 2.9 seconds, but some test drivers have recorded other, quite spectacular values: 2.6 seconds, even 2.5. Fabulous figures that probably make buyers of the incomparably far more expensive 918 nervous.

There is no end to the progress. Not even in the case of a car whose rear-mounted engine actually spells an indelible flaw. The aerodynamically improved LMP1 race cars, with which Porsche enjoyed incredible wins in Le Mans, point the way forward. In these race cars, 2-liter four-cylinder engines in combination with a basketball-sized electric motor generate a 1,000-bhp output highly efficiently by means of recuperation and the use of the exhaust gas flow. Weighing a mere 870 kg (1,918 lb.), these Le Mans racing cars are basic research on wheels, and the results will sooner or later find their way into series production.

This is why for Porsche, which has always preferred to center its marketing around its race successes, these latest triumphs are encouraging and define the marque. There is hardly a 911 purist around who is still going to get agitated if what will then perhaps only be a 2-liter engine at the rear features high-performance hybrid technology—in such a way that in the series models totally different consumption and acceleration levels are likewise conceivable. It is going to happen, and we can look forward to it. Even if we still cling to our air-cooled treasures in the garage.

The cars do not weigh anything anymore. A wing mirror is no heavier than an iPhone; the carbon-fiber rear chassis panel feels lighter than a crate of beer. And new in the 911 are a multimedia connectivity system (in this respect for a long time Porsche—how shall I put it?—lagged behind), a few fresh visual details relating to the air intake, the door handles, and the lights, not to mention any amount of assistance systems, available on request. For petrol heads, all that—the accessories, the fussiness—need not be. Following the rounds on the racetrack, all they want is a ruthless diet pared down to the bare minimum. Goodbye to any electronic frills! Goodbye to comfort, digital aids, seat adjustments, and center consoles! Goodbye to clocks on the dashboard. Goodbye to anything other than raw Porsche!

Nothing kills performance more than weight, and in that respect a lot is still conceivable with this car. With the lighter GT3 versions, the RS models, and perhaps too with a pure, indeed purist, 911 available again for performance-thirsty fanatics, who wish to find all the original features of the air-cooled model in what is now a turbo-charged water-cooled version. Precisely that is the reason for the 911 R and its success. In 2016 the test drivers soon had it down as the car they praised most. With this car, we start to come full circle. Porsche is reading its own history in order to find salient points for a profitable future. Only those who manage to seduce both the traditionalists and the open-minded will survive in times when driving as a symbol of freedom is being put into perspective by smartphones and rolling Google Apps. The 911 is taking on these latter-day rivals. Never lift!

Glossary

About the Author

Born in Nuremberg in 1967, Ulf Poschardt is a doctor of philosophy, the editor-in-chief of the German national newspapers *Die Welt* and *Die Welt am Sonntag,* and a Porsche driver. He was the editor-in-chief of the *Süddeutsche Zeitung* magazine and has written car columns for the Swiss weekly newspaper *Die Weltwoche.* He has published, among other titles, *DJ Culture* (1998), and the philosophical book *Über Sportwagen* (About Sports Cars, 2002).

Auto Union
Car company founded in 1932 and made up of four brands: Audi, Horch, DKW, Wanderer. Precursor to Audi.

Bildzeitung
German tabloid newspaper.

BKA
Bundeskriminalamt, Federal Office of Criminal Investigation.

CDU
Christian Democratic Union; the German liberal conservative party.

CSU
Christian Social Union in Bavaria; affiliated with the CDU.

Club of Rome
International think tank set up in 1968 to find ways to improve society around the world. Made up of intellectuals from diverse fields.

Cisitalia
Italian car company that made racing and sports cars. Existed from 1946 to 1963.

DKW
Car and motorcycle manufacturer founded in Germany in 1916. Initials stand for *Dampf-Kraft-Wagen* (steam-driven car). Became part of Auto Union in 1932.

Der Spiegel
Weekly news magazine famed for its investigative journalism.

Deutsche Mark, Deutschmark, DM
Currency of the Federal Republic from 1948 to 1990, and then from 1990 to 2002 in unified Germany.

Deutscher Werkbund
German Association of Craftsmen. Founded in Munich, 1907, it was important in the development of modern design, architecture, integrated crafts, and mass-production techniques.

Die Zeit
Centrist and liberal weekly broadsheet newspaper.

Federal Republic
West Germany. Also called the Bonn Republic.

FDP
Free Democratic Party; liberal party.

German Democratic Republic (GDR)
East Germany.

Hanseatic
Refers to the Hanseatic League, a historical confederation of trading cities. It was a guild created to protect the interests of merchants. Hamburg was part of this.

Hintertaunus
Area of the Taunus mountain range in Hesse, which is known for its spa towns frequented by the upper echelons of European society in days gone by.

Hitler-Stalin Pact
A pact of non-aggression between Germany and the Soviet Union made on 23 August, 1939, days before the Second World War.

kaizen
Strategy of continuous improvement, where individuals at all levels of a company work together.

East German Mark
Currency of GDR (East Germany) from 1948 to 1990.

Minister-President
Head of regional government in a German state.

Neckarsulm
Site of Audi HQ in Baden-Württemberg.

NSU
Founded in 1873, NSU was a German manufacturer of bikes, motorbikes, and cars. Later they were bought by VW and merged into Auto Union, which eventually became Audi. Not to be confused with the far-right terror group.

Pininfarina
Coachbuilder and car design firm headquartered in Turin, Italy. Founded 1930.

RAF
Rote Armee Fraktion (Red Army Fraction) aka the Baader-Meinhof gang. Leftwing terrorist group active in West Germany from the late 1960s. Spanned several generations.

Reichsmark
Currency in Germany from 1924 to 1948.

SPD
Social Democratic Party.

Swabia
Region of southwest Germany with its own culture, history, and dialect (Swabian German).

Ulm School of Design
School set up in 1953 by Max Bill, Otl Aicher, and Inge Scholl to teach progressive design. Closed in 1968.

Wanderer
Manufacturer of automobiles and military vehicles, founded as Winklhofer & Jaenicke in 1896. Incorporated into Auto Union.

Weissach
Site of Porsche Development Center and test track in Böblingen, Baden-Württemberg.

Wolfsburg
Site of VW HQ in Lower Saxony.

Zuffenhausen
Site of the Porsche factory in Northern Stuttgart, Baden-Württemberg.

Zündapp
Motorbike manufacturer founded in Nuremberg in 1917. Went bankrupt in 1984.

Acknowledgments

Very special thanks go to Dr. Jochen Wagner, the racing theologian; Dieter Landenberger, the director of the Porsche archive in Zuffenhausen who was inspiring and helpful in equal measure; and Tom Kraushaar, the publisher, editor, and unerring critic.

I would also like to thank the countless Porsche drivers and experts who have helped me with this book with their quotes, ideas, suggestions, film tips and suchlike. Above all Werner Sobek, Erwin Wurm, Albert Ostermaier, Moritz Rinke, Jerzy Skolimowski, Niklas Frings-Rupp, J. Philip Rathgen, Mateo Kries, Oliver Voss, Erik Spiekermann, Christian Lindner, Tobias Rehberger, Heinz "Cookie" Gindullis, Donald von Frankenberg, Dirk Maxeiner, Thomas Elsner, Alice Schwarzer, Peter Held, Leonora von Haften, Dr. Rainer Kaus, Dada Held, Jerry Seinfeld, André Schäfer, Hanns-Georg Rodek, Richard Kämmerlings, Matthias Müller, Ralf Bönt, Per Hinrichs, Kai Luehrs-Kaiser, Stefan Anker, Nikolaus Doll, Galerie Thaddaeus Ropac, Sascha Keilwerth, Rainer Schlegelmilch, Michael Mauer, Marley Fabis, Thomas "Marok" Marecki, Jörn Claussen, Helge Malchow, Tom Ising, Martin Fengel, the staff of the Porsche archive, and Franz Rother for his stoicism during our Mille Miglia adventure.

And most importantly of all: my wonderful family who lovingly endure this obsession.

Bibliography

» Aichele, Tobias. *Porsche Raritäten, Prototypen und Autos, die nie in Serie gingen.* Munich, 2009.

» Austen, Jörg, and Sigmund Walter. *Porsche 911: Die technische Dokumentation von 1963 bis 2009.* Stuttgart, 2008.

» Barthes, Roland. *Mythologies.* New York, 2012.

» Frankenberg, Donald von, and Richard von Frankenberg. *Mit Vollgas durchs Leben.* Bielefeld, 2009.

» Frankenberg, Richard von. *Porsche—the Man and his Cars.* Cambridge, MA, 1961.

» ———. *Schachspiel ohne Bedenkzeit. Warum Motorsport?.* Stuttgart, 1959.

» ———. *Die großen Fahrer von einst.* Stuttgart, 1967 (2nd edition).

» Fuths, Thomas. *Porsche 911. Die Geschichte einer Legende 1963–1990.* Rastatt, 1990.

» Häußermann, Martin. *Porsche 911, Die Prospekte seit 1964.* Bielefeld, 2012 (2nd revised edition).

» Henckmann, Wolfhart, and Konrad Lotter (ed.). *Lexikon der Ästhetik.* Munich, 1992.

» Hunger, Anton, and Dieter Landenberger. *Das Porsche Calendarium 1931–2008.* Munich/Zurich, 2008 (3rd revised edition).

» Landenberger, Dieter. *Porsche. Die Marke. Die Werbung. Geschichte einer Leidenschaft.* Cologne, 2008.

» Leffingwell, Randy. *The Complete Book of Porsche 911: Every Model Since 1964.* Minneapolis, 2011.

» Lewandowski, Jürgen. *Porsche 901: The Roots of a Legend.* Bielefeld, 2013

» Lewerenz, Frank, and Walter Röhrl. *Sportlich und sicher Autofahren mit Walter Röhrl.* Stuttgart, 2008.

» Osteroth, Reinhard. *Ferdinand Porsche. Der Pionier und seine Welt.* Reinbek, 2004.

» Piëch, Ferdinand. *Auto. Biographie.* Hamburg, 2002.

» Porsche, Susanne. *Ferrytales. Eine Retrospektive auf Ferry Porsche und seine große Idee.* Munich, 2005.

» Porsche AG and Anton Hunger (ed.). *Passion Porsche. Die Automobile im Porsche-Museum.* Munich/Zurich, 2009.

» Porsche Museum. *Ferry Porsche, 100 Years.* Stuttgart/Cologne, 2009.

» ———. *Porsche Clubs Worldwide.* Stuttgart, 2012.

» ———. *Porsche Ladies.* Stuttgart, 2010.

» ———. *Porsche Exclusive.* Stuttgart, 2011.

» Weibel, Peter. *Car Culture: Medien der Mobilität.* Karlsruhe, 2011.

» Wiedeking, Wendelin. *Don't Follow the Crowd: Suggesting a New Approach in Industry and Politics.* Munich, 2008.

Image Credits

» Götz Göppert Photography, Germany: p. 95
www.gotzgoppert.com

» Hermann Köpf, Germany: pp. 100/101
www.hermannkoepf.com

» Marcus Krueger: p. 225
www.photo-krueger.de

» Vincent Perraud: pp. 78, 121, 122/123, 134/135, 144/145, 162/163, 198/199, 232/233
www.vincentperraud.com

» Lauro Peter: pp. 214/215, 221
www.lauropeter.com

» Porsche Archiv, Porsche-Werkfoto: pp. 2, 5, 6/7, 9, 11, 12/13, 15, 16/17, 18, 20/21, 23, 24/25, 27, 28/29, 30/31, 32, 35, 36/37, 40, 42, 43, 45, 46/47, 49, 51, 52, 55, 56/57, 58, 60/61, 63, 64, 65, 66, 67, 68/69, 70/71, 73, 75, 81, 82/83, 84, 86/87, 89, 91, 96, 98/99, 103, 105, 106, 109, 111, 113, 114/115, 116, 118/119, 125, 126/127, 128/129, 131, 132/133, 137, 138, 142, 147, 148/149, 150/151, 153, 154/155, 157, 158/159, 161, 165, 172, 174/175, 176/177, 181, 182/183, 184/185, 186/187, 189, 190/191, 194/195, 197, 201, 202, 211, 212/213, 218/219, 228

» Andrew Ritter: p. 171
www.stanceworks.com

» Daniel Schaefer: pp. 38/39, 179, 209, 227
www.schaeferpictures.com

» Rainer W. Schlegelmilch: p. 77
www.schlegelmilch.com

» Guido Steenkamp: p. 167
www.guido-steenkamp.com

» Ronald Stoops: p. 193
www.ronaldstoops.com

» Studio Erwin Wurm: pp. 206/207
www.erwinwurm.at
© VG Bild-Kunst 2016, Erwin Wurm
Fat Convertible, 2005 mixed media

» Sjoerd Ten Kate: pp. 216/217
www.sjoerdtenkate.com
represented by Schierke Artists

» Bob Tilton: pp. 92, 141, 168/169, 230/231
www.werkcrew.com

» Jurrie Vanhalle: pp. 222/223
www.vjimages.be

» Jens Ziehe: p. 205
Tobias Rehberger, kao ka moo, 2000
Porsche 911 (handgefertigte Kopie)
© tobias rehberger, Sammlung Grässlin, St. Georgen,
Courtesy of neugerriemschneider, Berlin

Porsche 911

The Ultimate Sportscar as Cultural Icon

by Ulf Poschardt

Text by Ulf Porschardt
Edited by Robert Klanten and Ulf Porschardt

Editorial support by Maximilian Funk
Editorial management by Silvia Koch and Vanessa Obrecht
Translation from German by Colin Shepherd
Additional translation from German by Dr. Jeremy Gaines (pp. 234/235)
Copy-editing by Amy Visram
Proofreading by Benjamin Maurice Barlow

Creative direction design and cover by Ludwig Wendt
Layout by Léon Giogoli and Ludwig Wendt

Final drawing by Marcel Petersen
Production management by Vincent Illner

Typefaces: Euclid Flex by Swiss Typefaces,
Minion Pro by Robert Slimbach

Cover photography by Alexander Bermudez

Printed by Print Best OÜ, Viljandi, Estonia
Made in Europe

Published by Gestalten, Berlin 2017
ISBN 978-3-89955-687-2

The German edition is available under ISBN 978-3-608-94742-7

8th printing, 2025

Mariannenstrasse 9–10
10999 Berlin, Germany
hello@gestalten.com

For more information, and to order books, please visit www.gestalten.com

Bibliographic information published by the Deutsche Nationalbibliothek. The Deutsche Nationalbibliothek lists this publication in the Deutsche Nationalbibliografie; detailed bibliographic data are available online at www.dnb.de.

None of the content in this book was published in exchange for payment by commercial parties or designers; Gestalten selected all included work based solely on its artistic merit.

This book was printed on paper certified according to the standards of the FSC®.